The Holy Temple

The Holy Temple

Boyd K. Packer

Illustrations by Darrell Thomas

Bookcraft
Salt Lake City, Utah

Library of Congress Catalog Card Number: 80-69100
ISBN 0-88494-411-5

21th Printing, 1996

Lithographed in the United States of America
PUBLISHERS PRESS
Salt Lake City, Utah

Acknowledgments

Many have helped with this work. None is more appreciated than Roy W. Doxey. His fine scholarship, his lifelong interest in the subject of temples, and his deep spiritual insight have made him a valuable counselor. To him and to the many others not listed here I express my thanks.

Introduction

We approach the subject of the temples with deep reverence. The Lord told Moses from the burning bush, "Put off thy shoes from off thy feet, for the place whereon thou standest is holy ground." (Exodus 3:5.) Joshua also was bidden to "loose thy shoe from off thy foot; for the place whereon thou standest is holy." (Joshua 5:15.)

Perhaps it was not so much the ground itself as it was the nature of the interview that sanctified it. We know of places dedicated for such sacred purposes — the holy temples of The Church of Jesus Christ of Latter-day Saints. Each carries the designation, The House of The Lord. The work of the temples is transcendent in nature, its prospects so supernal that the mind of man could not have conceived it. Men could not have devised it, for it is above mortal kind. This work and the ordinances central to it came from Deity.

Therefore, as we together approach this sacred subject we will do so reverently. I will not describe the sacred ordinances and ceremonies of the temple in more detail than has previously been published by the Church. I desire rather to bring together those thoughts and concepts that will help you understand temples and the significance they have for the salvation and exaltation of the human family.

When you accept a temple recommend from your bishop and stake president to go to the temple, either for the first time or after a hundred times or more, when you enter therein you too stand on holy ground.

Contents

Part IV / Each A Savior

I

Your Temple Blessings

Elijah window in the Salt Lake Temple

*Behold, I will reveal unto you the Priesthood,
by the hand of Elijah the prophet, before the
coming of the great and dreadful day of the Lord.*

*And he shall plant in the hearts of the
children the promises made to the fathers, and
the hearts of the children shall turn
to their fathers.*

(Words spoken by Moroni, the angel, to Joseph
Smith the Prophet, while in his father's house
at Manchester, New York, on the evening of
September 21, 1823.)

The seen and the unseen worlds are closely connected. One assists the other. Those who fail to partake of the privileges and blessings of temple work deprive themselves of some of the choicest gifts within the keeping of the Church.
Temple work begins with genealogy.
(John A. Widtsoe)

1

Come to the Temple

If one of the temples might be singled out as being somewhat different from the rest it would be the Salt Lake Temple at the headquarters of the Church. Here are the council rooms of the First Presidency and the Quorum of the Twelve Apostles and of the First Quorum of the Seventy. Here each week the Brethren assemble to sit in council. First the Quorum of the Twelve Apostles meets; later in the morning the First Presidency arrives and the Council of the First Presidency and the Quorum of the Twelve Apostles is convened. Here the Brethren wrestle with the weighty matters of the kingdom of God upon the earth, for its management is upon their shoulders. Here, dressed in the proper way for temple ordinance work, they approach the altar in the true order of prayer to seek divine guidance and inspiration as they consider these matters. The Presidents of the Seventy meet in their council room as well.

Hidden away in the central part of the temple is the Holy of Holies, where the President of the Church may retire when burdened down with heavy decisions to seek an interview with Him whose Church it is. The prophet holds the keys, the spiritual keys and the very literal key to this one door in that sacred edifice.

Here on the fifth floor is the large assembly room, with the series of pulpits at each end like those constructed in the first temple at Kirtland, Ohio. Here special meetings have been held — solemn assemblies, special testimony meetings for leaders who have come on call from the Brethren. The missionaries used to be instructed here.

Here are the ordinance rooms and the sealing rooms. In some sealing rooms opposite walls are adorned with large mirrors so that one may stand near the altar and view on either side a corridor of diminishing images. It gives one the feeling of looking into infinity; into the eternities. For the images in that corridor never end. You can see as far as you can see, and you have the feeling that if you could move to the limit of your vision you yet could see on "forever."

And below the level of the gardens and streets that surround the temple is the baptismal font, where vicarious baptisms for the dead are performed, with young people acting as proxy for those who have gone beyond the veil.

As you move from room to room and set your hand to turn the knob you find that pioneer craftsmen have carefully fashioned the design of the latch and lock. The tribute "Holiness to the Lord" is engraved in circular fashion on each knob. When you enter this or any dedicated temple you are in the house of the Lord.

Jesus Christ Directs His Servants

Central to the message about temples is the fact that Jesus is the Christ, the Son of God, the Only Begotten of the Father; that

He lives; that He directs His servants upon this earth. It is His priesthood which has been restored, defined as the Holy Priesthood after the Order of the Son of God. (See D&C 107:2-4.) Before the foundation of the earth He was chosen. That event is dramatically portrayed by Elder Orson F. Whitney of the Quorum of the Twelve Apostles. Let me quote from "Elect of Elohim."

In solemn council sat the Gods;
    From Kolob's height supreme,
Celestial light blazed forth afar
    O'er countless kokaubeam.
And faintest tinge, the fiery fringe
    Of that resplendent day,
'Lumined the dark abysmal realm
    Where Earth in chaos lay.
. . . .

"Father!" the voice like music fell,
    Clear as the murmuring flow
Of mountain streamlet trickling down
    From heights of virgin snow.
"Father," it said, "since One must die,
    Thy children to redeem
From worlds all formless now and void,
    Where myriad life shall teem;

"And mighty Michael foremost fall
    That mortal man may be;
And chosen Savior yet must send,
    Lo, here am I — send me!
I ask, I seek no recompense,
    Save that which then were mine;
Mine be the willing sacrifice,
    The endless glory Thine!"
. . . .

Still rang that voice, when sudden rose
    Aloft a towering Form,
Proudly erect as lowering peak
    'Lumed by the gathering storm;
A presence bright and beautiful,
    With eye of flashing fire,

A lip whose haughty curl bespoke
  A sense of inward ire.

"Send me!" — coiled 'neath his courtly smile
  A scarce-concealed disdain —
"And none shall hence, from Heaven to Earth,
  That shall not rise again.
My saving plan exception scorns.
  Man's will? — nay, mine alone.
As recompense, I claim the right
  To sit on yonder Throne!"

Ceased Lucifer. The breathless hush
  Resumed and denser grew.
All eyes were turned; the general gaze
  One common Magnet drew.
A moment there was solemn pause —
  Listened Eternity,
While rolled from lips omnipotent
  The Father's firm decree:

"Jehovah, thou my Messenger!
  Son Ahman, thee I send!
And one shall go thy face before,
  While twelve thy steps attend.
And many more on that far shore
  The pathway shall prepare,
That I, the First, the last may come,
  And Earth my glory share.
  . . . .
"Go forth, thou chosen of the Gods,
  Whose strength shall in thee dwell!
Go down betime and rescue Earth,
  Dethroning Death and Hell.
On thee alone man's fate depends,
  The fate of beings all,
Thou shalt not fail, though thou art free —
  Free, but too great to fall.

"By Arm divine, both mine and thine,
  The lost shalt thou restore,
And man, redeemed, with God shall be,

As God forevermore.
Return, and to the parent fold
  This wandering planet bring,
And Earth shall hail thee Conqueror,
  And Heaven proclaim thee King."

'Twas done. From congregation vast,
  Tumultuous murmurs rose;
Waves of conflicting sound, as when
  Two meeting seas oppose.
'Twas finished. But the heavens wept;
  And still their annals tell
How One was choice of Elohim,
  O'er One who fighting fell.

                    (*Voices from the Mountains,* n.p., n.d.)

The Father came, Elohim, with his son, Jehovah or Jesus Christ, to open the dispensation of the fullness of times. In a lesson on delegation that few have noted, the Father in seven words commissioned the Son to represent him. In seven words it was done: "This is my Beloved Son, Hear Him." We are free not to do it. We are free to listen to one another. We are free to heed those of the world. We are free to listen to perverse or wicked spirits. But if we want to know what counsel would be given from Elohim Himself we must seek our direction always "in the name of the Lord Jesus Christ." The Church is named for Him, as it was anciently.

After the First Vision the Lord sent other heavenly messengers; at times of crucial moment He accompanied them to introduce them. This was true on April 3, 1836, when the house of the Lord had been completed and the keys were to be given; the Lord Himself appeared, standing upon the breastwork of the pulpit, to give consummate approval and authority for what was to occur.

Ordinances Performed Only in Temples

It is my hope to enlarge your understanding as to why the temples are built and as to why the ordinances and ceremonies are performed there; as to why we do some of the things we do with reference to the holy temples and why we do not do some other things concerning them. As I say in the introduction, I will not discuss the sacred ordinances and ceremonies of the temple further than has previously been published about them by the Church. But the things that are included in this book will, I hope, deepen your reverence for and appreciation of the holy temple.

We do not single out the one temple, the Salt Lake Temple, as being better in any respect than any of the others. It is bigger than most, but in its purpose, in the ceremonies that take place within, in the ordinances that are performed, and in the authority by which they are done it is the same as the others; exactly and precisely the same. The smallest of the temples in the most remote place on earth will be quite as much the house of the Lord as the one most central to the headquarters of the Church.

In the Church we build other buildings of many kinds. In them we worship, we teach, we find recreation, we organize. We can organize stakes and wards and missions and quorums and Relief Societies in these buildings or even in rented halls. But, when we organize families according to the order that the Lord has revealed, we organize them in the temples. Temple marriage, that sealing ordinance, is a crowning blessing that you may claim in the holy temple.

Redemption for the Dead

Around the turn of the century two missionaries were laboring in the mountain region of the southern part of the United States. One day, as they were walking along a ridge in the hill country, they saw people gathering in a clearing near a cabin some distance down the hillside. Because in the hill country the people were scattered, the missionaries did not often have a congregation to whom they might preach. They were attracted by this gathering and made their way down to the clearing.

They discovered that there was to be a funeral. A little boy had been drowned. His parents had sent for the minister to "say words" at the burial of the little fellow. The minister, who rode the circuit, only occasionally would visit these isolated families. But when there was to be a wedding, or when there was trouble, they would send for him.

The elders stayed in the background to watch the proceedings. The little fellow was to be buried in the grave already opened near the cabin. The minister stood before the grieving father and mother and the others gathered and began his funeral sermon. If the parents expected to receive consolation from this man of the cloth, they would be disappointed.

He scolded them severely for not having had the little boy baptized. They had put it off because of one thing or another, and now it was too late. He told them very bluntly that their little boy had gone to hell. He told them that it was their fault, that they were to blame — they had caused their son endless torment.

After the sermon was over and the grave was covered, the friends, neighbors, and relatives left the scene. The elders approached the grieving parents: "We are servants of the Lord," they told the sobbing mother, "and we have come with a message for you."

As the grief-stricken parents listened, the two teenage elders unfolded to their view something of a vision of the eternities. They read from the revelations and they bore to these humble, grief-stricken parents their testimony of the restoration of the keys for the redemption of both the living and the dead.

I do not berate the itinerant preacher. Indeed, I have some sympathy for him, for he was doing the best he knew how to do with such light and knowledge as he had received. But there is more than he had to give. There is the fullness of the gospel.

The elders came as comforters, as teachers, as servants of the Lord, as authorized ministers of the gospel of Jesus Christ. They came, having been "called of God by prophecy and by the laying on of hands by those who are in authority to preach the gospel and administer in the ordinances thereof."

One of those humble elders, when a very old man, told me of this experience. More than half a century had passed. He bore testimony and expressed his gratitude that we have so much to share. The path he pointed out to those humble folk was more than conversion and repentance and baptism; for, to those who will follow, in due time that path leads to the sacred rooms of the holy temple. There members of the Church who make themselves eligible can participate in the most exalted and sacred of the redeeming ordinances that have been revealed to mankind. There we may be washed and anointed and instructed and endowed and sealed. And when we have received these blessings for ourselves, we may officiate for those who have died without having had the same opportunity. In the temples the sacred ordinances are performed for the living and for the dead alike.

Without those sacred ordinances and the truth they represent, those humble elders might have given little more comfort than the poor minister who had no knowledge of the Restoration. But we in the Church have that knowledge, and it rests upon us as a great responsibility.

Privilege of Temple Attendance

It is a privilege to enter the holy temple. You should know the things that are required of you and understand the doctrine that underlies the work that is performed in the house of the Lord. This may inspire you to move forward with your individual part of that work. You will gain something of a vision of what lies ahead for those who participate in those sacred ordinances, for those who keep their covenants, and for those for whom they officiate.

As we proceed to review the subject of the holy temples and the blessings each of us may claim within them, do not be surprised if you notice some repetition. This is intended. You may find a particular concept or doctrinal point discussed in more than one context, a scripture or a statement from one of the prophets used in more than one chapter. For this no apology is offered. It is deliberate. For did not Moroni repeat three times in one night his message to the Prophet Joseph Smith and then return the next day to repeat it a fourth time?

You should come to the temple. You really should! It may be that you look forward to the once-in-a-lifetime privilege of going there to receive your own endowment, to receive your own blessings, and to enter into your own covenants with the Lord. It may be that you have been there once or twice already. It may be that you go frequently. It may even be that you are an officiator. Whatever the circumstances may be, you should come to the temple.

If you are eligible by the standards that are set, by all means you should come to receive your own blessings; and thereafter you should return again and again and again to make those same blessings available to others who have died without the opportunity to receive them in mortality.

You should *not* come to the temple until you are eligible, until you meet the requirements that the Lord has set, but you should come; if not now, as soon as you can qualify.

Transcendent Doctrine

The doctrine that underlies the work in the holy temple, more than any other thing, sets The Church of Jesus Christ of Latter-day Saints apart from and transcendent above every other religious organization on the face of the earth. We have something that no other religious denomination has. We can give something that they cannot extend.

What is represented by the humble elders comforting the grieving parents before that modest cabin is central to the doctrines of this Church and to the work that takes place in the holy temple. We have something to give that can be obtained in no other place. We have an answer to the question that can be found with none else.

A few years ago a mother came to my office seeking help and comfort with some weighty problems. She told me the story of her life before she joined the Church. It had been a hard life. She had been abandoned by her husband and left to raise a little boy. When he was nine years old he contracted a fatal disease. He came to know, in his little boy mind, that he would not live. And for the last two or three weeks of his life he would cling to his mother and say, "Mama, you won't forget me, will you? Mama, please don't forget me. Mama, I won't be forgotten, will I?"

I was deeply moved, for I sensed that exposed in the pleadings of this little boy is something of the feeling of every soul who has ever lived. We hope that, somehow at least, we will be remembered. We hope that there will be something about us worth remembering.

This mother would never forget her little boy. Our Heavenly Father does not forget, and he has provided, through the ministry of His Son, the way that all may be remembered and all can be redeemed.

The question on the mind of this little boy and the anguish in the hearts of those grieving parents can be satisfied only in the doctrines of this Church. The doctrines center on the holy temple.

When the Lord was upon the earth He made it very clear that there was one way, and one way only, by which man may be saved. "I am the way, the truth, and the life: no man cometh unto the Father, but by me." (John 14:6.) To proceed on that way, two things emerge as being firmly fixed. First, in His name rests the authority to secure the salvation of mankind; "for there is none other name under heaven given . . . whereby we must be saved." (Acts 4:12.) Second, there is an essential ordinance — baptism — standing as a gate through which every soul must pass to obtain eternal life.

The Lord was neither hesitant nor apologetic in proclaiming exclusive authority over those processes, all of them in total, by which we may return to the presence of our Heavenly Father. This ideal was clear in the minds of His apostles also, and their preaching provided for one way, and one way only, for men to save themselves.

Over the centuries men saw that many, indeed most, never found that way. This became very hard to explain. Perhaps they thought it to be generous to accept the idea that there are other ways. So they tempered or tampered with the doctrine.

This rigid emphasis on "one Lord and one baptism" was thought to be too restrictive and too exclusive, even though the Lord Himself had described it as being narrow, for "strait is the gate, and narrow is the way, which leadeth unto life." (Matthew 7:14.)

The Proselyting Assignment

Since baptism is essential, there must be an urgent concern to carry the message of the gospel of Jesus Christ to every nation, kindred, tongue, and people. That proselyting assignment came as a commandment from Him.

His true servants will be out to convert to the principles of the gospel all who will hear, and they will offer them that one baptism which He proclaimed as essential. The preaching of the gospel is evident to one degree or another in most Christian churches. Most of the adherents, however, are content to enjoy whatever they can gain from membership in their church without any real effort to see that others hear about it.

The powerful missionary spirit and the vigorous missionary activity in The Church of Jesus Christ of Latter-day Saints becomes a very significant witness that the true gospel and the authority are possessed in this church. We accept the responsibility to preach the gospel to every person on earth. And if the question is asked, "You mean you are out to convert the entire world?" the answer is, "Yes. We will try to reach every living soul."

Some who measure that challenge say quickly, "Why, that's impossible! It cannot be done!"

To that we simply say, "Perhaps, but we shall do it anyway."

Against the assertion that it cannot be done, we are willing to commit every resource that can be righteously accumulated to this work. Now, while our effort may seem modest when measured against the challenge, it is hard to ignore when measured against what is being accomplished, or even what is being attempted, elsewhere.

Presently we have tens of thousands of missionaries serving in the field—and paying for the privilege. Any one of them would be evidence enough if the source of the individual conviction that each carries were recognized.

We ask no relief of the assignment to seek out every living soul, teach them the gospel, and offer them baptism. And we are not discouraged, for there is a great power in this work, and that can be verified by anyone who is sincerely inquiring.

Baptism Must Be Offered Also to Dead

There is another characteristic that identifies the Lord's church and also has to do with baptism. There is a very provoking and a very disturbing question about those who died without baptism. What about them? If there is none other name given under heaven whereby man must be saved (and that is true), and they have lived and died without even hearing that name, and if baptism is essential (and it is), and they died without even the invitation to accept it, where are they now?

That question is hard to fathom. The itinerant preacher we spoke of earlier had no answer. That situation describes most of the human family.

There are several non-Christian religions larger than most of the Christian denominations, and together those religions are larger than all of the Christian denominations combined. Their adherents for centuries have lived and died and never heard the word *baptism*. What is the answer for them?

That is a most disturbing question. What power would establish one Lord and one baptism and then allow it to happen that most of the human family never comes within the influence of its doctrines? With that question unanswered, the vast majority of the human family must be admitted to be lost, including the little boy who drowned—and against any reasonable application of the law of justice, or of mercy, either. In those circumstances, how could Christianity itself be sustained?

If a church has no answer to this dilemma, how can it lay claim to be the Lord's church? Surely He is not willing to write off the majority of the human family because they were never baptized while on earth.

In all reason, those who admit in puzzled frustration that they have no answer to this question cannot lay claim to authority to administer the affairs of the Lord on the earth, or to oversee the work by which all mankind must be saved.

The Prophet Joseph Smith said very tersely:

> One dies and is buried, having never heard the Gospel of recon-
> ciliation; to the other the message of salvation is sent, he hears and
> embraces it, and is made the heir of eternal life. Shall the one become
> the partaker of glory and the other be consigned to hopeless perdi-
> tion? Is there no chance for his escape? Sectarianism answers "none."
> Such an idea is worse than atheism. The truth shall break down and
> dash in pieces all such bigoted Pharisaism; the sects shall be sifted,
> the honest in heart brought out, and their priests left in the midst
> of their corruption. (Joseph Smith, Jr., *History of the Church of
> Jesus Christ of Latter-day Saints*, ed. B. H. Roberts, 7 vols. [Salt
> Lake City: The Church of Jesus Christ of Latter-day Saints, 1949],
> 4:425-26; hereafter cited as *HC*.)

Since they had no answer concerning the fate of those who had not been baptized, many Christians came to believe that baptism itself was not critical in importance, and that the name of Christ may not be all that essential. There must, they supposed, be other names whereby man could be saved.

The answer to the puzzling challenge could not be invented by men. It had to be, and was, *revealed*. Revelation too is an essential characteristic of His church. Communication with Him through revelation was established when the Church was estab-lished. It has not ceased, and it is constant in the Church today.

Whenever I address myself to the question of those who died without baptism, I do so with the deepest reverence, for it touches on a sacred work. Little known to the world, we move obediently forward in a work that is marvelous in its prospects, transcendent above what man might have dreamed of, supernal, inspired, and true. In it is the answer.

In the earliest days of the Church the Prophet Joseph Smith was given direction through revelation that work should commence on the building of a temple akin to the temples that had been constructed anciently. There was revealed ordinance work to be performed there for the salvation of mankind.

Then another ancient scripture, ignored or overlooked by the Christian world in general, was understood and moved into prominence: "Else what shall they do which are baptized for the dead, if the dead rise not at all? Why are they then baptized for the dead?" (1 Corinthians 15:29.) Notice the way this verse is handled in other translations of the Bible.

> If the dead will not come back to life again, then what point is there in people being baptized for those who are gone? Why do it unless you believe that the dead will some day rise again? (The Living Bible.)
>
> Again, there are those who receive baptism on behalf of the dead. Why should they do this? If the dead are not raised to life at all, what do they mean by being baptized on their behalf? (The New English Bible.)
>
> Otherwise, if there is no such thing as a resurrection, what is the meaning of people getting baptized on behalf of their dead? If dead men do not rise at all, why do people get baptized on their behalf? (A New Translation of the Bible, Moffatt.)
>
> If the dead are not raised, what about those who have themselves baptized on behalf of the dead? If the raising of the dead is not a reality, why be baptized on their behalf? (The New American Bible.)

The whole point of this biblical passage is that baptism for the dead is meaningless unless there is to be a resurrection. This point is well expressed by the Reverend J. R. Dummelow: "The Resurrection alone gives an adequate motive for (a) baptism for the dead. . . ." (*A Commentary on the Holy Bible* [New York: Macmillan Company, 1936], page 919.)

Roy W. Doxey wrote:

If you assume that there is no validity to the practice of baptism for the dead as understood by the Corinthians, you will be unable to explain why Jesus in the interim between his death and resurrection went into the spirit world and preached the gospel. (1 Peter 3: 19-20; 4:6.) For what purpose? It is plain from Paul's writings that the purpose of the Savior's preaching to the spirits in prison was to give people who have never had an opportunity to receive the atoning sacrifice of Jesus in mortality an opportunity to hear the gospel, that vicarious baptism might then be performed for them.

When Paul discussed salvation regarding those who lived before the time of Christ, he gave us to understand clearly that though faith existed among many of these people, they were given the promise that God's people ("us") would provide the means whereby "they" (the dead) might receive salvation. "And these all, having obtained a good report through faith, received not the promise: God having provided some better thing for *us*, that *they without us* should not be made perfect." (Hebrews 11:39, 40; italics added.) [From an unpublished letter.]

Here, then, was the answer. With proper authority a mortal person could be baptized for and in behalf of someone who had not had that opportunity before passing on. That individual would then accept or reject the baptism in the spirit world, according to his own desire.

This work came as a great reaffirmation of something very basic that the Christian world now only partly believes — that there is life after death. Mortal death is no more an ending than birth was a beginning. The great work of redemption goes on beyond the veil as well as here in mortality.

The Lord said, "Verily, verily, I say unto you, The hour is coming, and now is, when the dead shall hear the voice of the Son of God: and they that hear shall live." (John 5:25.)

On October 3, 1918, President Joseph F. Smith was pondering on the scriptures, including this passage from Peter: "For for this cause was the gospel preached also to them that are dead, that they might be judged according to men in the flesh, but live according to God in the spirit." (1 Peter 4:6.)

There was opened to him a marvelous vision. In it he saw the concourses of the righteous in the spirit world. And he saw Christ ministering among them. Then he saw those who had not had the opportunity of the gospel in mortality, and those who had rejected the truth after receiving that opportunity. And he saw the work for their redemption. I quote from his record of this vision:

> I perceived that the Lord went not in person among the wicked and the disobedient who had rejected the truth, to teach them;
>
>   But behold, from among the righteous, he organized his forces and appointed messengers, clothed with power and authority, and commissioned them to go forth and carry the light of the gospel to them that were in darkness, even to all the spirits of men; and thus was the gospel preached to the dead. (D&C 138:29-30.)

We have been authorized to perform baptisms vicariously for the dead, so that, when they hear the gospel preached and desire to accept it, that essential ordinance will have been performed. They need not ask for any exemption from that essential ordinance. Indeed, the Lord Himself was not exempted from it.

Here and now, then, we move to accomplish the work to which we are assigned. We are busily engaged in that kind of baptism. We gather the records of our kindred dead, indeed insofar as possible the records of the entire human family; and in sacred temples, in baptismal fonts designed as those were anciently, we perform the sacred saving ordinances.

"Strange," one may say. It *is* passing strange. It is transcendent and supernal. The very nature of the work testifies that Jesus Christ is our Lord, that baptism is essential, that He taught the truth.

And so the question may be asked, "You mean you are out to make baptism available for all men?"

And the answer is simply, "Yes." For we have been commanded to do so.

"You mean for the entire human family? Why, that is impossible! If the preaching of the gospel to all who are living is a formidable challenge, then the vicarious work for all who have ever lived is impossible indeed."

To that we say, "Perhaps, but we shall do all that we can do."

We do not know how many will accept the ordinance. Some may not be eligible to accept it.

The principles and ordinances of the gospel all point to the celestial kingdom. The Lord has not given us direction as to the lower kingdoms, save to warn us that by falling short of the higher mark we will inherit a lesser reward.

Baptism is required for entrance into the celestial kingdom. Some who have lived may be disqualified from entering there. Such matters are settled beyond the veil.

The Lord has not shown us the way to judge those who have lived before. We are to do the work for them to the limits of our resources. We are to see that none will be denied the opportunity to choose because of our failure.

And once again we certify that we are not discouraged. We ask no relief of the assignment, no excuse from fulfilling it. Our effort today is modest indeed when viewed against the challenge. But we have come to know that our accomplishments, so far as they have gone, have been pleasing to the Lord. We do not suggest that the size of the effort should be impressive, for we are not doing nearly as well as we should be. But already we have collected hundreds of millions of names, and the work goes forward in the temples and will go on in other temples that will be built.

Those who thoughtfully consider the work inquire about those names that cannot be collected. "What about those for whom no record was ever kept? Surely you will fail there. There is no way you can search out those names."

To this I simply observe, "You have forgotten revelation." Already we have been directed to many records through that process. Revelation comes to individual members as they are led to discover their family records in ways that are miraculous indeed. And there is a feeling of inspiration attending this work that can be found in no other. When we have done all that we can do, we shall be given the rest. The way will be opened up.

Every Latter-day Saint is responsible for this work. Without this work, the saving ordinances of the gospel would apply to so few who have ever lived that the gospel could not be claimed to be true.

Probably no point of doctrine sets this Church apart from the other claimants as this one does. Save for it, we would, with all of the other churches, have to accept the clarity with which the New Testament declares baptism to be essential and then admit that most of the human family could never have it.

But we have the revelations. We have those sacred ordinances. The revelation that places upon us the obligation for this baptism for the dead is section 128 in the Doctrine and Covenants. Consider two or three of the closing verses of that section.

> Brethren, shall we not go on in so great a cause? Go forward and not backward. Courage, brethren; and on, on to the victory! Let your hearts rejoice, and be exceedingly glad. Let the earth break forth into singing. Let the dead speak forth anthems of eternal praise to the King Immanuel, who hath ordained, before the world was, that which would enable us to redeem them out of their prison. . . .
>
> Let the mountains shout for joy, and all ye valleys cry aloud; and all ye seas and dry lands tell the wonders of your Eternal King! And ye rivers, and brooks, and rills, flow down with gladness. Let the woods and all the trees of the field praise the Lord; and ye solid rocks weep for joy! . . .
>
> . . . Let us, therefore, as a church and a people, and as Latter-day Saints, offer unto the Lord an offering in righteousness; and let us present in his holy temple . . . a book containing the records of our dead, which shall be worthy of all acceptation. (D&C 128:22-24.)

Come to the Temple

But temple opportunities differ in the worldwide Church, and some members presently look toward the temple with very little hope that it will be their privilege to enter that holy house. Some live at such a distance from a temple and are so pressed financially that it does not seem possible for this blessing to be theirs. Others may be tied by bonds of marriage and by bonds of love to a companion who does not yet sense the meaning of the word *temple*. That companion may have little sympathy, and may even show antagonism, toward the yearning to enter the house of the Lord. Some may be frail in health and wonder if they will ever recover and be able to enter the temple. Some are aged and feel that in this life that dream will not be realized. And there are others whose lives are troubled, who are tainted with transgression and who have lived through a complicated history of mistake followed by mistake.

To all of you I say, "Come to the temple." If not now, come then. Pray fervently, set your lives in order, save whatever you can in hopes that that day may come. Start now that very difficult and sometimes very discouraging journey of repentance. For some of you at great distances the temples will come to you before you might come to them. I urge you all to keep your faith and your hope and determine that you will come — that you will be worthy and that you will come to the temple.

It has been my observation that the temple transforms the individual and makes abundantly worthwhile any efforts made to get there. Let me recount an experience.

In 1979 I dedicated a small chapel in San Andreas Itzapa, Guatemala. The chapel is located on the end of a street near the edge of the city. It is a modest chapel, but the thriving branch was joyous at moving from the makeshift shelter where they had been holding meetings. For the most part the branch members were very humble people with very little in the way of material blessings. My impression of the experience there centered on a tiny woman, the mother of the branch president.

Before the meeting she came forward. She did not come up to my shoulder. She had lost most of her teeth and she appeared to be very old. She was radiant! She looked different from most of the others. There was something about her that was just aglow. She looked clean and intelligent and happy. As she came to shake hands she embraced me. She hugged me very tightly with her head pressed against my chest, and the first words she spoke I understood, even with my meager knowledge of Spanish. "Yo a tengo a el templo" — I have been to the temple!

We conversed to the limits of my meager Spanish, and as she was about to return to her seat she pointed to the branch president and said, "This is my son. He also has been to the temple." He stood there in a white suit with his lovely wife, who was dressed in modest, appropriate, refined clothing. They impressed me — surely they would fit in at a reception of dignified community leaders in one of the large cities of Latin America. They were set apart — not only by virtue of his calling as a branch president, but by virtue of the fact that they had been to the temple.

I cannot imagine their financial sacrifice in getting to the temple. But I know something of the trip they must have taken on rickety buses, traveling sometimes day and night, north through the jungles of Central America, the full length of Mexico, across the deserts and mountains, through the border at Nogales and on to Mesa, Arizona — a trip of many days and many nights with no air conditioning, no comforts or conveniences. But what did it matter? They were going to the temple! I have organized stakes where not one of the officers had been to the temple — no member of the stake presidency, no members of bishoprics, no auxiliary officers. But they would get there — eight days and nights across the Andes from Santiago, Chile, through Argentina to Brazil.

I was told in South America how impressed some of the temple officials were with the spiritual dedication of the humble people who traveled from the far reaches of Latin America to come to the temple in Brazil. They were greatly impressed because many of the visitors apparently were determined to fast the entire time they were at the temple. And then one day we learned that it was not entirely a matter of devotion. They had so meager a budget to get them to the temple and return that, apart from their bus ticket, they had very little money, and they could not eat on those days simply because they could not afford it.

I hope these examples of dedication and sacrifice will touch the hearts of you for whom temple attendance is a much easier matter. Whether you need to put your personal life in order to obtain a temple recommend or whether you are just careless about this work and have allowed worldly matters to take precedence — whatever the reason, be moved to make the change. Firmly resolve now that you will do everything you can do to aid temple work and the genealogical work that supports it and to assist every living soul and every soul beyond the veil in every way you can with every resource at your disposal.

Come to the temple!

Trifle not
with sacred things.
(D&C 6:12.)

2

These Things Are Sacred

A careful reading of the scriptures reveals that the Lord did not tell all things to all people. There were some qualifications set that were prerequisite to receiving sacred information. Such things were to come "line upon line, precept upon precept," as people were able to receive them.

Temple ceremonies are not something that we try to limit to a restricted number of people. With great effort we urge every soul to qualify and prepare for the temple experience. Everyone who comes within the influence of the gospel is urged to prepare to go to the temple and participate fully in the sacred ordinances which are available there.

Our reluctance to speak of the sacred temple ordinances is not in any way an attempt to make them seem more mysterious or to encourage an improper curiosity about them. The ordinances and ceremonies of the temple are simple. They are beautiful. They are sacred. They are kept confidential lest they be given to those who are unprepared. Curiosity is not a preparation. Deep interest itself is not a preparation. Preparation for the ordinances includes preliminary steps: faith, repentance, baptism, confirmation, worthiness, a maturity and dignity worthy of one who comes invited as a guest into the house of the Lord.

In order that you may understand and respect the need to hold in confidence the detailed nature of the temple ceremonies, let us explore the question of why the Lord would direct us to refrain from talking about them outside of that sacred building. It is a matter of preparation. We must be prepared before we go to the temple. We must be worthy before we go to the temple. There are restrictions and conditions set. They were established by the Lord and not by man.

Preparation for Higher Instruction

Most educational programs require the completion of basic or prerequisite courses before one can register for advanced courses. At a university you cannot register for a graduate course in chemistry, or even an advanced course, until completing the basic or elementary courses. This principle of prerequisites is well understood in everyday life. It should not surprise anyone when it is applied to the ordinances of the gospel. That is common sense. Without the fundamental principles of chemistry, an advanced course may well be a mistake. To understand advanced chemistry, even a brilliant mind would need to know about basic elements, about atoms and molecules, about electrons and protons, about valence, compounds, properties—formulas and equations—about densities and solutions and suspensions and mixtures.

Chemistry might be called a vertical field. A foundation of information must be built before one can proceed upward. Someone may think himself a genius who could register for a graduate course in chemistry and, without the prerequisite courses or even an introduction to the fundamentals, survive and pull down a top grade. That would take a genius indeed! If you attempt to master the advanced course first, you will end in confusion. You will learn to dislike the subject, perhaps the teacher, and wonder about a school that would subject you to such misery.

This elementary principle of prerequisite courses applies to virtually every discipline and relates to virtually all subject matters. I recall taking a course in statistics in the early days of my master's program. It wasn't my favorite subject, for somewhere in elementary or secondary schooling I had missed some of the basics of mathematical computations. After considerable struggle I passed the course with an adequate grade. I avoided the subject after that, compensating in other areas. But finally, as it will, came the day of reckoning. Nine years later there stood between me and the degree of doctor of education a single course — *advanced* statistics. I struggled to remember things that really I hadn't previously learned, and it was a special kind of suffering. How I struggled with those formulas, writing them on the blackboard at night, trying to photograph them on my mind so I could produce an acceptable copy on a test paper before the instructor! I passed the course but I learned how important it is to learn *fundamentals* before moving to advanced work. This is true of most activities of life.

Now, not all of us are going to use the higher rules of statistics or chemistry. Most of us may manage quite well without having had an advanced course in these subjects. But there are some courses that must universally be mastered if we are to find happiness and fulfillment in life. Essential life activities must be mastered in the same way, fundamentals first and then more advanced ideals built on the foundations of the basic principles.

It should not seem unusual, then, that the Lord has decreed in His church that admission to the temple comes only after certain prerequisites have been filled. It should not seem unusual that certain preparation and worthiness should be established before these privileges are given.

Sacredness Requires Confidentiality

There are some blessings which can be bestowed only in the Lord's temple, and we do not talk of them outside the temple. But all who are worthy and qualify in every way may enter the temple, there to be introduced to the sacred rites and ordinances. This is not the secrecy of restrictiveness. Rather it is the sacredness required for covenants offered to all of God's children in His way. Clearly there is much difference between treating something as sacred and keeping something secret.

It is not unusual that the Lord told Joseph Smith, "Make not thy gift known unto any save it be those who are of thy faith. Trifle not with sacred things" (D&C 6:12).

It is not unusual that He repeated this counsel after He had shown Joseph Smith and Sidney Rigdon "great and marvelous . . . works of the Lord, and the mysteries of his kingdom" (D&C 76:114). Of these the Prophet recorded:

> Which he commanded us we should not write while we were yet in the Spirit, and are not lawful for man to utter;
> Neither is man capable to make them known, for they are only to be seen and understood by the power of the Holy Spirit, which God bestows on those who love him, and purify themselves before him;
> To whom he grants this privilege of seeing and knowing for themselves. (D&C 76:115-17.)

The Lord has every right and authority to direct that matters relating to the temple be kept sacred and confidential.

Questions about the temple ceremony usually meet with the response, "We are not free to discuss the temple ordinances and ceremonies." Those who have not been to the temple sometimes ask, "Why is it so secret?"

If "secret" means that others are permanently prevented from knowing of them, then *secret* is the wrong word. These things are *sacred*.

It was never intended that knowledge of these temple ceremonies would be limited to a select few who would be obliged
to ensure that others never learn of them. It is quite the opposite,
in fact. Those who have been to the temple have been taught an
ideal. Someday every living soul and every soul who has ever
lived shall have the opportunity to hear the gospel and to accept
or reject what the temple offers. If this opportunity is rejected, the
rejection must be on the part of the individual himself.

In the Church we continually stress the highest standards
of worthiness. The youth of the Church are urged to prepare
themselves for temple marriage. In the most reverent terms we talk
about temples and what they mean. And across the Church we
continually schedule meetings for married couples who have not
yet been to the temple. These meetings, under various titles,
embrace the theme of preparation for the temple.

When a member reports to the bishop seeking an initial temple
recommend, the bishop gives counsel regarding what will be
expected in the temple. Always this is in the most general terms.
While we make reference to washings and anointings, sealings
and endowments, we do not discuss the details.

In the Book of Mormon, Alma instructs Zeezrom in these
words:

> And now Alma began to expound these things unto him, saying:
> It is given unto many to know the mysteries of God; nevertheless
> they are laid under a strict command that they shall not impart only
> according to the portion of his word which he doth grant unto the
> children of men, according to the heed and diligence which they
> give unto him.
>
> And therefore, he that will harden his heart, the same receiveth
> the lesser portion of the word; and he that will not harden his heart,
> to him is given the greater portion of the word, until it is given unto
> him to know the mysteries of God until he know them in full.
>
> And they that will harden their hearts, to them is given the lesser
> portion of the word until they know nothing concerning his
> mysteries; and then they are taken captive by the devil, and led by
> his will down to destruction. Now this is what is meant by the chains
> of hell. (Alma 12:9-11.)

Sometimes nonmembers become very inquisitive as to what goes on in the temples. They quickly learn that members of the Church are not willing to talk about those matters, and they wonder what the nature of the ceremonies might be. Lacking knowledge, some have developed strange explanations about the work of our temples.

Some things concerning the temple ordinances have been published by apostates who seek to injure or destroy the Church. Their accounts do not assist understanding, partly because the accounts are usually distorted. In any case the temple ordinances cannot be understood without the feeling and the spiritual presence that surrounds them in the temple. They must make very dull reading indeed for the enemy who has no right to the Spirit of the Lord.

President Joseph Fielding Smith told of a person who directed an attack upon the Church and cited the so-called secrecy about temple ordinances as evidence that things were not in order. The critic quoted from the Savior's words in the New Testament: "Jesus answered him, I spake openly to the world; I ever taught in the synagogue, and in the temple, whither the Jews always resort; and in secret have I said nothing. Why askest thou me? ask them which heard me, what I have said unto them: behold, they know what I said." (John 18:20-21.)

Then, making reference to our unwillingness to discuss the temple ordinances, the critic said: "Christ was not afraid of any revealments. He stood there among His enemies, defying them to find any fault with His teachings." The critic asserted that Brigham Young was not willing to reveal "his doctrine and secret works" and asked the question, "Did he represent Christ?" (Joseph Fielding Smith, *Origin of the "Reorganized" Church and the Question of Succession* [Salt Lake City: The Church of Jesus Christ of Latter-day Saints, 1929], page 97.)

Members of the Church all over the world face similar questions. These questions need not disturb nor shake the faith of anyone. Those who take the position of this critic have not read the scriptures carefully. When we consider other statements of the Lord another dimension is added, for there are scriptures, equally as valid as John 18, which broaden our understanding and show us that the Lord did indeed restrict some information, giving it only to those who were prepared and qualified.

On the Mount of Transfiguration, Peter, James, and John saw the Lord transfigured before them. With Him were two personages whom they knew to be Moses and Elias (Elijah). An important point may be made in the present context. "And as they came down from the mountain, Jesus charged them, saying, *Tell the vision to no man,* until the Son of man be risen again from the dead." (Matthew 17:9; italics added.)

Commenting upon this subject, President Joseph Fielding Smith said:

> We are told that the Book of Mormon contains the fullness of the Gospel, yet the greater parts of the teachings of the Savior to that people are not yet revealed, because of the unbelief of the people. This from Third Nephi, the 26th chapter:
>
> "And now there cannot be written in this book even a hundredth part of the things which Jesus did truly teach unto the people;
>
> "But behold the plates of Nephi do contain the more part of the things which he taught the people.
>
> "And these things have I written, which are a lesser part of the things which he taught the people; and I have written them to the intent that they may be brought again unto this people, from the Gentiles, according to the words which Jesus hath spoken.
>
> "And when they shall have received this, which is expedient that they should have first, to try their faith, and if it shall so be that they shall believe these things then shall the greater things be manifest unto them.
>
> "And if it so be that they will not believe these things, then shall the greater things be withheld from them, unto their condemnation.
>
> "Behold, I was about to write them, all which were engraven upon the plates of Nephi, but the Lord forbade it, saying: I will try the faith of my people." (3 Nephi 26:6-11.) (*Origin of the "Reorganized" Church*, pages 99-100.)

In the same context President Smith made reference to the sealed portion of the Book of Mormon plates and quoted the following verses:

> Behold, I have written upon these plates the very things which the brother of Jared saw; and there never were greater things made manifest than those which were made manifest unto the brother of Jared.
>
> Wherefore the Lord hath commanded me to write them; and I have written them. And he commanded me that I should seal them up; and he also hath commanded that I should seal up the interpretation thereof; wherefore I have sealed up the interpreters, according to the commandment of the Lord.
>
> For the Lord said unto me: They shall not go forth unto the Gentiles until the day that they shall repent of their iniquity, and become clean before the Lord. (Ether 4:4-6.)

On one occasion the Prophet Joseph Smith was instructing some of the Brethren in the upper part of his store in Nauvoo. The room they were in was his "office," because it was there that, as he said, "I keep my sacred writings, translate ancient records, and receive revelations." The Brethren present included Brigham Young, Heber C. Kimball, and Willard Richards. He was "instructing them in the principles and order of the Priesthood, attending to washings, anointings, endowments and communication of keys pertaining to the Aaronic Priesthood, and so on to the highest order of the Melchizedek Priesthood, setting forth the order pertaining to the Ancient of Days, and all those plans and principles by which any one is enabled to secure the fullness of those blessings which have been prepared for the Church. . . ."

And then the Prophet Joseph said this:

> The communications I made to this council were of things spiritual, and *to be received only by the spiritual minded:* and there was nothing made known to these men but will be made known to all the Saints of the last days, so soon as they are prepared to receive, and a proper place is prepared to communicate them, even to the weakest of the Saints; therefore let the Saints be diligent in building the Temple, and all houses which they have been, or shall hereafter be, commanded of God to build; and wait their time with patience

in all meekness, faith, perseverance unto the end, knowing assuredly that all these things referred to in this council are always governed by the principle of revelation. (*HC*, 5:2; italics added.)

I quote again from President Joseph Fielding Smith:

In the book of Abraham (See Pearl of Great Price) published by the Prophet Joseph Smith in the Times and Seasons in 1842, is given a fac-simile of hieroglyphics with an accompanying translation by Joseph Smith, as far as he was permitted to translate. These figures are numbered from 1 to 20. Here are some of these translations and comments of the Prophet:

Figure 3.—Is made to represent God, sitting upon His throne, clothed with power and authority; with a crown of eternal light upon His head; representing also the grand *key-words* of the Holy Priesthood, as revealed to Adam, etc. Figure 7. — Represents God sitting upon His throne revealing through the heavens, the grand *key-words* of the Priesthood, as, also, the sign of the Holy Ghost unto Abraham, in the form of a dove. Figure 8.—*Contains writing that cannot be revealed unto the world, but is to be had in the Holy Temple of God.* Figures 9, 10, 11, the Prophet says "Ought not to be revealed at the present time; if the world can find out these numbers, so let it be. Amen." Figures 12 to 20, "Will be given in the own due time of the Lord." Then the Prophet concludes: "The above translation is given as far as we have any right to give, at the present time."

Here, then, we find things that were to be taught to the Saints in the Temple of the Lord, but were not to be revealed to the world; for they are sacred and holy, and can only be had in the Temple of God, for the Lord through Joseph Smith declared it.

Again, in verse 28 (see 124), the Lord says: "For there is not a place found on earth that he may come and restore again that which was lost unto you, or which he hath taken away, *even the fullness of the Priesthood.*" Therefore, we learn that only in the Temple of the Lord can the fullness of the Priesthood be received by His people. (*Origin of the "Reorganized" Church*, page 103.)

Temples Before and After Dedication

The restriction preventing nonmembers from visiting the dedicated temples does not suggest that there is anything about the building or its appointments that they should not see. Prior to the dedication of temples in each case an open house is held. This is continued for as many days as it is reasonably expected that people will want to tour the temple. Tours are arranged so that those who enter can see samples of most, if not all, of the rooms of the temple. The tours could visit every room in the temple except for the matter of convenience in conducting the tours. Therefore service areas and other areas of less interest to the visitors are generally not seen. Prior to the dedication of a temple the privilege to visit the temple is widely advertised with the hope that all within the area, member and nonmember, will visit the temple and become familiar with the building.

Even worthy members are not invited to the temple after dedication just to be in the building. Members with recommends do not go to the temple unless they have a specific purpose for going there, a specific ordinance in which to participate. There is a practical reason for not inviting everyone to come to the temples. If all who took a fancy to do so, whether nonmembers or members, were allowed to tour the temples, the temple work would be disrupted and delayed.

Consider the definition of the word *dedication* as it applies to temples. When a developer prepares a tract of land for the building of homes, he makes provision for streets. But the streets will not be the property of homeowners. These are deeded to the community. The process of deeding that property to the community is called dedication. A street that is "dedicated" becomes the property of the community, which has some responsibility to maintain it and to set the conditions under which the public might use it. In simple terms, the developer gives his ownership of that property to the community.

Something similar to that happens when we dedicate a temple. While members of the Church may have contributed the money to build the temple and may themselves have labored to construct it, it is not theirs once it is dedicated. The dedication of a temple, in a real way, gives the building and all of the landscaping and structures related to the temple site to the Lord. The temple itself becomes literally the house of the Lord. The word *temple* comes from the word *templum*, which is defined as the abode of Deity or simply the house of the Lord.

Elder James E. Talmage defines the temple as "a building constructed for and exclusively devoted to sacred rites and ceremonies." (James E. Talmage, *The House of the Lord* [Salt Lake City: Bookcraft, 1962], page 1.)

After a temple is dedicated we do not feel we own it. It is the Lord's house. He directs the conditions under which it may be used. He has revealed the ordinances that should be performed therein and has established the standards and conditions under which we may participate in them. He has full control over the authority of the priesthood by which the ordinances are performed and the standards pertaining to who may be ordained to the offices of the priesthood and under what conditions. Those who are called as sealers in the temple are set apart only by direct authority held by the President of the Church. This should illustrate the deep regard in which these ordinances are held and the limitations that the Lord has set upon who may perform them. It should not be surprising that there should be limitations as to those who may receive them and those who may witness them. It should not, therefore, seem strange that the temples are held sacred, for all who will prepare themselves by repentance, by baptism, by preparation in worthiness to meet the qualifications, may enter therein to participate in the ordinances offered in the house of the Lord. When we go there we go as His servants.

Few words in the revelations have more meaning for the temple ordinances and ceremonies than these words from the second chapter of First Corinthians.

> But as it is written, Eye hath not seen, nor ear heard, neither have entered into the heart of man, the things which God hath prepared for them that love him.
>
> But God has revealed them unto us by his Spirit: for the Spirit searcheth all things, yea, the deep things of God.
>
> For what man knoweth the things of a man, save the spirit of man which is in him? even so the things of God knoweth no man, but the Spirit of God.

Now we have received, not the spirit of the world, but the spirit which is of God; that we might know the things that are freely given to us of God.

Which things also we speak, not in the words which man's wisdom teacheth, but which the Holy Ghost teacheth; comparing spiritual things with spiritual.

But the natural man receiveth not the things of the Spirit of God; for they are foolishness unto him: neither can he know them, because they are spiritually discerned.

But he that is spiritual judgeth all things, yet he himself is judged of no man.

For who hath known the mind of the Lord, that he may instruct him? But we have the mind of Christ. (1 Corinthians 2:9-16.)

Without the spiritual atmosphere of the temple itself, and without the worthiness and preparation required of those who go there, the temple ceremonies would not be quickly understood and might be quite misunderstood. Therefore I am content with the restrictions the Lord has placed on them.

While we cannot discuss in detail the temple ordinances and ceremonies, there is much we *can* discuss in this book—and we will.

But the anointing which ye have received of him abideth in you, and ye need not that any man teach you: but as the same anointing teacheth you of all things, and is truth, and is no lie, and even as it hath taught you, ye shall abide in him.
(1 John 2:27.)

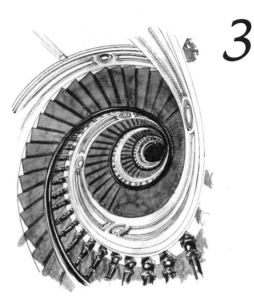

3

Taught from on High

Come to the temple to learn. The temple is a great school. It is a house of learning. In the temples the atmosphere is maintained so that it is ideal for instruction on matters that are deeply spiritual. The late Dr. John A. Widtsoe of the Quorum of the Twelve was a distinguished university president and a world-renowned scholar in his field. He had great reverence for temple work and said on one occasion:

The temple ordinances encompass the whole plan of salvation, as taught from time to time by the leaders of the Church, and elucidate matters difficult of understanding. There is no warping or twisting in fitting the temple teachings into the great scheme of salvation. The philosophical completeness of the endowment is one of the great arguments for the veracity of the temple ordinances.

Moreover, this completeness of survey and expounding of the Gospel plan, makes temple worship one of the most effective methods in refreshing the memory concerning the whole structure of the gospel.

Another fact has always appealed to me as a strong internal evidence for the truth of temple work. The endowment and the temple work as revealed by the Lord to the Prophet Joseph Smith fall clearly into four distinct parts: The preparatory ordinances; the giving of instruction by lectures and representations; covenants; and, finally, tests of knowledge. I doubt that the Prophet Joseph Smith, unlearned and untrained in logic, could of himself have made the thing so logically complete. (John A. Widtsoe, "Temple Worship," *The Utah Genealogical and Historical Magazine* 12 [April 1921]: 58.)

Temple Instruction Symbolic

Before going to the temple for the first time, or even after many times, it may help you to realize that the teaching of the temples is done in symbolic fashion. The Lord, the Master Teacher, gave much of His instruction in this way. That is why there is so much in the scriptures. That is why there is so much in the New Testament. That is why the teachings have so many applications to so many facets of our lives.

Many years ago I taught seminary with President Abel S. Rich. He was the second seminary teacher hired in the Church and was an authority on the gospel, well-versed in the scriptures. He had been a stake president, a mission president, and a community leader. He had taught the Book of Mormon for thirty-six years and had read it many, many times from cover to cover. He had read in and quoted from it frequently.

We shared an office at the seminary building. As a new teacher I needed careful preparation and would come an hour, sometimes two, before the opening of school to get my lessons in order. He invariably had preceded me there. During that fall he was reading the Book of Mormon again. I had difficulty in preparing my lessons because he would interrupt me. "Listen to this!" he would say, with some excitement in his voice. And then he would read a passage from the Book of Mormon. "Isn't that marvelous!" he would exclaim. "I wonder when they put that in there?"

It was a new book to him and it will be new as many times as any of us can read it, for the scope of it touches the eternities.

The temple ceremony is like that. It constantly is renewing itself in the minds of those who participate. Have you ever wondered why it is that many patrons of the temple can go session after session, week after week, month after month, year after year, and never become bored or tired or resistant? At the end of that time they are quite as anxious to go as they were in their beginning days.

That is a testimony indeed. By that time, you might imagine, they could have the entire endowment memorized. Yes, they could, and I suppose some of them do, particularly those who are temple workers. How, then, could they continue to learn? The answer to that lies in the fact that the teaching in the temple is symbolic. As we grow and mature and learn from all of the experiences in life, the truths demonstrated in the temple in symbolic fashion take on a renewed meaning. The veil is drawn back a little bit more. Our knowledge and vision of the eternities expands. It is always refreshing.

To quote again from Elder Widtsoe's article:

> The wonderful pedagogy of the temple service, especially appealing to me as a professional teacher, carries with it evidence of the truth of temple work. We go to the temple to be informed and directed, to be built up and to be blessed. How is all this accomplished? First by the spoken word, through the lectures and conversations, just as we do in the class room, except with more elaborate care, then by the appeal to the eye by representations by living, moving beings; and by pictorial representations [and, we would now add, filmed presentations] in the wonderfully decorated rooms. . . . Meanwhile the recipients themselves, the candidates for blessings, engage actively in the temple service. . . . Altogether our temple worship follows a most excellent pedagogical system. I wish instruction were given so well in every school room throughout the land, for we would then teach with more effect than we now do.

For these reasons, among many others, I've always felt that temple work is a direct evidence of the truth of the work reestablished by the Prophet Joseph Smith. It may be that the temple endowment and the other temple ordinances form the strongest available evidence of the divine inspiration of the Prophet Joseph Smith. ("Temple Worship," page 59.)

Spiritual truths are sometimes very difficult to teach. The most conclusive certification of man's intelligence is his ability to re-create in symbolic form the world in which he lives. He has produced the alphabet of the language, which is a system for sound and for writing. Through it he is able to write and then to read his writing. He can also verbalize the symbols and write and read and speak — all in symbols. But in using the symbols of language we become used to restricting some things to dimensions. We convey ideas by describing them in terms of size, shape, color, texture, weight, position, and a number of other features.

The reason the teaching of the gospel ofttimes is so difficult is that ideals in the gospel are such intangible things as faith, repentance, love, humility, reverence, obedience, modesty, and so forth. The dimensions of size and shape and color and texture just do not serve us there.

In teaching the gospel we do not re-create the material world around us; we deal with the intangible world within us. It is far easier to re-create the visible, tangible world around us in alphabetical symbols than to re-create the spiritual ideals and have them understood. And yet it can be done, and it can be done most effectively by using symbols.

Again quoting from Elder Widtsoe's comments:

We live in a world of symbols. We know nothing, except by symbols. We make a few marks on a sheet of paper, and we say that they form a word, which stands for love, or hate, or charity, or God or eternity. The marks may not be very beautiful to the eye. No one finds fault with the symbols on the pages of a book because they are not as mighty in their own beauty as the things which they represent. We do not quarrel with the symbol G-O-D because it is not very beautiful, yet represents the majesty of God. We are glad to have symbols, if only the meaning of the symbols is brought home to us. I speak to you tonight; you have not quarreled very much with my manner of delivery, or my choice of words; in following the meaning of the thoughts I have tried to bring home to you, you have forgotten words and manner. There are men who object to Santa Claus, because he does not exist! Such men need spectacles to see that Santa Claus is a symbol; a symbol of the love and joy of Christmas and the Christmas spirit. In the land of my birth there was no Santa Claus, but a little goat was shoved into the room, carrying with it a basket of Christmas toys and gifts. The goat of itself counted for nothing; but the Christmas spirit, which it symbolized, counted for a tremendous lot.

We live in a world of symbols. No man or woman can come out of the temple endowed as he should be, unless he has seen, beyond the symbol, the mighty realities for which the symbols stand. ("Temple Worship," page 62.)

If you will go to the temple and remember that the teaching is symbolic you will never go in the proper spirit without coming away with your vision extended, feeling a little more exalted, with your knowledge increased as to things that are spiritual. The teaching plan is superb. It is inspired. The Lord Himself, the Master Teacher, in His own teaching to His disciples taught constantly in parables, a verbal way to represent symbolically things that might otherwise be difficult to understand. He talked of the common experiences drawn from the lives of His disciples, and He told of hens and chickens, birds, flowers, foxes, trees, burglars, highwaymen, sunsets, the rich and the poor, the physician, patching clothes, pulling weeds, sweeping the house, feeding pigs, threshing grain, storing into barns, building houses, hiring help, and dozens of other things. He talked of the mustard seed, of the pearl. He wanted to teach his hearers, so he talked of simple things in a symbolic sense. None of these things is mysterious or obscure, and all of them are symbolic.

Light and Truth from Temple Ceremony

The temple ceremony will not be understood at first experience. It will be partly understood. Return again and again and again. Return to learn. Things that have troubled you or things that have been puzzling or things that have been mysterious will become known to you. Many of them will be the quiet, personal things that you really cannot explain to anyone else. But to you they are things known.

In the temple we face the sunlight of truth. The light of the temple, that understanding, shines upon us as does the light of the sun. And the shadows of sin and ignorance and error, of disappointment and failure, fall behind us. Nowhere quite equals the temple.

I learned something about our responsibility as patrons of the temple from an experience I have recorded elsewhere:

> A number of years ago I served on a stake high council in Brigham City. On one occasion the stake presidency and members of the high council and their wives attended an evening temple session in the Logan Temple. One of the workers was participating in the instruction for the first time and did very poorly. He had difficulty in remembering his part and was obviously nervous and flustered. He mixed up his presentation in a way that in other places would have been considered humorous. He struggled through, however, and was gently coached and corrected by those who were with him. As much dignity and reverence was maintained as would be possible considering his difficulty.
>
> After the session was over, the brethren from the stake presidency and the high council were standing on the walkway from the temple, waiting for our wives to meet us. One of the brethren commented in some amusement that he surely wouldn't have wanted to be that man, that night. "He really went through an ordeal," he said. "It was like being put on trial before all those people."
>
> President Vernal Willey, characteristically a quiet man, said with some firmness, "Hold on, brethren, let's get one thing straight here. It wasn't that man that was on trial here tonight. We were." (*Teach Ye Diligently* [Salt Lake City: Deseret Book Co., 1975], page 288.)

What we gain *from* the temple will depend to a large degree on what we take *to* the temple in the way of humility and reverence and a desire to learn. If we are teachable we will be taught by the Spirit, in the temple.

The temple itself becomes a symbol. If you have seen one of the temples at night, fully lighted, you know what an impressive sight that can be. The house of the Lord, bathed in light, standing out in the darkness, becomes symbolic of the power and the inspiration of the gospel of Jesus Christ standing as a beacon in a world that sinks ever further into spiritual darkness.

That light is symbolic too of another kind of light — spiritual light. The first temple to be dedicated in this dispensation was that in Kirtland, Ohio. It had been built at great cost and sacrifice to the relatively small number of members of the Church in that day. The design of the temple was preliminary. It was built as a house wherein the Lord could reveal Himself to His servants, where other heavenly beings could restore priesthood keys essential to the salvation of mankind, and where the faithful Saints would be blessed with an increase of spiritual power and enlightenment. The dedication of the temple was attended by a marvelous spiritual manifestation, some features of which were witnessed by many who were not members of the Church.

There are in the standard works no fewer than 128 references to *light* used symbolically to represent things that are spiritual. Here are samples from each of the standard works. From the Old Testament:

> Thy word is a lamp unto my feet, and a light unto my path. (Psalm 119:105.)

> The Lord is my light and my salvation; whom shall I fear? the Lord is the strength of my life; of whom shall I be afraid? (Psalm 27:1.)

In the New Testament, perhaps the classic reference is in John:

> Then spake Jesus again unto them, saying, I am the light of the world: he that followeth me shall not walk in darkness, but shall have the light of life. (John 8:12.)

From the Doctrine and Covenants:

> Behold, I am Jesus Christ, the Son of God. I am the life and the light of the world. (D&C 11:28.)

> The glory of God is intelligence, or, in other words, light and truth. Light and truth forsake that evil one.

Every spirit of man was innocent in the beginning; and God having redeemed man from the fall, men became again, in their infant state, innocent before God.

And that wicked one cometh and taketh away light and truth, through disobedience, from the children of men, and because of the tradition of their fathers.

But I have commanded you to bring up your children in light and truth. (D&C 93:36-40.)

From the Book of Mormon:

And I will also be your light in the wilderness; and I will prepare the way before you, if it so be that ye shall keep my commandments; wherefore, inasmuch as ye shall keep my commandments ye shall be led towards the promised land; and ye shall know that it is by me that ye are led. (1 Nephi 17:13.)

For the reward of their pride and their foolishness they shall reap destruction; for because they yield unto the devil and choose works of darkness rather than light, therefore they must go down to hell. (2 Nephi 26:10.)

Of the many references to light contained in the Pearl of Great Price, none is more symbolic than the light that attended the Father and the Son in the First Vision, a light that caused the suffocating darkness to release the boy Prophet and to depart.

We frequently talk in the Church of the light of revelation, the light of inspiration, the light of the gospel, the light of truth, the light of testimony, the inner light; all in an effort to use something we know — physical light and darkness — to stand symbolically for spiritual things that are otherwise difficult to describe. The light of the temple fits well into such manner of teaching. Although the temple is but a building framed up of the same materials used to build other buildings, it is not the same. It is separated from all of the others by the intensity of the light of which we have been speaking.

How much spiritual light we may absorb as part of the learning process depends on our receptivity. The Prophet Joseph Smith described the challenge of teaching the Saints concerning spiritual matters relating to the sacred work we are discussing.

But there has been a great difficulty in getting anything into the heads of this generation. It has been like splitting hemlock knots with a corn-dodger for a wedge, and a pumpkin for a beetle. Even the Saints are slow to understand.

I have tried for a number of years to get the minds of the Saints prepared to receive the things of God; but we frequently see some of them, after suffering all they have for the work of God, will fly to pieces like glass as soon as anything comes that is contrary to their traditions: they cannot stand the fire at all. How many will be able to abide a celestial law, and go through and receive their exaltation, I am unable to say, as many are called, but few are chosen. (*HC*, 6:184-85.)

We are now more than a century removed from 1844, when the Prophet gave that appraisal, and we have had the benefit of further revelations since that time plus a climate of their acceptance by Church members. We also now have the temple and all that means in our learning experience. Interestingly, not only spiritual but also what we think of as temporal learning develops in us through the temple experience. The instruction given in the endowment provides a firm perspective, a point of reference by which a person may gauge all his learning and wisdom, both spiritual and temporal; by which he may gather things together, determine their true meaning and significance, and fit them into their proper places.

It is at the temple that we may begin to see into the eternities. Go to the temple to learn, and you will be fulfilling on your part the commandment given by the Lord when He said:

And I give unto you, who are the first laborers in this last kingdom, a commandment that you assemble yourselves together, and organize yourselves, and prepare yourselves, and sanctify yourselves; yea, purify your hearts, and cleanse your hands and your feet before me, that I may make you clean;

That I may testify unto your Father, and your God, and my God, that you are clean from the blood of this wicked generation; that I may fulfil this promise, this great and last promise, which I have made unto you, when I will.

Also, I give unto you a commandment that ye shall continue in prayer and fasting from this time forth.

And I give unto you a commandment that you shall teach one another the doctrine of the kingdom.

Teach ye diligently and my grace shall attend you, that you may be instructed more perfectly in theory, in principle, in doctrine, in the law of the gospel, in all things that pertain unto the kingdom of God, that are expedient for you to understand;

Of things both in heaven and in the earth, and under the earth; things which have been, things which are, things which must shortly come to pass; things which are at home, things which are abroad; the wars and the perplexities of the nations, and the judgments which are on the land; and a knowledge also of countries and of king-doms —

That ye may be prepared in all things when I shall send you again to magnify the calling whereunto I have called you, and the mission with which I have commissioned you. (D&C 88:74-80.)

In observing this commandment you will be seeking out light and truth for yourself and your family. "The glory of God is intelligence, or, in other words, light and truth. Light and truth forsake that evil one." And again, "I have commanded you to bring up your children in light and truth." (D&C 93: 36-37, 40.)

This light and truth is knowledge from on high. When you have the opportunity to attend an endowment session in the temple or to witness a sealing, ponder the deeper meaning of what you see demonstrated before you. And in the days following your visit keep these things on your mind; quietly and prayerfully review them and you will find that your knowledge will increase. Remember the statement by the Prophet Joseph Smith, "A man is saved no faster than he gets knowledge." (*HC*, 4:588.) And, of course, he particularly meant gospel knowledge.

When I taught the Church History course in seminary I learned that the most useful procedure was to present during the first week of school the entire course in brief form. This consisted of a concise discussion of the ministry of Christ, the great apostasy, the restoration of the gospel, the early days of the Church, the persecutions of the Saints, the ultimate move west to the valleys of the mountains, and the expansion of the Church from there throughout the world. This touched in abridged form all we would consider during the course. I learned from the students that, when we followed this procedure, during the year they always knew where we were. They knew where any lesson fit into the great panorama of events.

One of the great values of the temple experience is that it does the same thing with our lives. It presents the broad, sweeping panorama of God's purposes relating to this earth. Once we have been through the temple (and we can return and refresh our memories) the events of life fit into the scheme of things. We can see in perspective where we are, and we can quickly see when we are off course.

So look toward the temple. Point your children toward the temple. From the days of their infancy, direct their attention to it, and begin their preparation for the day when they may enter the holy temple.

Meantime, be teachable yourself, be reverent. Drink deeply from the teachings—the symbolic, deeply spiritual teachings—available only in the temple.

Be ye clean, that bear the vessels of the Lord.
(D&C 38:42; 133:5; 3 Nephi 20:41; Isaiah 52:11.)

4

Worthy to Enter

Once you have some feeling for the value of temple blessings and for the sacredness of the ordinances performed in the temple, you would be hesitant to question the high standards set by the Lord for entrance into the holy temple.

You must possess a current recommend to be admitted to the temple. This recommend must be signed by the bishop of your ward and the president of your stake. In the mission field, of course, the branch president, the district president, and the mission president have responsibility for issuing temple recommends. Only those who are worthy should go to the temple. The bishop has the responsibility of making inquiries into our personal worthiness. This interview is of great importance to you as a member of the Church, for it is an occasion to explore with an ordained servant of the Lord the pattern of your life. If anything is amiss in your life, the bishop will be able to help you resolve it. Through this procedure, as you counsel with the common judge in Israel, you can declare or can be helped to establish your worthiness to enter the temple with the Lord's approval.

The interview should be private in each instance. The bishop and stake president are reminded that in conducting these interviews they should realize and make it clear that they are representing the Lord in determining the worthiness of individuals to enter His holy house.

The Temple Recommend Interview

President N. Eldon Tanner, first counselor in the First Presidency, spoke to the general priesthood meeting about interviews. His counsel has meaning both for the Church leaders who conduct the interview and for the members who are to be interviewed. Consider carefully this counsel:

> With all this evil present in the world today, it is most important that those who are responsible conduct proper interviews.
>
> Let us always remember that our main purpose, assignment, and responsibility is to save souls.
>
> It is important that those we interview realize that they are *spirit children of God* and that *we love them,* and *let them know that we love them* and are interested in their welfare and in helping them succeed in life.
>
> It is a great responsibility for a bishop or a stake president to conduct a worthiness interview. There is equal responsibility, however, upon the member who is interviewed. Careful, searching interviews need to be conducted always individually and privately. . . .
>
> Let [the member] know that if there is something amiss in his life, there are ways to straighten it out. There is a great cleansing power of repentance. . . .
>
> Remember, the interview is based on consideration, on sympathy and love. This is so important. Let the people know we love them and are only trying to help them.
>
> You bishops and stake presidents might approach an interview for a temple recommend something like this:

"You have come to me for a recommend to enter the temple. I have the responsibility of representing the Lord in interviewing you. At the conclusion of the interview there is provision for me to sign your recommend; but mine is not the only important signature on your recommend. Before the recommend is valid, you must sign it yourself.

"When you sign your recommend, you make a commitment to the Lord that you are worthy of the privileges granted to those who hold such a recommend. There are several standard questions that I will ask [because you are instructed to do that]. You are to respond honestly to each one."

An associate of mine mentioned that some years ago, when he held a position in his ward, he went to the bishop for a temple recommend.

The bishop was busy and said, "Now, I know you very well, and I will not have to ask you the questions before signing your recommend."

This member responded: "Bishop, don't you have the responsibility to ask those questions? It is my privilege to answer them. I need to answer those questions to you and to the Lord and would appreciate your putting each question to me."

And so it is. The Lord gives the privilege to members of the Church to respond to those questions in such interviews. Then if there is something amiss, the member can get his life in order so that he may qualify for the priesthood advancement, for a mission, or for a temple recommend.

Now, after you have put those required questions to the applicant, you may wish to add something like this: "One who goes into the house of the Lord must be free from any *unclean, unholy, impure, or unnatural practice.*"

. . . We who lead the Church are responsible to see that you are taught in plainness. . . .

Surely no holder of the priesthood would feel worthy to accept advancement in the priesthood or sign his temple recommend if any impure practice were a part of his life.

If, perchance, one of you has been drawn into any degrading conduct, cast it away from you so that when you are subject to a worthiness interview you can answer to yourself, and to the Lord, and to the interviewing priesthood officer that you are worthy.

Remember, you who conduct worthiness interviews are representatives of the Lord and you must conduct the interviews as the Lord himself would conduct them.

That is, there must be nothing immodest or degrading in your interview. Our interviews are not to be indelicate, or offensive, or pornographic in any way.

May I say here that occasionally we receive reports that a bishop or a stake president has been very indiscreet or indelicate in an interview, especially of married members.

It is not in order for a priesthood leader to list in detail ugly, deviant, or bestial practices and then cross-examine a member of the Church as to whether or not such things are practiced.

One of the General Authorities once interviewed a young man who had gone into the mission home who had made confession of a transgression which disqualified him from missionary service.

The General Authority was amazed at the sordid nature of what the young man had done and asked, "Where on earth did you get the idea to do things like this?" He was shocked when the young man answered, "From my bishop."

During a preliminary interview for the young man's mission, the bishop had said, "Have you ever done this? Have you ever done that?" describing every unworthy and depraved act he could think of. Such things had never before entered the young man's mind, but they were in his mind now! The adversary put in his way the opportunity and the temptation — and he fell!

Brethren, our interviews must be conducted in love, in modesty. Ofttimes things can be corrected if you ask: "Would there be a reason you may feel uncomfortable or perhaps even dishonest to the Lord if you were to sign your own temple recommend?

"Would you like a little time to get some very personal things in order before you sign it? Remember, the Lord knows all things and will not be mocked. We are trying to help you. Never lie to try to obtain a call, a recommend, or a blessing from the Lord."

If you approach the matter as outlined above, the member has the responsibility to interview himself. The bishop or stake president has the right to the power of discernment. He will know whether or not there is something amiss that ought to be settled before a recommend is issued.

How blessed we are to have the gift of discernment available to us as officers in the priesthood!

On occasion a bishop or a stake president will receive a confession from a member of the Church concerning a transgression that took place many, many years ago. That individual should have made confession long since but did not and, therefore, has suffered unnecessarily.

It is not always necessary to conduct a court in such cases. That is up to the bishop. You are entitled to inspiration and guidance, particularly if the individual has demonstrated through his conduct over the years that that mistake is not characteristic of his life.

How marvelous that inspiration and revelation may accompany us in our duties! Brethren, be worthy of that.

We frequently hear accounts of how bishops and stake presidents, motivated by consideration and love, have been inspired in conducting interviews and have been able, where problems were present, to help members of the Church correct their course in life so that they became completely worthy to fulfill missions, to be advanced in the priesthood, or to enter the house of the Lord. And that's what we are trying to do — help . . . through love and understanding and interest, to do those things which are necessary in their lives for them to enjoy the blessings of the faithful.

Again I say, what a blessing that we have discernment and revelation and inspiration to guide us in our main purpose, which is to save souls, yes, even our own, and to help prepare our members to understand the purpose of their mission here upon the earth, and to prepare themselves to go back into the presence of our Heavenly Father! ("The Blessing of Church Interviews," *Ensign* [November 1978]: 40-43.)

The interview for a temple recommend is conducted privately between the bishop and the Church member concerned. Here the member is asked searching questions about his personal conduct and worthiness and about his loyalty to the Church and its officers. The person must certify that he is morally clean and is keeping the Word of Wisdom, paying a full tithing, living in harmony with the teachings of the Church, and not maintaining any affiliation or sympathy with apostate groups. The bishop is instructed that confidentiality in handling these matters with each interviewee is of the utmost importance.

Acceptable answers to the bishop's questions will ordinarily establish the worthiness of an individual to receive a temple recommend. If an applicant is not keeping the commandments or there is something unsettled about his life that needs putting in order, it will be necessary for him to demonstrate true repentance before a temple recommend is issued.

Benefits of the Interview

Members of the Church might well cherish the great privilege of going before the bishop for an interview — and not just when everything is all right, when you can say with a deep personal satisfaction that your life is in order. Particularly is this a privilege when some things are not right and there is an opportunity for a member of the Church to put his life in order.

> Wash you, make you clean; put away the evil of your doings from before mine eyes; cease to do evil;
>
> Learn to do well; seek judgment, relieve the oppressed, judge the fatherless, plead for the widow.
>
> Come now, and let us reason together, saith the Lord: though your sins be as scarlet, they shall be as white as snow; though they be red like crimson, they shall be as wool. (Isaiah 1:16-18.)

Sometimes it is difficult to talk about mistakes. But it is a great blessing in the Church for us to have the privilege of cleansing ourselves. One of the steps of repentance is to make proper confession, confession to the Lord in the normal course. And there are some things where confession to the bishop is a requirement.

Repentance is something like soap. It can cleanse us from our transgressions. Yet some people stay unclean when it is not necessary to do so.

What a privilege it is to be able to go to the bishop for a temple recommend! If we are fully repentant, it is an opportunity to put out from our lives things that may be amiss.

After the bishop has conducted such an interview, a member of the stake presidency likewise interviews each of us before we go to the temple. If we are going for the first time, ordinarily the stake president personally conducts the interview. It may be, on subsequent occasions, that he must delegate to one of his counselors that responsibility in order to attend to the many duties connected with presiding over the several thousand members in the stake.

I have come to know, in interviewing people who have made mistakes in their lives, that a very convincing evidence of repentance is that they are willing to do whatever is required of them. Occasionally, when a bishop is hesitant to issue a temple recommend, a member will resist the bishop and perhaps argue with him. That very attitude is a signal that the bishop may well need to consider very, very carefully whether or not someone with that spirit should be given the privilege of entering the house of the Lord. It indicates that member may not be quite ready.

Surely, when you appear to be interviewed for a temple recommend you would accept the judgment of him who is designated as the judge in Israel, who is responsible to represent the Lord in determining whether or not it is proper for you to enter this sacred place.

President John Taylor counseled members to consider very seriously the matter of worthiness interviews. Note that in his day, besides the bishop and the stake president, a member also had to be approved by the President of the Church before being admitted to the temple.

> In the first place people desirous to go and attend to ordinances in these houses must have a recommendation from their Bishop. That is one of those. . . . facts that must be faced. Then when they have obtained this recommendation from the Bishop, it must be endorsed by the President of the Stake, and after that have the sanction of the President of the Church. This is quite an ordeal for many men to go through. For men and women who are upright, virtuous and honorable, it is a very simple matter; there is no difficulty in their way at any time; but to those who have been careless of their duties, who have departed from the laws of God, and who have tampered with, or violated the ordinances of the Gospel — to such people it is a critical time.
>
> However, there is something far more difficult than that yet to come. That is only a starting point in these matters. The things that are ahead are a great deal more difficult to accomplish. What are they? The time will come when we shall not only have to pass by those officers whom I have referred to — say, to have the sanction and approval of our Bishop, of the President of the Stake and of the President of the Church — but we are told in this book [the Book of Doctrine and Covenants] that we shall have to pass by the angels and the Gods. We may have squeezed through the other; we may

have got along tolerably well, and been passed and acted upon, and sometimes a "tight squeak" at that; but how will it be when we get on the other side, and we have the angels and the Gods to pass by before we can enter into our exaltation? If we cannot pass, what then? Well, we cannot, that is all. And if we cannot, shall we be able to enter into our exaltation? I think not. What do you think about it? (*The Gospel Kingdom*, comp. G. Homer Durham [Salt Lake City: Bookcraft, 1964], pages 290-91.)

Be grateful for the lofty standards of the Church. Remember the admonition of the Lord through the prophet Isaiah (52:11): "Be ye clean, that bear the vessels of the Lord."

Enter this door as if the floor within were gold;
And every wall of jewels all of wealth untold;
As if a choir in robes of fire were singing here;
Nor shout nor rush but hush . . . for God is here.
(From "Words of Life," page 45.)

5

First and Every Time

You may be preparing to go to the temple for the first time to receive your endowments. This may precede your temple marriage. It may be that you are returning to witness the marriage of a loved one. It may be that you are returning to do ordinance work for the dead. Whatever your circumstance may be, there are some practical things that you may wish to consider and some principles that may help you as you go there.

Because we sometimes overlook the obvious, I wish to point out several things that may seem to be very ordinary. However, consider these suggestions on deportment for temple attenders. If you need to make some improvement in your attitude or in your conduct, seek to put yourself in the proper spirit for temple blessings.

If you are going to the temple for the first time it is quite normal for you to be a little unsettled. We are naturally anxious about the unknown. We often become nervous over new experiences.

Be at peace. You are going to the temple. You will have someone to assist you at every turn. You will be carefully guided—be at peace.

Deportment in the Temple

When we enter the temple we should be reverent. Any conversations that are necessary ought to be conducted in very subdued tones. During the periods of instruction, of course, we are completely reverent and quiet.

There are few places now that offer an opportunity to meditate in quiet reverence. Before entering the temple to begin the ordinance work, the companies frequently will assemble in the chapel in the annex portion of the building. Here the members wait until the full company is assembled. Generally in life we would become impatient with waiting. To be first in a room and then be compelled to wait for the last to enter before proceeding would in other circumstances cause irritation. In the temple it is just the opposite. That waiting is regarded as a choice opportunity. What a privilege it is to sit quietly without conversation and direct the mind to reverent and spiritual thoughts! It is a refreshment to the soul.

Temples have become very busy places. As the Church grows, and more members come to receive their own ordinances or to participate in work for the dead, the temple may become a bit crowded. Surely no one would say "overcrowded!" In these circumstances the management of a temple becomes an increasingly important function. It requires that every person entering the temple contribute by responding to directions—by refraining from conversations, by acting in a reverent and disciplined fashion. The word *discipline* sometimes touches a slightly rebellious chord in our natures. Remember that it comes from the word *disciple*.

President Harold B. Lee was a man of quiet response to things that were humorous. Yet he enjoyed a very alert sense of humor and always had a ready story with some humorous twist to it. On one occasion while I was traveling with him he said that Elder Charles A. Callis had told him many years ago that loud laughter was a symptom of a vacant mind. He said, "I took that seriously, and since then I've tried to respond more quietly when I have been amused, not with an outburst of laughter."

When you come to the temple, remember that you are a guest in the house of the Lord. It is a time of joy, but a time of quiet joy. Sometimes when I perform a temple marriage it is necessary to remind the relatives and friends that their expressions of love and congratulations, and their greetings to family members whom they have not seen for a long period of time, should be given in a very quiet and subdued tone. Loud talking and loud laughter are not fitting in the house of the Lord.

Consider these verses from section 88 of the Doctrine and Covenants:

> Remember the great and last promise which I have made unto you; cast away your idle thoughts and your excess of laughter far from you. (D&C 88:69.)

> Therefore, cease from all your light speeches, from all laughter, from all your lustful desires, from all your pride and light-mindedness, and from all your wicked doings. (D&C 88:121.)

Accept the direction of the workers in the temple. Someone will guide you as you proceed.

Occasionally a Church member will ask for special privileges or adjustments in temple procedure, or for special people to attend him. Remember that the temple is a place for complete unselfishness and cooperation. Let your visit there be on the Lord's terms rather than on yours.

Sometimes a member coming to the temple has requested administration for an infirmity or sickness. The member may feel that a blessing given in the temple will somehow be more powerful than a blessing given at the chapel or in a home. But this is not the purpose of the temples. Administrations to those who are sick or otherwise afflicted will be quite as powerful and effective if given in a home or at the chapel as they would be in the temple. The Brethren in times past have suggested that members not come to the temple for their administrations.

Occasionally members will ask special privileges at the temple, wanting to be together as a family or as a couple in one of the rooms for very private prayer and contemplation. These purposes also can be accomplished outside of the temple. With temples busily but reverently moving the companies through the ordinance work, such special requests would be difficult to honor. The fact that a person's quiet personal purposes can be achieved outside of the temple should be the consideration in this context.

Appropriate Authority Should Perform Ordinance

This matter of asking for special consideration or accommodation at the temple brings to mind a principle. Members who come to temples near Church headquarters frequently write or call General Authorities asking if they will perform the marriage ceremony. It seems they feel that there would somehow be additional authority and the ordinance would somehow be more binding in that case, or that there is additional prestige or perhaps honor attached to having the marriage ceremony pronounced by one of "the Brethren."

When I was first called as a General Authority it was a common thing for the Brethren to spend a good portion of their time in the temple performing temple marriages. As the Church grew, the General Authorities received additional responsibilities. In those days there were only two or three overseas stakes; now there are hundreds. It became more and more difficult to schedule marriages without conflicting with other meetings that we were required to attend. We found that many members of the Church were anxious to have a General Authority perform their sealings.

I was quite relieved when we had a letter from the First Presidency suggesting that the General Authorities leave the performing of sealing ordinances to the regularly ordained temple sealers. We were, of course, free to perform those for our own families and for others who may be very close to us for one reason or another. But we were counseled that our other duties were to take precedence over performing temple marriages. In that way the vital meetings held at Church headquarters were not constantly interrupted, as previously they had been.

We have been reminded of this counsel a time or two in the years since then, and a letter has been sent to the areas surrounding Church headquarters asking that members not request the General Authorities to perform their temple marriages. This instruction has been a disappointment to some who have been anxious that some "favorite" General Authority perform the marriage in their case.

This desire to have the "highest" possible official perform an ordinance—a General Authority or a temple president—brings us to a principle important for every member of the Church to learn. It applies to temples, as it applies to all of the ordinances of the Church. Perhaps we can illustrate it best by discussing the ordinance of administering to the sick.

The revelation says:

> And whosoever among you are sick, and have not faith to be healed, but believe, shall be nourished with all tenderness, with herbs and mild food, and that not by the hand of an enemy.
>
> And the elders of the church, two or more, shall be called, and shall pray for and lay their hands upon them in my name; and if they die they shall die unto me, and if they live they shall live unto me. (D&C 42:43-44; see also D&C 66:9; 84:68; 124:98.)

In times of need, members of the Church naturally want the highest spiritual power available to them. It is natural for them, if they are close to Church headquarters or in a country where one of the General Authorities is a resident, to call upon them to perform the blessing, or to want the stake president or mission president or bishop to bless them.

Many years ago, long before I was one of the General Authorities of the Church, I had something to do with the construction of a chapel. President McKay had accepted the invitation to dedicate the building. (This, too, is another of the functions of Church authorities that is subject to the principle we are discussing.)

During the dedication, a young person who was critically ill and not expected to live was brought to the chapel and carried into one of the rooms. When the service was over a relative of the individual approached President McKay and explained the unfortunate plight of this person and asked if the President would give him a blessing.

I was standing with President McKay. Elder Spencer W. Kimball also was present. To my surprise, President McKay said, "Dear sister, if I performed all of the blessings for the sick that I am requested to do, I would not have the time nor the strength to do those things that only I can do with the authority of the office that I hold." He then turned to one of the local leaders and appointed him to give the blessing.

Although he was very kindly in his explanation and later extended a special blessing to the family, I did not understand why he declined to bless that person then. I thought he could almost have pronounced the blessing in the time it took to assign it to someone else. Why did he not do it?

As the years unfolded and I became more acquainted with Church administration, I learned. Indeed, it would be possible to fill the schedule of the President of the Church or other General Authorities with duties and responsibilities that many other holders of the priesthood could do quite as well. Some of them perhaps they could do even better. This is surely true when our local brethren are close to their people and know and understand their needs. Sometimes there are underlying needs that are not obvious to those who are not acquainted with the circumstances but are well understood by those who know the individuals concerned.

How glorious it is that the priesthood in the Lord's church is not confined to a few professional ministers who are trained in special seminaries and are thought to be the only ones competent to perform the sacred rites of the church!

Men are called from all walks of life who hold the priesthood and are given authority. Often they are unschooled, inexperienced, and certainly not trained in a professional ministry. That may seem dangerous to the prelates of the other churches and appear in their minds to be an awful problem fraught with the possibility of mismanagement and bungling of every kind. It is in truth a very strength to the Church. For the Lord said in the first section of the Doctrine and Covenants that it was His desire "that every man might speak in the name of God the Lord, even the Savior of the world" (verses 2 and 20).

In the Church, therefore, we are quite content to call Church members to office to administer and direct and teach and carry on the work of the Lord. Keep that principle in mind as you prepare to go to the temple. Keep it in mind after you have been there a hundred times or more. Remember, you may go to the temple for your own wedding, or for that of a son or a daughter or a grandchild, and find a very ordinary man, not distinguished by being prominent in the world, standing at the altar dressed in white, officiating in the most sacred ordinances of the gospel. This is the very strength and the power of the Church. The Church is not jeopardized by the standard the Lord has set. Indeed, to do the opposite would be dangerous, for we would be moving along that road that led to the great apostasy in ancient times.

The Temple Wedding

Let me include a few words of counsel to those planning to go to the temple to be married.

It takes time to plan a temple marriage. It is worthy of careful planning. Not infrequently young couples who fall in love determine that they are going to be married and insist, against the pleadings of parents, that they want to be married right away, in just a week or two. The plea by parents for more time to prepare is sometimes interpreted by the young couple as being a disapproval of their marriage. They are afraid that if they wait something will interfere. Some young couples show themselves to be very immature and unkind when they press for immediate arrangements that can be met only with great difficulty and often result in an experience that is much less memorable than it might have been under other circumstances.

I have observed that, if things are too hurried or too pressured, something seems missing from the first visit to the temple, or from the wedding day in the temple. This first time through the temple or the sealing on a wedding day is a once-in-a-lifetime experience. It is worth preparing for. It is so significant that we should not let the little details of preparation, the little housekeeping chores, detract from it. For that reason, everything should be done beforehand. It can be a great frustration for some essential thing to be left untended until that day.

Occasionally when I am invited to speak in a meeting I like to get to the building before the people begin to arrive. Generally there are a few early comers, then most of the people come gathering just a short time before the meeting is to commence. Some few rush in at the last minute, and always there are a few tardy ones. If you go to a meeting early and sit in the chapel quietly and watch the people arrive, you see that they bring something with them. The spiritual temperature warms up and the room is changed as it is transformed from an empty room to a congregation, an audience of brothers and sisters who have come with a sense of expectancy. I find that I make a better presentation when I can do this; that it is as though something is given me to make me more qualified and inspired.

Now, in our busy days we cannot always do this when going

to a meeting. But when I can I like to do it, and my family know that I am always quite restless to get there not just on time but early—and occasionally very early. It is because I am seeking something I need. And whatever is brought about by this approach to a meeting is doubly important when we go to the temple. This is especially true when we are going for the first time. We should get there early, very early.

As you see, this early attendance is not just for protection, for making sure that the recommends and other things are in order and that we can adapt ourselves to the new experience. It is more than that. It is to get into the right place in time to get calmly into the right spirit—to get ourselves prepared for what is to take place.

So when you go to the temple, be on time—in fact, be early. It is important.

We have been speaking in terms of the participants in the temple experience, but there are occasions when a temple wedding is being planned and some very close members of the family are not qualified for temple recommends. It may be that the groom or the bride is a convert and his or her parents are not yet in the Church; or, that they are too new in the Church to qualify for a temple recommend. Or it may be that the parents are members of the Church but one of them is not living the gospel standards sufficiently to receive a temple recommend. These limitations loom large at times of temple marriages. These are the times when families should be very close together, when they should be drawn together to share in these sacred moments of life. The withholding of a temple recommend to one who is not qualified, or the inability to invite a nonmember friend or relative to witness the sealing, can quickly present problems. This might cause unhappiness and contention at the very moment when there is a great need to have things serene, to have the greatest harmony.

What do we do in cases like that? I know what we would not do, and that is apply pressure upon a bishop. The bishop, by the standard he is obliged to keep as a common judge in Israel, could not in good faith issue a recommend to one not qualified. To do so could be a great disservice to the individuals involved. And it would not be fair to the bishop himself.

I repeat the statement, "I, the Lord, am bound when ye do what I say, but when ye do not what I say, ye have no promise." (D&C 82:10.)

When a temple marriage is scheduled and one of the parents or a very close relative is not able to enter the temple, careful planning may well make that an opportunity instead of a problem. Consider these suggestions. Invite the nonmember parent, or the member who is not eligible for a temple recommend, to come to the temple with the wedding party. There is a spirit and influence on the temple grounds that is not found in other places. Many of the temples have visitors centers. The temple grounds in every case are beautifully kept. All in all it is a place of peace and serenity.

Arrange to have someone wait with that family member. Surely you would not leave the person alone. I have known instances in which family members who were quite eligible to enter the temple to witness the marriage were content instead to spend the time on the temple grounds with those who could not. Here in the surroundings of the temple they have been able to explain the desire of the young couple to be sealed in the house of the Lord.

There can be great influence exerted at this time that may not have been possible otherwise. For instance, at some of the larger temples tours are conducted. Planning ahead may provide some special attention tailored to fit the need of a close family member who for one reason or another is not able to enter the temple. The disappointment and even resentment, sometimes bitterness, on the part of the nonmember parents or ineligible-member parents can be greatly softened in these ways.

The young couple must understand that their parents may have looked forward to the wedding day during the entire lives of the bride and groom. Their desire to attend the wedding, and their resentment when they cannot, is a sign of parental attachment. It is not to be resented by the young couple. It is to be understood and planned for carefully as a part of the wedding.

There are some cases of course in which the ineligible parent is offended and will not be placated. In those cases the young couple will just have to make the best of it. The question may come up: Well, then, should we be married civilly so that they can witness the marriage, then we would wait for the necessary year before entering the temple? But that would not be the ideal solution. Prayerful and careful planning in most cases can make the problem transform itself into an opportunity that ultimately will bring the family closer together than it previously had been.

Some years ago, when the General Authorities were more involved than now in performing temple marriages, a young couple from Brigham Young University called and asked if I would perform their marriage. I agreed to do so. A day or two later, they called to indicate that they were planning a double wedding. There were two young men who had been companions in the mission field and were very close to one another. They had determined that they would be married on the same day. They therefore had called to advise me that there would be two couples to be married on that occasion and they had called the temple to arrange for the largest sealing room.

I declined the invitation and said that I would prefer not to perform the double marriage. I pointed out that, while they were very close now, in the years ahead the two young men would find their separate ways as they went to seek their fortunes. They would keep in touch for the first few years, but as the children came and they became turned to normal life activities it was quite likely that their lives would find separate paths. I told them that in looking back on their wedding day they would want to remember it as a very personal and a very private matter. It should be shared only by the intimate family members and friends.

They were not responsive to that suggestion, and they called a day or so later saying that they had arranged for a second sealing room. Their idea was that, after one marriage ceremony had been performed, the wedding party could move in to be witnesses to the wedding in the other room. Again I declined, saying that I would prefer not to perform this sealing under those circumstances. I strongly recommended that each of them have a separate marriage ceremony, and that if they had it on the same morning they should not try to have one set to the time needs or to the circumstances that were important to the other. They finally agreed to comply with my counsel.

Some time ago a letter was issued from the Brethren suggesting that large groups of friends, ward members, and so on not be invited to witness a marriage. Wedding groups should be small, comprising only the members of the two families and some few who are very close to the couple. On occasions a wedding has been announced in the ward with the invitation that all should try to attend to give support and encouragement to the couple being married. That is what a reception is for. A wedding reception is to provide a time for greeting the friends and the well-wishers. The temple marriage itself should be sacred and should be shared only by those who have a very special place in the lives of those being married. In our own family, when our children have been married our wedding contingent has always been small even though we are a large family. The number of adults eligible to enter the temple has grown as our children have married. But even with our large family we have generally been able to perform our sealings in the smaller sealing rooms in the temple.

We do not quote the words of the sealing ordinance outside of the temple, but we may describe the sealing room as being beautiful in its appointment, quiet and serene in spirit, and hallowed by the sacred work that is performed there.

Before the couple comes to the altar for the sealing ordinance it is the privilege of the officiator to extend, and of the young couple to receive, some counsel. These are among the thoughts that a young couple might hear on this occasion.

"Today is your wedding day. You are caught up in the emotion of your marriage. Temples were built as a sanctuary for such ordinances as this. We are not in the world. The things of the world do not apply here and should have no influence upon what we do here. We have come out of the world into the temple of the Lord. This becomes the most important day of your lives.

"You were born, invited here by parents who prepared a mortal tabernacle for your spirit to inhabit. Each of you has been baptized. Baptism, a sacred ordinance, is symbolic of a cleansing, symbolic of death and resurrection, symbolic of coming forward in a newness of life. It contemplates repentance and a remission of sins. The sacrament is a renewal of the covenant of baptism, and we can, if we live for it, retain a remission of our sins.

"You, the groom, were ordained to the priesthood. You had first conferred upon you the Aaronic Priesthood and probably have progressed through all the offices thereof — deacon, teacher, and priest. Then the day came when you were found worthy to receive the Melchizedek Priesthood. That priesthood, the higher priesthood, is defined as the priesthood after the holiest order of God, or the Holy Priesthood after the Order of the Son of God. You were given an office in the priesthood. You are now an elder.

"Each of you has received your endowment. In that endowment you received an investment of eternal potential. But all of these things, in one sense, were preliminary and preparatory to your coming to the altar to be sealed as husband and wife for time and for all eternity. You now become a family, free to act in the creation of life, to have the opportunity through devotion and sacrifice to bring children into the world and to raise them and foster them safely through their mortal existence; to see them come one day, as you have come, to participate in these sacred temple ordinances.

"You come willingly and have been judged to be worthy. This union can be sealed by the Holy Spirit of Promise."

Wherefore, I now send upon you another Comforter, even upon you my friends, that it may abide in your hearts, even the Holy Spirit of promise; which other Comforter is the same that I promised unto my disciples, as is recorded in the testimony of John.

This Comforter is the promise which I give unto you of eternal life, even the glory of the celestial kingdom. (D&C 88:3-4.)

"To accept one another in the marriage covenant is a great responsibility, one that carries with it blessings without measure."

A bride and groom will quite likely be so emotionally involved with the wedding that they may not listen carefully — they may not really hear the words of the sealing ordinance. While we may not repeat those words outside of the temple, we may return on occasions to witness a wedding. It is a generous Lord who has authorized us to do this. On these occasions, when we are not so personally involved, we may listen carefully to the words of the ordinance.

Come to the temple. Renew the instruction given there. This is a blessing which you may claim in the holy temple.

*For he hath clothed me with the garments of
salvation, he hath covered me with the robe of
righteousness.*
(Isaiah 61:10.)

6

Dressed in White

When we do ordinance work in the temple we wear white
clothing. This clothing is symbolic of purity and worthiness and
cleanliness.

Upon entering the temple you exchange your street clothing
for the white clothing of the temple. This change of clothing takes
place in the locker room, where each individual is provided with
a locker and a dressing space that is completely private. In the
temple the ideal of modesty is carefully maintained. As you put
your clothing in the locker you leave your cares and concerns and
distractions there with them. You step out of this private little
dressing area dressed in white and you feel a oneness and a sense of
equality, for all around you are similarly dressed.

If you are going to the temple for the first time, counsel with your bishop. When he issues you a recommend he will explain something of the nature of the clothing that will be required in the temple. Obtaining this clothing need not be a worry to you. You can either buy it from a Relief Society Distribution Center or rent it at the temple. In the latter case a very modest fee is required which covers only the cost of laundering the clothing.

As with the ceremonies and ordinances of the temple, outside of the temple we say very little about the clothing worn inside. We can say that it, like the ceremonies, has great symbolic meaning.

There are three main considerations for you which relate to clothing and the temples. First, there is the clothing that you wear, your own clothing, going to and coming from the temple. The image you present at this time, I'm sure, is important to the Lord. Your dress and grooming are signals as to how deeply you revere the privilege of going to the temple.

The next consideration is the temple clothing itself. As I have indicated, we will not discuss that here. When you are eligible to go to the temple your bishop can counsel with you on this matter.

The third matter is the garment worn at all times by those who are endowed. This we will discuss later in the chapter.

Proper Grooming for Temple Attenders

It is a mark of reverence and respect when the Church member visits the temple dressed and groomed in such a way that he would not be uncomfortable in the presence of the Lord. Suppose for a moment that you are invited to be the guest in the home of a prominent and highly respected leader. You are given to understand that you will mingle with distinguished guests who have received similar invitations. The invitation is an indication that the host holds you in very high regard. You realize that many others would highly prize such an invitation, but for one reason or another they have not likewise been invited and therefore are not able to attend. Under those circumstances I doubt that you would arrive in old work clothes or dressed as you do for recreation. I doubt that a man would go unshaven, or a woman with her hair unkempt.

People of dignity and refinement, upon receiving an invitation to an important gathering, frequently make inquiry as to what dress would be in order. Would you not prepare carefully for such a special occasion? You might even purchase new clothing in the hope that your appearance would not detract from the dignified nature of the setting.

Care would also be shown for the pressing and cleaning of your clothes. You would feel uncomfortable if you were not properly attired.

The opportunity to visit the temple might be compared to such an invitation.

There is one occasion only when members of the Church are invited into the temple proper in "street" clothing, and that is when they witness a temple marriage. In that case only the shoes are removed, and these are replaced with white footwear. Years ago the Brethren authorized this to be so for the convenience of those family members and friends who would not be going through an endowment session immediately prior to the marriage.

I have been puzzled and a little saddened at times, when attending the temple, to find that some have come to witness marriages or to attend a session in the temple dressed as though they were going to a picnic or an athletic event.

The privilege to enter the temple deserves more from us than that. I am sure that it is pleasing to the Lord when we bathe our bodies and put on clean clothing, however inexpensive the clothing may be. We should dress in such a way that we might comfortably attend a sacrament meeting or a gathering that is proper and dignified.

Some time ago on a cold winter morning I was on my way to the airport at a very early hour. I stopped at an intersection near the Salt Lake Temple. Although the light changed to green, I waited while a very old man laboriously made his way across the slick street; because of his crippled condition, the time allowed by the signal was not sufficient to see him across the street safely. He was carrying a small suitcase. Obviously he was going to the temple. I was impressed that he was a regular attender at the temple. He came, no doubt, from a very modest room or apartment somewhere in central city. He was dressed in a dark suit with a white shirt, very carefully groomed.

As I pondered on his crippled condition I imagined how very difficult it must have been for him to get moving in the morning. I knew from experience how painful it is for some people with arthritis or other crippling limitations to clothe themselves. And yet, there he was, going at the invitation of the Lord to the temple. For him there would be no loose and informal dress. He took his invitation seriously. I will not forget what he taught me.

On occasions, when I have performed a marriage in the temple, there has been one there to witness it who obviously has paid little attention to the counsel that the Brethren have given about dress and grooming, about taking care not to emulate the world in the extremes of style in clothing, in hair length and arrangement, etc. I have wondered why it is that if such a person was mature enough to be admitted to the temple he would not at once be sensible enough to know that the Lord could not be pleased with those who show obvious preference to follow after the ways of the world.

How could a recommended member attend the temple in clothing that is immodest or worldly? How could one groom himself in such a way that the style of hair is not in keeping with refinement and dignity? The crippled old brother taught me again that even in coming to and going from the temple we may show respect in the manner of our dress.

When you have the opportunity to go to the temple to participate in the temple ceremonies or to witness a sealing, remember where you are. You are a guest in the house of the Lord. You should groom yourself and clothe yourself in such a way that you would feel comfortable should your Host appear.

The Garment

Those who hold and share in the blessings of the priesthood should have their bodies covered as was revealed to the Prophet Joseph Smith when the endowment ceremony was given to him.

It is interesting to note that those who officiated in the Tabernacle in Moses' time wore special garments and their bodies were anointed.

> And he put upon him the coat, and girded him with the girdle, and clothed him with the robe, and put the ephod upon him [*ephod* is defined in the dictionary as "an official garment for the high priest"], and he girded him with the curious girdle of the ephod, and bound it unto him therewith. (Leviticus 8:7.)

Members who have received their temple ordinances thereafter wear the special garment or underclothing. Garments are manufactured by an agency of the Church—and are generally available to members throughout the world through a distribution program operated by the Relief Society.

The garment represents sacred covenants. It fosters modesty and becomes a shield and protection to the wearer.

The wearing of such a garment does not prevent members from dressing in the fashionable clothing generally worn in the nations of the world. Only clothing that is immodest or extreme in style would be incompatible with wearing the garment. Any member of the Church, whether he or she has been to the temple or not, would in proper spirit want to avoid extreme or revealing fashions.

There may be occasions when endowed members of the Church face questions on the garment. For instance, there are some occasions when nonmembers who perform certain services for Church members who wear the garment have a legitimate reason for showing an interest in why we wear this type of underwear.

On one occasion I was invited to speak to the faculty and staff of the Navy Chaplains Training School in Newport, Rhode Island.

The audience included a number of high-ranking naval chaplains from the Catholic, Protestant and Jewish faiths. A class of chaplains then being trained were also invited to the meeting. My invitation asked me to explain the tenets of the Church and to respond to questions the chaplains might have. The idea was for them to learn more about what they might do for Latter-day Saint servicemen in their chaplaincy service, particularly in remote areas where such men were out of contact with the Church. At the time there was a need for them to be informed, because the Vietnam War was then in full fury.

In the question-and-answer period one of the chaplains asked, "Can you tell us something about the special underwear that some Mormon servicemen wear?" The implication was, "Why do you do that? Isn't it strange? Doesn't that present a problem?"

I knew of course that the matter of the garment was a concern to Latter-day Saint servicemen who had been to the temple. Since they generally were living in open barracks, on occasions their underclothing was visible to the other men. Naturally they sometimes were questioned about it, and on some occasions uncharitable fellows ridiculed them. It was also true that chaplains as well as military medical personnel had to minister to a sick or injured Latter-day Saint serviceman in circumstances wherein the matter of the patient's underclothing became part of their responsible interest in that Church member.

The same is true of morticians who prepare for burial the bodies of members of the Church who have died or have been killed, either in the military or in civilian life. If the dead person has been endowed in the temple it is the proper thing that the body be clothed in the garment and in temple clothing for burial. So there are several circumstances in which nonmembers may have a legitimate reason to take an interest in the garment or special underclothing that is worn by members of the Church who have been endowed. Those who have received their endowment know what the garment symbolizes and the sacred nature of the covenants connected with it. But it is important to satisfy the inquiry of those who are legitimately interested, to the point at least of having them understand that this is a matter of very deep significance to us in the Church.

To the chaplain who made the inquiry I responded with a question: "Which church do you represent?" In response he named one of the Protestant churches.

I said, "In civilian life and also when conducting the meetings in the military service you wear clerical clothing, do you not?" He said that he did.

I continued: "I would suppose that that has some importance to you, that in a sense it sets you apart from the rest of your congregation. It is your uniform, as it were, of the ministry. Also, I suppose it may have a much more important place. It reminds you of who you are and what your obligations and covenants are. It is a continual reminder that you are a member of the clergy, that you regard yourself as a servant of the Lord, and that you are responsible to live in such a way as to be worthy of your ordination."

The chaplains all seemed to consent to this appraisal of the value of their own clerical clothing.

I then told them: "You should be able to understand at least one of our reasons why Latter-day Saints have a deep spiritual commitment concerning the garment. A major difference between your churches and ours is that we do not have a professional clergy, as you do. The congregations are all presided over by local leaders. They are men called from all walks of life. Yet they are ordained to the priesthood. They hold offices in the priesthood. They are set apart to presiding positions as presidents, counselors, and leaders in various categories. The women, too, share in that responsibility and in those obligations. The man who heads our congregation on Sunday as the bishop may go to work on Monday as a postal clerk, as an office worker, a farmer, a doctor; or he may be an air force pilot or a naval officer. By our standard he is as much an ordained minister as you are by your standard. He is recognized as such by most governments. We draw something of the same benefits from this special clothing as you would draw from your clerical vestments. The difference is that we wear ours under our clothing instead of outside, for we are employed in various occupations in addition to our service in the Church. These sacred things we do not wish to parade before the world."

I then explained that there are some deeper spiritual meanings as well, connecting the practice of wearing this garment with covenants that are made in the temple. We wouldn't find it necessary to discuss these—not that they are secret, I repeated, but because they are sacred.

I told them that if they would accept baptism into The Church of Jesus Christ of Latter-day Saints and live in harmony with its teachings, they too could share in all of the blessings connected with the holy temple.

They found that answer completely satisfying. They made a comment or two about it along the lines of understanding now why the Latter-day Saint men in the military service were so careful about this matter. They could then see that to ridicule that practice was, in a sense, to ridicule Christian clergy in general. I have found from making this explanation to military chaplains and to Christian ministers generally, individually and on occasions in large gatherings where the question has come up, that it is a dimension they had not previously considered. Having received this explanation, they tend to become more protective of the members of the Church who are wearing the garment.

Young Church members who are athletes sometimes have a problem in locker rooms where their style of underclothing is a matter of interest to, and sometimes comment from, their fellow players.

I have heard many of them say that, once they make a simple explanation such as the one I have given, it is usually accepted by their teammates. Not infrequently if a comment is then made that is not in good taste some of their teammates jump quickly to the defense of the Church member. Out of respect for the standards we keep they offer their protection of our right to live the covenants we have made.

The garment, covering the body, is a visual and tactile reminder of these covenants. For many Church members the garment has formed a barrier of protection when the wearer has been faced with temptation. Among other things it symbolizes our deep respect for the laws of God—among them the moral standard.

Meditation in the Temple

Consider these interesting verses from the New Testament:

After this I beheld, and, lo, a great multitude, which no man could number, of all nations, and kindreds, and people, and tongues, stood before the throne, and before the Lamb, clothed with white robes, and palms in their hands;

And cried with a loud voice, saying, Salvation to our God which sitteth upon the throne, and unto the Lamb.

And one of the elders answered, saying unto me, What are these which are arrayed in white robes? and whence came they?

And I said unto him, Sir, thou knowest. And he said to me, These are they which came out of great tribulation, and have washed their robes, and made them white in the blood of the Lamb. (Revelation 7:9-10, 13-14.)

The Lord said in the Old Testament, and again to the Prophet Joseph Smith (Psalm 46:10 and D&C 101:16), "Be still, and know that I am God." There is such a thing as learning to listen spiritually. There is such a thing as having pure intelligence poured into the mind. In the temple the meditation and contemplation that comes from a quietly observed reverence frequently results in such a pouring-in of intelligence and spiritual learning. And no small part of the atmosphere that makes this possible is the temple clothing and the spirit in which the wearer views it.

It may seem to some to be a very bold doctrine that we talk of — a power which records or binds on earth and binds in heaven. Nevertheless, in all ages of the world, whenever the Lord has given a dispensation of the priesthood to any man by actual revelation, or any set of men, this power has always been given. (D&C 128:9.)

7

The Power to Seal

If we would understand both the history and the doctrine of temple work we must understand what the sealing power is. We must envision, at least to a degree, why the keys of authority to employ the sealing power are crucial — crucial not just to the ordinance work of the temples but to all ordinance work in all the Church throughout the world.

For many centuries it has been the practice all over the world to use an official seal to certify that a document or a proceeding is indeed authoritative. The word *seal*, used in that context, becomes synonymous for endorse or confirm, to license, to favor, to ratify, to accredit, to authorize, to advocate, and to *bind*. Everywhere in the world this system is used. Governments have their official seal, sometimes called the great seal. It was common in earlier eras in the courts of kings. In those courts it was a position of the greatest responsibility and honor to be designated as the keeper or the clerk of the great seal. To have custody of the seal was an office of unequalled trust.

We see the use of seals everywhere. When a signature is notarized, an impression is made upon the paper with a seal. When a license is obtained from a municipality or a state, from a federation or an association, somewhere upon it is impressed the official seal of the organization. You find it on the diploma issued by universities, on legal documents that process through the courts, and on many other papers.

The use of a seal is a visible means of signifying that the document is authoritative, that it is worthy of respect and recognition, that its effect is binding.

Seal is the right word, therefore, to be used to represent spiritual authority. In this case it is not represented by an imprint, by a wax impression, by an embossment, or by a ribbon; nor by an engravement on a signet, or by a stamp, or by a gold design pressed onto a document. The seal of official authority relating to spiritual matters, like other things spiritual, can be identified by the influence that is felt when the sealing power is exercised.

Priesthood Keys and Sealing Power

The sealing power represents the transcendent delegation of spiritual authority from God to man. The keeper of that sealing power is the Lord's chief representative here upon the earth. That is the position of consummate trust and authority. We speak often of holding the key to that sealing power in the Church.

Much of the teaching relating to the deeper spiritual things in the Church, particularly in the temple, is symbolic. We use the word *keys* in a symbolic way. Here the keys of priesthood authority represent the limits of the power extended from beyond the veil to mortal man to act in the name of God upon the earth. The words *seal* and *keys* and *priesthood* are closely linked together.

In 1976 an area general conference was held in Copenhagen, Denmark. Following the closing session, President Kimball expressed a desire to visit the Vor Frue Church, where the Thorvaldsen statues of the Christus and of the Twelve Apostles stand. He had visited this some years before. Others of us had also seen it but some had not, and he felt we should all go there.

The church was closed for renovation, nevertheless arrangements were quickly made for us to be admitted for a few minutes. There were just a few of us.

To the front of the church, behind the altar, stands the familiar statue of the Christus with his arms turned forward and somewhat outstretched, the hands showing the imprint of the nails, the wound in his side clearly visible. Along each side stand the statues of the Apostles, Peter at the front on the right side of the church, and the other Apostles in order. It is not a large building, and these beautiful statues make an impressive sight indeed.

Most of the group were near the rear of the chapel, where the custodian, through an interpreter, was giving some explanation. I stood with President Kimball, Elder Rex Pinegar, and President Bentine, the stake president, before the statue of Peter. In his hand, depicted in marble, is a set of heavy keys. President Kimball pointed to them and explained what they symbolized. Then, in an act I shall never forget, he turned to President Bentine and with unaccustomed sternness pointed his finger at him and said with firm, impressive words, "I want you to tell every Lutheran in Denmark that they do not hold the keys! I hold the keys! We hold the real keys and we use them every day."

This declaration and testimony from the prophet so affected me that I knew I would never forget it — the influence was powerfully spiritual and the impression was physical in its impact as well.

We walked to the other end of the chapel where the rest of the group were standing. Pointing to the statues, President Kimball said to the kind custodian who was showing us the building, "These are the dead Apostles. Here we have the living Apostles." Pointing to me he said, "Elder Packer is an Apostle." He designated the others and said, "Elder Monson and Elder Perry are

Apostles, and I am an Apostle. We are the living Apostles. You read about seventies in the New Testament, and here are living seventies, Brother Pinegar and Brother Hales."

The custodian, who to that time had shown no particular emotion, suddenly was in tears.

As we left that little chapel where those impressive sculptures stand, I felt I had taken part in an experience of a lifetime.

The word *key* is symbolic. The word *sealing* is symbolic. Both represent, I repeat, the consummate authority on this earth for man to act in the name of God.

I have found that many members of the Church have a very limited view of what the sealing power is. Since it is used most frequently in connection with temple marriages, the word *seal* has come to mean, in the minds of many Church members, simply that — sealing two people in the eternal marriage bond. It is also used to designate the ordinance by which children who have not been born in the covenant are "sealed" to their parents. Other members of the Church have the idea that the sealing authority that Elijah brought had to do solely with baptism for the dead.

The authority is much more inclusive than that. The keys of the sealing power are synonymous with the keys of the everlasting priesthood.

> When Jesus came into the coasts of Caesarea Philippi, he asked his disciples, saying, Whom do men say that I the Son of man am?
>
> And they said, Some say that thou art John the Baptist: some, Elias; and others, Jeremias, or one of the prophets.
>
> He saith unto them, But whom say ye that I am?
>
> And Simon Peter answered and said, Thou art the Christ, the Son of the living God.
>
> And Jesus answered and said unto him, Blessed art thou, Simon Barjona: for flesh and blood hath not revealed it unto thee, but my Father which is in heaven.
>
> And I say also unto thee, That thou art Peter, and upon this rock I will build my church; and the gates of hell shall not prevail against it.
>
> And I will give unto thee the keys of the kingdom of heaven; and whatsoever thou shalt bind on earth shall be bound in heaven: and

whatsoever thou shalt loose on earth shall be loosed in heaven. (Matthew 16:13-19.)

Peter was to hold the keys. Peter was to hold the sealing power, that authority which carries the power to bind or seal on earth or to loose on earth and it would be so in the heavens. Those keys belong to the President of the Church—to the prophet, seer, and revelator. That sacred sealing power is with the Church now. Nothing is regarded with more sacred contemplation by those who know the significance of this authority. Nothing is more closely held. There are relatively few men who hold this sealing power upon the earth at any given time—in each temple are brethren who have been given the sealing power. No one can get it except from the prophet, seer, and revelator and President of The Church of Jesus Christ of Latter-day Saints. It is more closely held than any other authority. I am an Apostle and in company with fourteen other men now living hold all of the keys. I have the sealing power. It was given to me at the time of my ordination, as is true of all the Brethren who hold membership in the First Presidency and the Quorum of the Twelve. I can seal and I can loose according to the directions given by the President of the Church. But I cannot give this authority to another. If another is to have it, he must get it from that one man on the earth who has the right to exercise all the keys of the priesthood. We know from the revelations that there will be but one at a time on the earth who has this right.

Three clear statements follow regarding the sealing power as binding on all that we do for the living and the dead.

> Whenever the fulness of the gospel is on earth, the Lord has agents to whom he gives power to bind on earth and seal eternally in the heavens. (Matt. 16:19; 18:18; Hela. 10:3-10; D&C 132: 46-49.) This *sealing power*, restored in this dispensation by Elijah the Prophet (D&C 2:1-3; 110:13-16), is the means whereby "All covenants, contracts, bonds, obligations, oaths, vows, performances, connections, associations, or expectations" attain "efficacy, virtue, or force in and after the resurrection from the dead." (D&C 132:7.)

All things that are not sealed by this power have an end when men are dead. Unless a baptism has this enduring seal, it will not admit a person to the celestial kingdom; unless an eternal marriage covenant is sealed by this authority, it will not take the participating parties to an exaltation in the highest heaven within the celestial world.

All things gain enduring force and validity because of the sealing power. So comprehensive is this power that it embraces ordinances performed for the living and the dead, seals the children on earth up to their fathers who went before, and forms the enduring patriarchal chain that will exist eternally among exalted beings. (Bruce R. McConkie, *Mormon Doctrine*, 2d ed. [Salt Lake City: Bookcraft, 1966], page 683.)

Why was Elijah reserved? What keys did he hold? What keys did he bestow on Peter, James and John? Exactly the same keys that he bestowed upon the head of Joseph Smith and Oliver Cowdery. And what were they? Some of you may be saying the keys of baptism for the dead. *No, it was not that.* Some of you may be thinking it was the *keys of the salvation* of the dead. No, it was not that. That was only a portion of it. The keys that Elijah held were the *keys of the everlasting priesthood, the keys of the sealing power, which the Lord gave unto him. And that is what he came and bestowed upon the head of Peter, James and John*, and that is what he gave to the Prophet Joseph Smith; and that included a ministry of sealing for the living as well as the dead — and it is not confined to the living and it is not confined to the dead, but includes them both. (Joseph Fielding Smith, *Elijah, the Prophet and His Mission*, [Salt Lake City: Deseret Book Co., 1957], pages 29-30; italics added.)

These keys of the binding, or sealing power, which were given to Peter, James, and John in their dispensation, are keys which make valid *all* the ordinances of the gospel. They pertain more especially to the work in the temples, both for the living and for the dead. *They are the authorities which prepare men to enter the celestial kingdom and to be crowned as sons and heirs of God.*

These keys hold the power to *seal husbands and wives for eternity* as well as for time. They hold the power to seal children to parents, the key of adoption, by which the family organization is made intact forever. This is the power which will save the obedient from the curse in the coming of the great and dreadful day of the Lord. Through these keys the hearts of the children have turned to their fathers. (Joseph Fielding Smith, *Doctrines of Salvation,* 3 vols. [Salt Lake City: Bookcraft, 1954-56], 2:119.)

It is well worth considering this sacred power and learning what we may learn about it — including how we got it. To understand how this sacred power was delivered to the Church we must go back to ancient times, to the prophet Elijah. In the following chapters we will do this, following that thread of gospel history to our day and to you.

Please go with us. Whether you are new to or well familiar with the temple experience, you will not understand clearly what happens to you in the temple unless you know something of this history, of this doctrine, and of this sealing power.

PART

II

In Ages Past

And again, verily I say unto you, how shall your washings be acceptable unto me, except ye perform them in a house which you have built to my name?

For, for this cause I commanded Moses that he should build a tabernacle, that they should bear it with them in the wilderness, and to build a house in the land of promise, that those ordinances might be revealed which had been hid from before the world was.

——————

(D&C 124:37-38.)

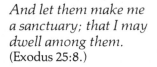

*And let them make me
a sanctuary; that I may
dwell among them.*
(Exodus 25:8.)

8

Temples in Ancient Israel

It is not too much to ask those going to the temple to acquaint themselves with the beginnings of temple work. It is important to know that the keys of authority to perform this work have been delivered to us from ancient times. We can learn much from knowing how those keys were restored. One day each of us will have to know the doctrine connected with this work.

It will be my purpose in the next few chapters to give just an overview of that doctrine from scriptural history and from the revelations on the doctrines connected with the holy temple. I think you will find it interesting reading. First we will consider temples built in ancient times.

It is not our purpose to discuss in any detail the history of these ancient temples. Elder James E. Talmage in his comprehensive work, *The House of the Lord*, goes into much detail on this. His book is well worth obtaining and reading.

In a revelation the Lord spoke to the Saints in Nauvoo in these words: "I command you, all ye my saints, to build a house unto me; and I grant unto you a sufficient time to build a house unto me." And then in sober declaration He warned, "and if you do not these things at the end of the appointment ye shall be rejected as a church, with your dead, saith the Lord your God." (D&C 124:31, 32.) President Joseph Fielding Smith explained this matter:

> This passage [Sec. 124:31-35] has been misinterpreted by some, especially by enemies of the Church who profess a belief in the mission of the Prophet Joseph Smith, but do not accept the doctrine of salvation for the dead. A careful reading of these verses will show that it was not the failure to build a house, but the failure to perform the ordinances for the dead in the house after it was prepared for those ordinances that would cause the rejection. In the months when the saints were without a Temple the Lord granted them the privilege of baptizing for their dead in the Mississippi River, but with the understanding that this was a special privilege which would end when they had been given sufficient time to prepare a place in the Temple where this ordinance could be performed. For baptism for the dead, as well as other ordinances for the dead, are to be performed in a house built to the name of the Lord and for that holy purpose. Therefore we find the members of the Church engaging in baptisms for the dead in the river from the time the privilege was granted until the time arrived when the font in the house of the Lord was prepared for that ordinance, and when that time arrived all baptisms for the dead in the river ceased by divine command. The Lord said: [Sec. 124:32-33, quoted.]
>
> *And if ye do not these things at the end of the appointment* [v. 32], obviously does not mean "if ye do not build a temple at the *end* of the appointment," as our critics infer it does, but it refers to the *ordinances* that were to be performed in the Temple, and the failure on the part of the Saints to perform these ordinances for their dead was the thing that would cause their rejection with their

dead, and not the failure to build the Temple, which was merely the edifice in which the saving principles were to be performed. This is in harmony with the teachings of the Prophet Joseph Smith, who said that if we neglect the salvation of our dead, we do it at the peril of our own salvation! Why? Because we without them cannot be made perfect. (D&C 128:15.) [*Salvation Universal,* 1912, page 22, as quoted in Roy W. Doxey, *Latter-day Prophets and the Doctrine and Covenants,* 4 vols. (Salt Lake City: Deseret Book, 1978), 4:265-66.]

The temple was to be a "holy house, which my people are always commanded to build unto my holy name." There were times when the people had no way to build a temple and He demanded that they do less than He expected of them in Nauvoo. Speaking of one of the sacred ordinances, He said, "For this ordinance belongeth to my house, and cannot be acceptable to me, only in the days of your poverty, wherein ye are not able to build a house unto me." (D&C 124:30.)

Ancient Tabernacle and Temples

Anciently the Lord's covenant people were commanded to build sanctuaries—sacred places that were not regarded as ordinary places of assembly but as sacred enclosures, consecrated for solemn ceremonies. As soon as they were delivered from Egypt, the Israelites were commanded to build a tabernacle, and the design was given to them by revelation in detail. The kind of wood to be used, the design of it, the fabrics of leather and linen and other materials, and the kind of metals to be used were all explained to them. There was an outer court and an inner court; the tabernacle itself, with two rooms; an outer room called the Holy Place; and then, separated by a veil, an inner sanctuary—the Most Holy Place, or the Holy of Holies.

The tabernacle served as the center of worship and as the focal point of the Israelites' communication with God while they were in the wilderness. In due time the Holy Land was delivered to them. David, the king, sought to build a temple to the Lord but the prophet Nathan told him that he was wanting in some spiritual dimensions and that instead his son Solomon would build the temple. The temple of Solomon, finished about 1005 B.C., would be a symbol for temples for thousands of years.

The center part of the plan in the temple of Solomon beyond the various courts, the Holy Place and the Holy of Holies, was a duplicate of the design in the tabernacle, but in size just double.

It is not the building itself but the visitations of the Spirit that sanctify. When the people stray from the Spirit their sanctuary ceases to be the house of the Lord. So it was with Solomon's temple. The building was despoiled and the vessels and artifacts were carried into Egypt and into Babylon. When the Jews returned from captivity another temple was built, known in history as the Temple of Zerubbabel, remembered for the man who directed its construction. It was dedicated in 515 B.C. It did not compare in splendor with the temple of Solomon, but it was a temple nonetheless.

The purpose of the building, not the splendor of it, is the measure of whether it would qualify for the designation *temple*. This temple too, though it stood for five hundred years, lost its sacred purpose; and, under the corroding pressures of men and nature and time, it stood little more than a wreck at the close of the Old Testament epoch.

About sixteen years before the birth of Christ, the first Herod, the king of Judea, determined to reconstruct the decayed temple of Zerubbabel; and when the Lord pursued His earthly ministry the temple of Herod stood and was regarded by Him as a sacred structure. He taught reverence for it and drove the moneychangers from it. He prophesied the destruction of it. And like the temples that preceded it, this one too lost its purpose and in A.D. 70 was destroyed by the Romans in the conquest of Jerusalem under the emperor Titus.

There is record also of the temples being built in the western hemisphere by the Nephites. Nephi said of the first Nephite temple, "And I, Nephi, did build a temple; and I did construct it after the manner of the temple of Solomon save it were not built of so many precious things; for they were not to be found upon the land, wherefore, it could not be built like unto Solomon's temple. But the manner of the construction was like unto the temple of Solomon; and the workmanship thereof was exceeding fine." (2 Nephi 5:16.)

There is mention of a temple in Zarahemla (Mosiah 1:18) and one in Bountiful (3 Nephi 11:1). The Lord came to the area of this latter temple after His resurrection. For two hundred years or so after this visit, the people lived in total righteousness.

Then came the generations of darkness when no temples were to be found upon the earth. Men who read of ancient temples must have looked forward, yearning for that day when the morning once more would break, the shadows flee, and Zion's standard be unfurled; and the dawning of a brighter day would with majesty rise upon the world.

Much has been written by others about these ancient temples, especially those in Jerusalem. We move now from the temple of Solomon, in the Kingdom of Judah, to the court of Ahab, king of the sister nation of Israel. There began the ministry of Elijah the prophet. We will follow his ministry through to the temples in our day.

Elijah was the last Prophet that held the keys of the Priesthood, and who will, before the last dispensation, restore the authority and deliver the keys of the Priesthood, in order that all the ordinances may be attended to in righteousness. (Joseph Smith.)

9

Elijah the Prophet

Biblical scholars of the past have often given but passing attention to Elijah the prophet. They did not have the revelations that run a thread from his ancient ministry across the centuries to every living soul. But two of them, McClintock and Strong, who produced a great cyclopedic work of biblical history in the nineteenth century, appraised Elijah in these words:

> Elijah the Tishbite, the Elias of the New Testament, a character whose rare and sudden, and brief appearances, undaunted courage and fiery zeal—the brilliance of whose triumphs—the pathos of whose despondency—the glory of whose departure, and the calm beauty of whose reappearance on the Mount of Transfiguration throws such a halo of brightness around him as is equalled by none of his compeers in the sacred history. (*Cyclopedia of Biblical and*

Theological and Ecclesiastical Literature [New York: Harper and Bros., 1895], page 144.)

This tribute is not extreme—not when you come to know, to a degree, about Elijah. How these authors should have marveled, had they lived now and had certain testimony that Elijah returned to deliver the sacred sealing power so that the fulness of the priesthood could be held by men, so that all things could be done in order!

Elijah and his ministry are worthy of a book. Here we will give but an overview. This is important to an understanding of the temples and why we build them.

Elijah and Elias

One question about Elijah needs to be clear at the outset. The New Testament refers to Elijah by the name *Elias*. For example, James 5:17, "Elias was a man subject to like passions as we are." The reason we are sure that this refers to Elijah is that *Elias* is the Greek translation of the Hebrew name *Elijah*. We will be quoting other New Testament verses containing the name *Elias*. When they refer to an individual's name, they could not mean anyone but the Elijah of the Old Testament.

The use of *Elias* to describe *Elijah* should not be hard for moderns to understand. After all, the name *John* in English, goes into German as *Johann*; the name *Roberto* comes back from Spanish as *Robert*. Today we have two General Authorities with the same name in different languages: Howard W. *Hunter* of the Quorum of the Twelve Apostles and Jacob *de Jager* of the First Quorum of the Seventy. *De Jager* in Dutch means "the Hunter." So the Elijah of the Old Testament comes to us in the New Testament under the name *Elias*, just as *Jeremiah* comes to us as *Jeremias* in the New Testament. (Matthew 16:14.)

There are two other meanings to the word *Elias*. There was a prophet named Elias, a separate man from Elijah. We know little about him, but he himself, as a separate individual, has appeared in this dispensation, as we shall note later.

And finally there is the third meaning of the name *Elias*. It has become synonymous with the word *forerunner*, or one who prepares the way. The Prophet Joseph Smith said: "The spirit of Elias is first, Elijah second, and Messiah last. Elias is a forerunner to prepare the way, and the spirit and power of Elijah is to come after, holding the keys of power, building the Temple to the capstone, placing the seals of the Melchisedec Priesthood upon the house of Israel, and making all things ready; then Messiah comes to His Temple, which is last of all." (*HC*, 6:254.)

He also said that "the spirit of Elias was a going before to prepare the way for the greater, which was the case with John the Baptist. He came crying through the wilderness, 'Prepare ye the way of the Lord, make His paths straight.' " (*HC*, 6:250.)

Some have become confused because the name of John the Baptist is connected with that of Elias. But that can be understood if we remember that he was *an* Elias, a forerunner, one who prepares the way.

It should not seem strange to us to put names together in that way, for do we not say of a budding artist with great talent, "He is a real Michelangelo"? Or do we not speak of some scientist of exceptional genius as being "an Einstein"? No one would assume from such expressions that we thought the person to be a reincarnation of Michelangelo or of Einstein. Names, at times, become something of a title. A liberator is referred to as a George Washington or as an Abraham Lincoln. It is just a common way to speak. Therefore, it should not seem unusual that John the Baptist was called *an* Elias.

Elder Bruce R. McConkie explains it in this way:

> According to the plan and program of the Lord, the dispensation of the fulness of times is "the times of restitution of all things, which God hath spoken by the mouth of all his holy prophets since the world began." (Acts 3:21.) This restoration is to be effected by *Elias*. Before the winding up of the Lord's work, the promise is: *"Elias truly shall first come, and restore all things."* (Matt. 17:11.) With these ancient scriptures before us, these questions arise: *Who is the promised Elias who was to come and restore all things? Has*

this work of restoration taken place? Or is it something that is yet future?

Correcting the Bible by the spirit of revelation, the Prophet restored a statement of John the Baptist which says that *Christ is the Elias who was to restore all things.* (*Inspired Version*, John 1:21-28.) By revelation we are also informed that *the Elias who was to restore all things is the angel Gabriel* who was known in mortality as Noah. (D. & C. 27:6-7; Luke 1:5-25; *Teachings*, p. 157.) From the same authentic source we also learn that *the promised Elias is John the Revelator.* (D. & C. 77:9, 14.) Thus there are three different revelations which name Elias as being *three different persons.* What are we to conclude?

By finding answer to the question, by whom has the restoration been effected, we shall find who Elias is and find there is no problem in harmonizing these apparently contradictory revelations. *Who has restored all things? Was it one man? Certainly not. Many angelic ministrants have been sent from the courts of glory to confer keys and powers, to commit their dispensations and glories again to men on earth.* At least the following have come: Moroni, John the Baptist, Peter, James and John, Moses, Elijah, Elias, Gabriel, Raphael, and Michael. (D. & C. 13; 110; 128:19-21.) Since it is apparent that no one messenger has carried the whole burden of the restoration, but rather that each has come with a specific endowment from on high, it becomes clear that *Elias is a composite personage. The expression must be understood to be a name and a title for those whose mission it was to commit keys and powers to men in this final dispensation.* (*Doctrines of Salvation*, vol. 1, pp. 170-174.) [*Mormon Doctrine*, page 221; some italics added.]

In summary, then, *Elias* is the Greek translation of the Hebrew name *Elijah* and is used in the New Testament to designate Elijah, the prophet of the Old Testament. Elias is the name of another man, a prophet of whom we know little. And Elias is a title, meaning forerunner, or one who prepares the way.

Prophets "Ordinary" Men

It was about 875 years before Christ when the prophet Elijah first strode onto the stage of human history. He is introduced as simply, "Elijah the Tishbite, who was of the inhabitants of Gilead." (1 Kings 17:1.) Some scholars feel he may have been born in Tishbe, a place in Galilee, and that he later went to Gilead, beyond the Jordan, which was then a land of wilderness.

The few details we can glean from the record concerning Elijah's appearance, what he looks like, call up the word *ordinary*. It was true then, as it is true now, that the prophets were "ordinary men." Paul of Tarsus, the tent-maker, said it was true in his day, and he used words similar to those of James: "We also are men of like passions with you, and preach unto you that ye should turn from these vanities unto the living God." (Acts 14:15.)

Those references, and there are others we could cite, teach a lesson worth fixing in our minds. The prophets and the Apostles—for Apostles are prophets as well—are not uncommon men either in their backgrounds or in their physical appearance. They come from various walks of life. Some may be short of stature, others impressively tall, but in general appearance they are like other men.

It is said that we can learn much from history if we will move in our minds from the here and now to the then and there. We realize that the scenery and the costumes change somewhat, but beyond that everything is the same. Some of the past actors in the human drama held different titles, and the social structure of their day was not quite like ours today, but the feelings, the emotions, the relationships, the passions, and particularly the spiritual processes, were the same then as now.

Details mentioned about Elijah describe him in terms that are by no means uncommon. On one occasion the emissaries of the king reported that they had met a man and talked with him. Though they were not given a name, in reporting the encounter they described him as being "an hairy man, and girt with a girdle of leather about his loins." (2 Kings 1:8.) The king deduced from that that they had met Elijah. The description fits also the traditional image of John the Baptist (see Mark 1:6), who centuries later became a major participant in the early scenes of the New Testament.

As well as wearing a girdle of skin about his loins, Elijah wore a mantle, a very common article of clothing in that day. Generally it was simply a sheepskin. If rolled tightly, it would form something of a staff. In one moment of great emotion, when Elijah heard the still, small voice, he "wrapped his face in his mantle." (1 Kings 19:13.)

We could extract other details from the Old Testament, but none of them suggests that Elijah was uncommon in appearance, either in stature or in clothing.

I repeat this as a lesson worth learning: The prophets, as they walk and live among men, are common, ordinary men. Men called to apostolic positions are given a people to redeem. Theirs is the responsibility to lead those people in such a way that they win the battles of life and conquer the ordinary temptations and passions and challenges. And then, speaking figuratively, it is as though these prophets are tapped on the shoulder and reminded: "While you carry such responsibility to help others with their battles, you are not excused from your own challenges of life. You too will be subject to passions, temptations, challenges. Win those battles as best you can."

Some people are somehow dissatisfied to find in the leading servants of the Lord such ordinary mortals. They are disappointed that there is not some obvious mystery about those men; it is almost as if they are looking for the strange and the occult. To me, however, it is a great testimony that the prophets anciently and the prophets today are called out from the ranks of the ordinary men. It should not lessen our faith, for example, to learn that Elijah was discouraged at times, even despondent. (See 1 Kings 19:4.)

This calling forth of ordinary men for extraordinary purposes is as evident during the Savior's earthly mission as in former and later eras. Centuries after Elijah, when Christ called the Twelve, except for them all coming from the same nation they were so diverse that scholars have often commented on the difficulty of welding together into a united, motivated group such totally different individuals drawn from the ranks of the common folk.

Elijah Seals the Heavens

Elijah first appears in the court of Ahab, the king of Israel. "Ahab," the Old Testament tells us, "did more to provoke the Lord God of Israel to anger than all the kings of Israel that were before him." (1 Kings 16:33.)

Ahab had forsaken the faith of his fathers and had allowed the Northern Kingdom to adopt the worship of calves instead of the God Jehovah. And Ahab, "as if it had been a light thing for him to walk in the sins of Jeroboam" (1 Kings 16:31), married the daughter of the king of Zidon. Jezebel—a name that in modern times is a term used to describe a domineering, wicked woman—introduced into Israel the worship of the Phoenician god Baal. Baal was worshipped in high places, that is, clearings on high mountain tops. The worship of Baal is described by scholars as being festive and gay, and it is said that there were licentious and impure rites connected with it. Baal-worship turned away from the virtues of righteousness and goodness and humility to venerate power and mere strength.

Elijah condemned the wicked king, who had authority to correct all of this, and invoked the name of the Lord in sealing the heavens. "As the Lord God of Israel liveth, before whom I stand, there shall not be dew nor rain these years, but according to my word."

Notice that he did not set some preliminary condition and say, "When you've done this or when you've done that, the rains will come again." He said that they would come only "according to my word." That declaration represents the fact that Elijah, who was a prophet and who was possessed of the authority of the priesthood, also was in possession of considerable power as well.

Elijah was warned to flee from the presence of the king. He went eastward and hid by the brook Cherith, and there the ravens fed him. Eventually the brook dried up. Thus Elijah himself was not immune from the trials the Lord had caused him to call forth upon the people by sealing the heavens so there would be no rain. This too illustrates a principle that members of the Church should consider. In later years the Lord counseled his disciples to stay in the world, even though they were to be not of the world. A life of righteousness does not necessarily lift from any soul the trials and difficulties, suffering and concerns of life. But the righteous do have some protection and blessings, and there is power working in their behalf.

It was the Lord who had warned Elijah to flee from Ahab, to preserve his life. And again "the word of the Lord came unto him, saying, Arise, get thee to Zarephath, which belongeth to Zidon, and dwell there: behold, I have commanded a widow woman there to sustain thee."

This was the widow who was willing to share the last handful of meal from her barrel and the little oil from her cruse. She had intended to "dress it for me and my son, that we may eat it, and die." But at Elijah's request she fed him first, "And the barrel of meal wasted not, neither did the cruse of oil fail, according to the word of the Lord, which he spake by Elijah." Later the widow's son was stricken with a sore sickness, and "there was not breath left in him." Through the power of the priesthood Elijah restored him to life. (1 Kings 17:1-24.)

Jezebel had caused Israel's prophets to be slain. The word *prophet*, here, might be understood in the light of what the Prophet Joseph Smith said:

> If any person should ask me if I were a prophet, I should not deny it, as that would give me the lie; for, according to John, the testimony of Jesus is the spirit of prophecy; therefore, if I profess to be a witness or teacher, and have not the spirit of prophecy, which is the testimony of Jesus, I must be a false witness; but if I be a true teacher and witness, I must possess the spirit of prophecy, and that constitutes a prophet; and any man who says he is a teacher or preacher of righteousness, and denies the spirit of prophecy, is a liar, and the truth is not in him; and by this key false teachers and impostors may be detected. (*HC*, 5:215-16.)

Obadiah, the governor in the house of Ahab, was a righteous man, and to preserve them from Jezebel he hid a hundred of the prophets in caves and supplied them with bread and water. Later, after the drouth had been plaguing the country for over three years, Obadiah finally found Elijah and arranged for a meeting with King Ahab. The king greeted Elijah with the question: "Art thou he that troubleth Israel?" And Elijah answered, "I have not troubled Israel; but thou, and thy father's house, in that ye have forsaken the commandments of the Lord, and thou hast followed Baalim."

Elijah asked Ahab to gather the people at Mount Carmel and to have the priests of Baal there also. When they were gathered, Elijah addressed the people. "How long halt ye between two opinions? If the Lord be God, follow him: but if Baal, then follow him. And the people answered him not a word."

Elijah challenged the priests of Baal to build a sacrificial altar and to place a bullock upon it, and then to have their god send down fire to consume the offering. All day long they tried, pleading and shouting to their god, leaping upon the altar, cutting themselves with knives and lancets, doing everything they could think of to cause the fire to descend. At noon Elijah mocked them. "Cry aloud: for he is a god; either he is talking, or he is pursuing, or he is in a journey, or peradventure he sleepeth, and must be awaked." But evening came, and neither voice nor fire had answered their exertions.

Now it was Elijah's turn. Using twelve stones he repaired the altar of the Lord which had been broken down, made a trench around it, and had it drenched three times with water. Then, at the time of the evening sacrifice, he called upon the Lord. Immediately fire came down and consumed the offering, the altar, and even the stones.

After that demonstration, the priests of Baal were taken to the brook Kishon and there slain.

Now Elijah went up to the top of Mount Carmel and sat on the ground with his face between his knees. In due time his servant reported that there was a little cloud out of the sea, like a man's hand. And then the rains came. (1 Kings 18:1-46.)

When Jezebel heard of her loss of the priests of Baal, she was furious. She vowed that Elijah would not live beyond the next day, and once again he fled. Again he was miraculously fed. Elijah hid in a cave to keep from being slain. He was discouraged. "I, even I only, am left," he said, "and they seek my life, to take it away."

The Voice of the Spirit

Then came an experience for Elijah that is a signal lesson for every Latter-day Saint. He was told to go and stand before the Lord upon the mountain. And there he witnessed a "great and strong wind" that rent the mountains and "brake in pieces the rocks."

"But the Lord was not in the wind."

Then came an earthquake. "But the Lord was not in the earthquake: and after the earthquake a fire; but the Lord was not in the fire."

And then it happened! "After the fire [came] a still small voice." (1 Kings 19:1-12.)

That voice is described elsewhere in scripture:

> And it came to pass when they heard this voice, and beheld that it was not a voice of thunder, neither was it a voice of a great tumultuous noise, but behold, it was a still voice of perfect mildness, as if it had been a whisper, and it did pierce even to the very soul. (Helaman 5:30.)

> And it came to pass that while they were thus conversing one with another, they heard a voice as if it came out of heaven; and they cast their eyes round about, for they understood not the voice which they heard; and it was not a harsh voice, neither was it a loud voice; nevertheless, and notwithstanding it being a small voice it did pierce them that did hear to the center, insomuch that there was no part of their frame that it did not cause to quake; yea, it did pierce them to the very soul, and did cause their hearts to burn. (3 Nephi 11:3.)

> Behold, thus saith the Lord unto the elders whom he hath called and chosen in these last days, by the voice of his Spirit. (D&C 52:1.)

We could come away from our study of Elijah with no more important lesson than to recognize how the Lord communicates with his children here upon the earth: through the still, small voice that is so difficult to describe to one who has never experienced it and is almost unnecessary to describe to one who has. That sweet, quiet voice of inspiration that comes more as a feeling than it does as a sound. That process through which pure intelligence can be spoken into the mind and we can know and understand and have witness of spiritual things. The process is not reserved for the prophets alone, but every righteous seeking soul who will qualify and make himself worthy can have that manner of communication, even as a gift.

In Elijah's interview he was told that he was not alone, that the Lord had left "seven thousand in Israel, all the knees which have not bowed unto Baal, and every mouth which hath not kissed him." (1 Kings 19:18.) Elijah also was instructed to anoint a new king over Syria and a new king over Israel. He was told who they were to be, and then he was told to find Elisha, the son of Shaphat, to be the prophet to succeed him.

Elijah's Prophecies Fulfilled, Successor Chosen

Elijah found Elisha plowing with twelve yoke of oxen — another demonstration that prophets come from the ranks of ordinary men. Elijah cast his mantle upon him, and Elisha followed him thereafter.

King Ahab and Queen Jezebel demonstrated their wickedness by causing Naboth to be slain in order that they could take possession of his vineyard. Through the promptings of the Spirit, news of this came to Elijah. He returned, and Ahab greeted him with these words: "Hast thou found me, O mine enemy?" And Elijah answered, "I have found thee: because thou hast sold thyself to work evil in the sight of the Lord." (1 Kings 21:20.)

Elijah then pronounced upon Ahab a terrible penalty, for he said that he would "take away thy posterity." Naboth had been slain by a wall, and Elijah now prophesied to Ahab that the dogs would lick his blood in that self-same spot. And of the wicked queen he said, "The dogs shall eat Jezebel by the wall of Jezreel." (1 Kings 21:21, 23.)

Ahab repented for a short time, but the Old Testament carries the detailed account of the battles and of the wounding and of the death of Ahab, and describes how the chariot in which he was riding was washed at the pool of Samaria and his armor was washed, and the dogs licked the blood, and how all the detail of Elijah's prophecy was fulfilled, as was the prophecy concerning Jezebel.

Ahaziah succeeded Ahab as king and had confrontations with the prophet Elijah not dissimilar to those of his father. And the prophecies Elijah had pronounced upon Ahab and his posterity were fulfilled.

The time came when the ministry of Elijah in Israel was complete. Elijah knew that he soon would be taken, and when they were together Elijah said to Elisha, "Ask what I shall do for thee, before I be taken away from thee. And Elisha said, I pray thee, let a double portion of thy spirit be upon me." (2 Kings 2:9.)

That request for a double portion of the spirit of Elijah provokes me to deep thought, for the spirit of Elijah, as we still may learn, is something so moving and so powerful, and something tied so closely to the most sacred authority of the priesthood, that obviously it would be glorious to be under the constant influence of even a part of that spirit, let alone a double portion.

Elijah was prompted to set a condition; for that portion, that double portion, was not, I believe, his to give. The answer to that appeal would be in the hands of the Lord, and Elijah simply replied that if Elisha should see him as he was taken, his request would be granted. "And Elisha saw it," for it happened that "as they still went on, and talked, that, behold, there appeared a chariot of fire, and horses of fire, and parted them both asunder; and Elijah went up by a whirlwind into heaven." (2 Kings 2:11-

12.) The mantle fell from Elisha and he took up the one that had fallen from Elijah. He smote the waters of the Jordan and they parted, and he went over.

Elijah Translated

Elijah was truly remarkable. The prophecies he made, as recorded in the Old Testament, were fulfilled during his lifetime. We have no record of his making prophecies concerning these last days, as we do in the case of most of the Old Testament prophets—Isaiah, Jeremiah, Daniel, Amos, and others—but we do have an account of what he did. In this he is quite like Moses. We have but little record of prophecies that Moses may have given concerning the last days or the ultimate fate of the earth. We know what he did in his lifetime.

Elijah and Moses were similar in another important respect. They were both translated—taken from the earth without experiencing mortal death. The Book of Mormon mentions Moses in connection with the departure of Alma: "The saying went abroad in the church that [Alma] was taken up by the Spirit, or buried by the hand of the Lord, even as Moses. But behold, the scriptures saith the Lord took Moses unto himself." (Alma 45:19.) There were things that both Elijah and Moses must pass on to others in the flesh in the generations that were still to come, and they would come back to earth to do that before experiencing the change from mortality to resurrected being.

The Prophet Joseph Smith had this to say about translated beings: "Translated bodies cannot enter into rest until they have undergone a change equivalent to death. Translated bodies are designed for future missions." (*HC,* 4:425.)

On an earlier occasion he said:

> Many have supposed that the doctrine of translation was a doctrine whereby men were taken immediately into the presence of God, and into an eternal fullness, but this is a mistaken idea. Their place of habitation is that of the terrestrial order, and a place prepared for such characters He held in reserve to be ministering

angels unto many planets, and who as yet have not entered into so great a fullness as those who are resurrected from the dead. (*HC*, 4:210.)

The recorded event requiring the later appearance of Elijah and Moses in the flesh as translated beings was the Savior's transfiguration on the mount. From President Joseph Fielding Smith we have this explanation.

When Moses and Elijah came to the Savior and to Peter, James and John upon the Mount, what was their coming for? Was it just some spiritual manifestation to strengthen these three apostles? Or did they come merely to give comfort unto the Son of God in his ministry and to prepare him for his crucifixion? No! That was not the purpose. I will read it to you. The Prophet Joseph Smith has explained it in the Church History, Vol. 3, 387, as follows:

"The priesthood is everlasting. The Savior, Moses, and Elias [Elijah, in other words], gave the keys to Peter, James and John, on the Mount when they were transfigured before him. The Priesthood is everlasting—without beginning of days or end of years; without father, mother, etc.

If there is no change of ordinances, there is no change of Priesthood. Wherever the ordinances of the Gospel are administered, there is the Priesthood. . . ."

From that we understand why Elijah and Moses were preserved from death—because they had a mission to perform, and it had to be performed before the crucifixion of the Son of God, and therefore it could not be done in the spirit. They had to have tangible bodies. Christ is the first fruits of the resurrection; therefore if any former prophet had a work to perform preparatory to the mission of the Son of God, or to the dispensation of the Meridian of Time, it was essential that they be preserved to fulfill that mission in the flesh. For that reason Moses disappeared from among the people and was taken up into the mountain, and the people thought he was buried by the Lord; the Lord preserved him, so that he could come at the proper time and restore his keys, on the heads of Peter, James and John, who stood at the head of the dispensation of the Meridian of Time. He reserved Elijah from death that he might also come and bestow his keys upon the heads of Peter, James and John and prepare them for their ministry. (*Elijah, the Prophet and His Mission*, pages 27-29.)

Malachi Prophesies Elijah's Return

Following the account of Elijah's being caught up, the name *Elijah* does not appear in the Old Testament again until the next to the last verse of the last chapter in that book. Four and a half centuries were to pass after Elijah's time before Malachi the prophet would speak.

Malachi's words concerning Elijah were few. But this prophecy represents the central theme of this book, for in the last verses of his message we begin to follow a golden thread that reaches to every Latter-day Saint — indeed, to every human soul.

> Behold, I will send you Elijah the prophet before the coming of the great and dreadful day of the Lord:
>
> And he shall turn the heart of the fathers to the children, and the heart of the children to their fathers, lest I come and smite the earth with a curse. (Malachi 4:5-6.)

When we consider the brevity of this last Old Testament reference to Elijah the extent of the traditions that are connected with it is remarkable.

The Old Testament closes there. In the King James version that closing is signified by the statement, "The End of the Prophets," a statement that is true only as it applies to completing the Old Testament records, because the ministry of Elijah was hardly begun.

Behold, I will send you Elijah the prophet before the coming of the great and dreadful day of the Lord.
(Malachi 4:5.)

10

Elijah to Return

The single reference in Malachi stating that Elijah would return was somehow reinforced with a fixed tradition that has lasted through the centuries. In the Jewish tradition there was a certain belief that he would appear again. He was expected. In the Talmud "he is recorded as having often appeared to wise and good rabbis—at a prayer, in the wilderness, or on their journeys—generally in the form of an Arabian merchant." (*Cyclopedia of Biblical Literature*, page 150.) At the circumcision of a child, a seat was always placed for Elijah. During certain prayers the door of the house was kept open, that Elijah might enter.

In the celebration of the Feast of the Passover, an extra place is set for Elijah. The tradition is observed even in our day.

The door is opened and the fourth and last cup of wine is filled. An additional cup, the Cup of Elijah the Prophet, is set on the table. The company rises as if to greet him. Elijah in Jewish tradition is the long expected messenger of the final redemption of mankind from all oppression. (*Passover Haggadah*, Christian Friends Bulletin of the Anti-Defamation League of B'nai B'rith, March 1954.)

At the dedication of the Orson Hyde Park in Jerusalem in 1979, Elder LeGrand Richards of the Quorum of the Twelve Apostles had a conversation with the mayor of Jerusalem. Elder Richards told the mayor of having visited a synagogue that day and having observed a large armchair suspended from the ceiling above the altar. He had asked the rabbi what the chair was for. (He said he already knew what it was for, but that he asked the question to see if the modern-day rabbi still held to the tradition.) The rabbi informed him that the chair was for Elijah, and that upon Elijah's return it would be lowered from the ceiling so that he might occupy it. Elder Richards then bore testimony to the mayor that the tradition was not only true but had been fulfilled.

Traditions About Elijah's Return

These and other traditions and references all center on the fact that Elijah would indeed return. There is something very significant about Elijah to the Jewish people.

Traditions about Elijah exist among the Muhammadans as well. For Elijah is said to have drunk of the fountain of life, "by virtue of which he still lives, and will live to the day of judgment." (*Cyclopedia of Biblical Literature*, page 150.)

Four hundred years after Malachi uttered his prophecy came the forerunner of the Savior's earthly ministry, John the Baptist. He came from Gilead, beyond the Jordan. There were some things characteristic of him that were reminiscent of Elijah. It was not surprising that the people should ask if he were Elijah. They expected Elijah to return.

John replied that he was not Elijah, nor was he the Messiah. He was later referred to as *an* Elias. This is in the frame of meaning mentioned earlier, a forerunner, or one who prepares the way. Although John the Baptist was not Elijah or Elias, he was like them in some ways. He was *an* Elias; a messenger, a forerunner.

In the Inspired Version of the Bible, the Prophet Joseph Smith translated Matthew 17, verses 10 to 14, in this way:

> And Jesus answered and said unto them, Elias truly shall first come, and restore all things, as the prophets have written.
>
> And again I say unto you that Elias has come already, concerning whom it is written, Behold, I will send my messenger, and he shall prepare the way before me; and they knew him not, and have done unto him, whatsoever they listed.
>
> Likewise shall also the Son of man suffer of them.
>
> But I say unto you, Who is Elias? Behold, this is Elias, whom I send to prepare the way before me.
>
> Then the disciples understood that he spake unto them of John the Baptist, and also of another who should come and restore all things, as it is written by the prophets.

Elijah did come again in that day. Peter, James and John went up onto the mountain with the Lord and there He was transfigured before them. And then they saw, with the Lord, two personages whom they knew to be Moses and Elias (Elijah). It is significant indeed that these two ancient prophets who had so much in common, who held keys, whose ministries were of great moment to us, should appear together transfigured with the Lord.

This appearance, however, did not fulfill completely the prophecy of Malachi. The prophecy stated that Elijah would come before the great and dreadful day of the Lord should come, before the world should be burned as an oven, before all the proud and all that do wickedly should be burned up.

So the waiting was not over and the traditions were not fulfilled. We have evidence of this, for after the Crucifixion, in

A.D. 34, the Lord appeared on the American continent. He ministered to the Nephites and taught them of the prophecy and tradition that Elijah would return. In the twenty-fourth chapter of 3 Nephi we find a record of the Lord dictating to them the words of Malachi, commanding them that they should write those words, and expounding the prophecies to them.

> And it came to pass that he commanded them that they should write the words which the Father had given unto Malachi, which he should tell unto them. And it came to pass that after they were written he expounded them. And these are the words which he did tell unto them, saying: Thus said the Father unto Malachi. (3 Nephi 24:1.)

And He gave them the third and the fourth chapters of Malachi as they are contained in the King James Version of the Bible, concluding with the prophecy:

> Behold, I will send you Elijah the prophet before the coming of the great and dreadful day of the Lord;
> And he shall turn the heart of the fathers to the children, and the heart of the children to their fathers, lest I come and smite the earth with a curse. (3 Nephi 25:5-6.)

We have, then, these records concerning the return of Elijah:

Malachi the prophet had prophesied clearly, four hundred years before Christ, that Elijah would be sent before the great and dreadful day of the Lord came, and that his ministry would include the turning of the hearts of the fathers to the children and the hearts of the children to the fathers.

When John the Baptist appeared on the scene, some thought him to be Elijah. When the Lord asked his disciples at Caesarea Philippi what people were saying about Him—"Whom do men say that I . . . am?"—the response was, "They think you are John the Baptist" [who by then was beheaded], or, "that you are Elias." (See Matthew 16:13-14.) Other references in the New Testament touch upon the subject.

And when the Lord appeared to the Nephites, He wove this thread—the coming of Elijah and the turning of the hearts of

the fathers to the children and of the children to their fathers—
into the fabric of their scripture.

In addition to scriptural records and inferences, the traditions of the Jews and those of the Muhammadans and some
references in the Talmud kept very much alive the expectation
that Elijah would return. In the Muhammadan tradition, Llyas
is said to have drunk of the fountain of life, "by virtue of which
he still lives, and will live to the day of judgment." He is, by
some, confounded with St. George, and with the mysterious el-
Khidr, one of the most remarkable of the Moslem saints. (See
Lane's *Arabian Nights*, introduction, note 2; also *Lane's Selections from Kuran*, pages 221-22.)

But it does not end there. In both the Greek and the Latin
churches, Elijah has been canonized. Among the Greeks he is
the patron of elevated spots, and many mountains in Greece
are called by his name. And in the early church there was a
commemoration and a service for his day, observed on July 20,
in both the Greek and the Latin churches. And in the Latin
church the order of the Carmelites has celebrated Elijah as the
founder of their order.

In modern-day Jerusalem, Temple Hill, or the Place of the
Rock, is a religious shrine to Islam, to Christianity, and to
Judaism. All three great religions hold tie to this place. All three,
likewise, have a common thread in a tradition that Elijah the
prophet would return.

The biblical scholars would wrestle with the question of
Elijah the prophet and his return to the earth. Their common
answer, which seemed to them the only possible one, was that
he did return—on the Mount of Transfiguration. But, as mentioned before, that did not satisfy completely the prophecies of
Malachi. Thus for centuries it was to remain an enigma.

The fulfillment of the prophecies concerning Elijah would
await the Restoration.

The Power Restored

From window in the Salt Lake Temple

And again, what do we hear? Glad tidings from Cumorah! Moroni, an angel from heaven, declaring the fulfilment of the prophets — the book to be revealed. A voice of the Lord in the wilderness of Fayette, Seneca county, declaring the three witnesses to bear record of the book! . . . The voice of Peter, James, and John in the wilderness between Harmony, Susquehanna county, and Colesville, Broome county, on the Susquehanna river, declaring themselves as possessing the keys of the kingdom, and of the dispensation of the fulness of times!

And again, the voice of God in the chamber of old Father Whitmer, in Fayette, Seneca county, and at sundry times, and in divers places. . . . And the voice of Michael, the archangel; the voice of Gabriel, and of Raphael, and of divers angels, from Michael or Adam down to the present time, all declaring their dispensation, their rights, their keys, their honors, their majesty and glory, and the power of their priesthood; giving line upon line, precept upon precept.

———

(D&C 128:20-21.)

So, in accordance with this, my determination to ask of God, I retired to the woods to make the attempt. It was on the morning of a beautiful, clear day, early in the spring of eighteen hundred and twenty. (Joseph Smith.)

The Morning Breaks

Elijah was to return "before the coming of the great and dreadful day of the Lord." That very expression suggests the latter days of the earth. And it would be in the latter days, as Nebuchadnezzar's dream and the prophet Daniel's interpretation indicated, that the Lord would set up his kingdom for the last time. (See Daniel 2.)

The Lord made careful preparation for this event. After centuries of darkness and error, the gloom began to lift gradually as questioning minds and courageous hearts asserted themselves in the Reformation, which was to break the hold of Christendom's monopolistic church. Concurrently the newly discovered land of America was being colonized. Within two or three centuries, the yearnings for freedom affected every Western country, finding their greatest flowering in America and their sublimest written expression in the inspired Constitution of the United States of America. Now there was a new nation specifically founded in political, personal, and religious freedom. The time was ripe and the place was ready.

The First Vision

The Reformers had done well with their limited resources, but naturally the differing interpretations of their common authority—the Bible—produced disagreement and doctrinal diversity. When a religious revival hit the region of Manchester, New York, in the early nineteenth century, the clamor and contention of the various ministers left the fourteen-year-old Joseph Smith in confusion as to which church was right. He recorded:

> While I was laboring under the extreme difficulties caused by the contests of these parties of religionists, I was one day reading the Epistle of James, first chapter and fifth verse, which reads: *If any of you lack wisdom, let him ask of God, that giveth to all men liberally, and upbraideth not; and it shall be given him.*
>
> At length I came to the conclusion that I must either remain in darkness and confusion, or else I must do as James directs, that is, ask of God. I at length came to the determination to "ask of God," concluding that if he gave wisdom to them that lacked wisdom, and would give liberally, and not upbraid, I might venture. (Joseph Smith—History: 11, 13; hereafter cited as JS-H.)

Thus it came that on a spring day in 1820 he knelt in prayer in the woods near his home to ask the crucial question—Which church is right? When he began to offer up his petition, the first thing that happened was that he was overwhelmed by a great power of darkness. He described this as not an imaginary force but the influence of a real being from the unseen world which had such marvelous power as he never before had felt in any being. So total was this power that he was about to abandon himself to it, when he, in a sense, turned a key of deliverance, for he called upon the name of the Lord. As soon as he had done so a light descended; and as soon as the light was there, he was released from the power of darkness.

To me there has always been a lesson in that experience. While light and virtue and truth at times will not endure the presence of darkness and evil and will not, by choice, stay in their presence, ultimately the powers of darkness cannot endure the presence of light.

By analogy, this can be demonstrated to a degree with electricity. We are able to run a wire into a room and through a system of connections and switches turn on a light. The instant that happens, the darkness is gone. Some little of it may hide as shadows under the furniture; but, wherever the light can penetrate, the darkness must vanish.

In other words, we have the capacity to introduce light into a room; and, as we do, darkness must dissipate. I do not know of anyone who can do the opposite — that is, introduce such darkness into a room that light will vanish.

The ultimate power rests with the Lord and with His priesthood, with His servants. That idea should be an encouragement to members of the Church when they are intruded upon by forces that are evil and dark. Ultimately the power of light can hold them in abeyance.

Joseph Smith tells us:

> When the light rested upon me I saw two Personages, whose brightness and glory defy all description, standing above me in the air. One of them spake unto me, calling me by name and said, pointing to the other — *This is My Beloved Son. Hear Him!* (JS-H: 17.)

From the Lord Jesus Christ Himself, the young Joseph received his answer: He was to join none of the existing churches because "they teach for doctrines the commandments of men." He was told that the fullness of the gospel would at some future time be made known to him.

The Gospel Restored

This glorious visitation was the first of many heavenly manifestations to the Prophet Joseph Smith. A few years later, in September 1823, in response to another fervent prayer he was visited by an angel, Moroni, who in four visits over a period of a few hours instructed him on the coming forth of the kingdom. In particular he told Joseph of the Book of Mormon plates hidden in the nearby Hill Cumorah and of his calling to translate them under direction of the Spirit. He received these plates four years later, in September 1827; and after many vicissitudes he completed the translation in June 1829.

That translation sparked another angelic ministration. As Joseph and his scribe, Oliver Cowdery, came across references to baptism in the plates, they wanted to know more about it. Inquiring of the Lord in prayer on the banks of the Susquehanna River near Harmony, Pennsylvania, on May 15, 1829, they were visited by the resurrected John the Baptist, who laid his hands on their heads and conferred upon them the Aaronic Priesthood, as follows:

> Upon you my fellow servants, in the name of Messiah I confer the Priesthood of Aaron, which holds the keys of the ministering of angels, and of the gospel of repentance, and of baptism by immersion for the remission of sins; and this shall never be taken again from the earth, until the sons of Levi do offer again an offering unto the Lord in righteousness. (D&C 13.)

Now they had authority to baptize—and under the angel's instruction they proceeded to baptize each other.

The two men had not long to wait for a further addition of priesthood authority, for a week or two later Peter, James, and John appeared to them and conferred upon them the Higher or Melchizedek Priesthood including the holy apostleship. Thus ordained, they were now qualified to set up the kingdom of God on earth when the Lord should so direct them.

So it was that, on April 6, 1830, they gathered in the log house of Peter Whitmer, Senior, in Fayette, New York, and established the Church of Jesus Christ under divine direction. They prayed; they confirmed and bestowed the gift of the Holy Ghost upon those who had previously been baptized; they partook of the sacrament; and they ordained men to priesthood offices. There was a great outpouring of the Spirit, so that all rejoiced and some prophesied.

Others present at the meeting received baptism shortly after this, and from then on the new church grew continually. The great latter-day work had been launched, and none would be able to halt its progress.

There was more to be given. Much more. The Lord told Peter that he would build his church upon the rock of revelation, and that the gates of hell would not prevail against it. He said to Peter, "I *will* give unto thee the keys of the kingdom of heaven: and whatsoever thou shalt bind on earth shall be bound in heaven: and whatsoever thou shalt loose on earth shall be loosed in heaven." (Matthew 16:19; italics added.) The word *will* makes it clear that the Savior had not given those keys to Peter at the time he spoke. That would come in the future.

It was six days later that He took Peter, James, and John "up into an high mountain apart, and was transfigured before them: and his face did shine as the sun, and his raiment was white as the light. And, behold, there appeared unto them Moses and Elias [Elijah] talking with him." (Matthew 17:1-3.)

Peter proposed the building of three tabernacles—indicating that he sensed a visitation of that kind to be of the most sacred nature.

A bright cloud overshadowed them and they heard the voice of God the Father, Elohim, responding as He would later to Joseph in the grove: "This is my beloved Son, in whom I am well pleased; hear ye him." (Matthew 17:5.)

In 1830, much was yet to be given to Joseph and his

followers. The most sacred of these additions were worthy of a "tabernacle" or a "temple."

That little band of followers was to grow. While yet but few in number, they began — in spite of trials in the extreme — to build, for the first time in the dispensation of the fullness of times, a holy temple.

*For thou knowest that we have done this work
through great tribulation; and out of our poverty
we have given of our substance to build a house to
thy name, that the Son of Man might have a place
to manifest himself to his people.*
(D&C 109:5.)

12

A Place Prepared

Kirtland, Ohio, and the surrounding area occupies a prominent and honored position in the history of the Restoration.

Embarking on the first mission outside of the state of New York, Oliver Cowdery and the recently baptized Parley P. Pratt and two others proselyted the area in late 1830 on their way to Missouri. Many received baptism with gladness, among them future leaders Sidney Rigdon and Edward Partridge. In response to the Lord's commandment the body of the Saints from New York state moved there early in 1831, and it became the center of Church activity for about seven formative years until the end of 1837, when the center of Church activity moved to the Missouri settlements.

Many scenes that enrich our history, both inspiring and otherwise, were enacted in and around Kirtland. Here Joseph Smith produced his inspired translation of the Bible. Here the School of the Prophets met in an eleven-by-fourteen foot room above the Whitney store. In Hiram the Prophet was dragged from his bed by a mob and tarred and feathered. From Kirtland the Zion's Camp march set off on its thousand-mile trek to Missouri. Here the first Quorum of the Twelve Apostles was called and ordained and the Quorum of the Seventy was organized. And here apostasy took shape and spread with such power as to eventually compel the Prophet and other leaders to flee to Missouri.

An important measure of the contribution of the Kirtland period is the wealth of doctrine and instruction the Lord revealed there through the Prophet Joseph Smith. No less than sixty-five of the sections in our current Doctrine and Covenants were received in the Kirtland area, plus ten or eleven others received in other places during the Kirtland years. They include the revelation on health, known as the Word of Wisdom (section 89), two major revelations on priesthood (84 and 107), several on the temporal welfare of the Saints, the glorious truths of the "Olive Leaf" (88), and the magnificent vision of the three degrees of glory (76).

The Kirtland Temple

But Kirtland's most significant contribution to our present consideration is the house of the Lord the Saints built there out of their poverty and sacrifice — the Kirtland Temple. This was the first temple of the present dispensation. The command to build it came at the end of 1832:

> Organize yourselves; prepare every needful thing; and establish a house, even a house of prayer, a house of fasting, a house of faith, a house of learning, a house of glory, a house of order, a house of God. (D&C 88:119.)

> Verily I say unto you, it is my will that you should build a house. If you keep my commandments you shall have power to build it. (D&C 95:11.)

It appears that serious construction work on the temple began on June 5, 1833, when "George A. Smith hauled the first load of stone for the Temple, and Hyrum Smith and Reynolds Cahoon commenced digging the trench for the walls of the Lord's house, and finished the same with their own hands." (*HC*, 1:353.) The temple committee and others were soon busily occupied in obtaining stone, brick, lumber and other materials; funds were solicited; labor was donated for the construction; and the sisters provided food and clothes for the workers. The cost of the temple is estimated at $200,000, a very large sum in those days. Almost all of it was given at considerable sacrifice. At the last, many of the women donated precious china to be ground up and added to the surfaces of the stuccoed plaster walls to give them sparkle.

The design and construction of the Kirtland Temple was different from that of all other latter-day temples because its purpose was different. While already in 1836 certain ordinances had been introduced in a limited way which later would form part of the regular temple ordinances, the sacred ordinances and ceremonies performed in today's temples were not done in this first temple. The priesthood keys necessary for this work were yet to be restored. This temple was built as a holy place in which that restoration was to take place.

In addition this temple had another special but connected purpose. The sacrifice the Saints had made to build it, the spiritual power they had built in the process, and their continued ardent desires to do the Lord's will had fitted them for the spiritual manifestations which would "endow [them] with power from on high" (D&C 95:8). When the Saints were empowered by those manifestations, the missionaries would go forth with new zeal and success to spread the gospel, and their womenfolk at home would have the strength and endurance to match those efforts.

The main floor of the Kirtland Temple was basically a house of worship. The Saints met there for Sabbath services, general conferences of the Church, fast meetings (then held on the first Thursday of the month), and so on.

There were other refinements, to take account of the special nature of this building. At both the east and west ends of the main floor were three ascending rows of three pulpits, one row behind the other, the Melchizedek Priesthood pulpits at one end and Aaronic Priesthood pulpits at the other. The seats in the hall were reversible, so that the audience could face either way. Further, white canvas curtains (referred to as veils) could be dropped which divided the room into four areas for separate meetings as desired. All this was in accord with the Lord's instructions to Joseph Smith.

> And let the lower part of the inner court be dedicated unto me for your sacrament offering, and for your preaching, and your fasting, and your praying, and the offering up of your most holy desires unto me, saith your Lord. (D&C 95:16.)

It was following a sacrament meeting that the glorious event for which the building was erected took place. Fittingly it occurred on a Sunday.

We saw the Lord standing upon the breastwork of the pulpit, before us; and under his feet was a paved work of pure gold, in color like amber. (D&C 110:2.)

13

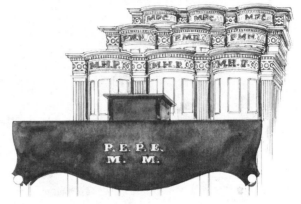

"We Saw the Lord...."

The day of the returning came! It was on a Sunday afternoon, April 3, 1836. A sacrament meeting had been held in the Kirtland Temple. The first temple of this dispensation was not like those to be built later. It was not arranged to accommodate the sacred ordinances that would be revealed once the temple had been dedicated. The Saints had extended themselves and sacrificed to build a temple, without fully comprehending the monumental contribution they were making to the history of mankind. They built to the extent of the light and knowledge that had been given to them at that point. Another line, another precept, and they had provided a building sufficient for the restoration of those keys which, when held, would open the heavens so that the revelations on the sacred ordinances might be poured out upon them.

The temple had been dedicated, the solemn assemblies had been held, the faithful had attended in numbers beyond expectation. The Saints perhaps approached the spring of 1836 as though events of sufficient power and inspiration had already been poured out upon them to last through the years ahead. But there was more to come, much more.

The Prophet described that afternoon, April 3, 1836, in these simple terms:

> In the afternoon, I assisted the other Presidents in distributing the Lord's Supper to the Church, receiving it from the Twelve, whose privilege it was to officiate at the sacred desk this day. After having performed this service to my brethren, I retired to the pulpit, the veils being dropped, and bowed myself, with Oliver Cowdery, in solemn and silent prayer. (*HC*, 2:435.)

The Savior Introduces Three Heavenly Beings

From the previous description of the temple we can visualize the veils having been dropped to cover the end of the large room where the pulpits of the Melchizedek Priesthood stand. Joseph and Oliver were behind the veil, separated in privacy from any others who may have been in the building. They completed their "solemn and silent prayer." The Prophet recorded, "After rising from prayer, the following vision was opened to both of us." (D&C 110, introduction.)

I remind you that they were standing in full capacity, alert and present, when these remarkable events unfolded in such a succession that as one glorious vision faded, another burst upon them. All of this is described in the sixteen short verses of section 110 of the Doctrine and Covenants as follows:

> The veil was taken from our minds, and the eyes of our understanding were opened.
>
> We saw the Lord standing upon the breastwork of the pulpit, before us; and under his feet was a paved work of pure gold, in color like amber.

His eyes were as a flame of fire; the hair of his head was white like the pure snow; his countenance shone above the brightness of the sun; and his voice was as the sound of the rushing of great waters, even the voice of Jehovah, saying:

I am the first and the last; I am he who liveth, I am he who was slain; I am your advocate with the Father.

Behold, your sins are forgiven you; you are clean before me; therefore, lift up your heads and rejoice.

Let the hearts of your brethren rejoice, and let the hearts of all my people rejoice, who have, with their might, built this house to my name.

For behold, I have accepted this house, and my name shall be here; and I will manifest myself to my people in mercy in this house.

Yea, I will appear unto my servants, and speak unto them with mine own voice, if my people will keep my commandments, and do not pollute this holy house.

Yea the hearts of thousands and tens of thousands shall greatly rejoice in consequence of the blessings which shall be poured out, and the endowment with which my servants have been endowed in this house.

And the fame of this house shall spread to foreign lands; and this is the beginning of the blessing which shall be poured out upon the heads of my people. Even so. Amen.

After this vision closed, the heavens were again opened unto us; and Moses appeared before us, and committed unto us the keys of the gathering of Israel from the four parts of the earth, and the leading of the ten tribes from the land of the north.

After this, Elias appeared and committed the dispensation of the gospel of Abraham, saying that in us and our seed all generations after us should be blessed.

After this vision had closed, another great and glorious vision burst upon us; for Elijah the prophet, who was taken to heaven without tasting death, stood before us, and said:

Behold, the time has fully come, which was spoken of by the mouth of Malachi—testifying that he [Elijah] should be sent, before the great and dreadful day of the Lord come—

To turn the hearts of the fathers to the children, and the children to the fathers, lest the whole earth be smitten with a curse—

Therefore, the keys of this dispensation are committed into your hands; and by this ye may know that the great and dreadful day of the Lord is near, even at the doors.

And so it had happened. Elijah had returned. Or we might say it had happened again. For, as we have related, some eighteen hundred years previously Moses had appeared with Elijah on the Mount of Transfiguration. They had conveyed the keys of the priesthood to Peter, James, and John. The Lord Himself had made the introduction, as he now had in the Kirtland Temple.

President Joseph Fielding Smith commented on the coincident observance by the Jews on this day:

> It was, I am informed, on the third day of April, 1836, that the Jews, in their homes at the Paschal feast, opened their doors for Elijah to enter. On that very day Elijah did enter—not in the home of the Jews to partake of the Passover with them—but he appeared in the house of the Lord, erected to his name and received by the Lord in Kirtland, and there bestowed his keys to bring to pass the very thing for which these Jews, assembled in their homes, were seeking. (*Doctrines of Salvation*, 2:101.)

Now, once again the Lord Himself appears, leaving no doubt as to His identity. "I am the first and the last; I am he who liveth, I am he who was slain; I am your advocate with the Father."

What would it be worth to have announced to you, as was announced to Joseph and Oliver on this occasion, "Behold, your sins are forgiven you; you are clean before me; therefore, lift up your heads and rejoice"?

The rejoicing the Lord referred to was extended beyond those two brethren to His people in the thousands and tens of thousands who would rejoice in consequence of what would be accomplished that Sabbath day.

"Yea the hearts of thousands and tens of thousands shall greatly rejoice in consequence of the blessings which shall be poured out, and the endowment with which my servants have been endowed in this house." Consider these other references to endowment, or the conferring of spiritual power: D&C 38:32, 38; 39:15; 43:16; and 95:8-9.

At this time the Lord prophesied that the "fame of this house shall spread to foreign lands." (D&C 110:10.) That, under the circumstances then existing, was at best improbable. The Church members were but a handful of Saints living and scattered in the rural areas of a new land. But despite the persecution and struggles and trials of those early days, there are congregations now spread literally across the world, and tens of thousands of missionaries bear witness at every door where they are welcome.

Significance of Elijah's Return

As provoking to scholars as the prophecy was that Elijah would return, an even greater mystery to them concerns what Malachi said Elijah was to do, and what would take place if he did not in fact return. "And he shall turn the heart of the fathers to the children and the heart of the children to their fathers, lest I come and smite the earth with a curse." (Malachi 4:6.)

What does it mean to turn the hearts of the fathers to the children and the hearts of the children to their fathers? Why should that be so significant that, if it failed to be brought about, the Lord would "smite the earth with a curse"?

Those verses have intrigued the clergymen and scholars for centuries. They have not known where to turn to find the answer.

The answer came when the dispensation of the fulness of times was ushered in.

We can turn back to the history of the Prophet. During the three and a half years following the First Vision he experienced a testing, a tempering, a preparation. And then, on September 21, 1823, he sought the Lord in fervent prayer. He was in his small bedroom in the modest farm home in rural Palmyra, New York. He opened the record of this experience with these words:

> While I was thus in the act of calling upon God, I discovered a light appearing in my room, which continued to increase until the room was lighter than at noonday, when immediately a personage appeared at my bedside, standing in the air, for his feet did not touch the floor. (JS-H: 30.)

The angel introduced himself by name. He was Moroni, who had lived anciently on the American continent. He told Joseph Smith of a work that Joseph was to do, and of the existence of the Book of Mormon plates and the Urim and Thummim, and he showed him where they were.

The angel Moroni then commenced quoting prophecies from the Old Testament.

> He first quoted part of the third chapter of Malachi; and he quoted also the fourth or last chapter of the same prophecy, though with a little variation from the way it reads in our Bibles. Instead of quoting the first verse as it reads in our books, he quoted it thus:
>
> *For behold, the day cometh that shall burn as an oven, and all the proud, yea, and all that do wickedly shall burn as stubble; for they that come shall burn them, saith the Lord of Hosts, that it shall leave them neither root nor branch.*
>
> And again, he quoted the fifth verse thus: *Behold, I will reveal unto you the Priesthood, by the hand of Elijah the prophet, before the coming of the great and dreadful day of the Lord.*
>
> He also quoted the next verse differently: *And he shall plant in the hearts of the children the promises made to the fathers, and the hearts of the children shall turn to their fathers. If it were not so, the whole earth would be utterly wasted at his coming.* (JS-H: 36-39.)

He quoted also the eleventh chapter of Isaiah and the third chapter of Acts, the twenty-second and twenty-third verses, precisely as they stand in the New Testament. He told Joseph Smith that Christ was the prophet referred to, "but the day had not yet come when 'they who would not hear his voice should be cut off from among the people,' but soon would come." (JS-H: 40.)

The angel also quoted Joel, the second chapter, verses 28 through 32. And then, the Prophet tells us, "he quoted many other passages of scripture, and offered many explanations which cannot be mentioned here." (JS-H: 41.)

The statement of Malachi concerning Elijah was treated differently from all the others given him on that occasion. It was separated out, considered of unique importance, and registered in a way different from all the rest. The Prophet did not, perhaps, understand the full significance of Moroni repeating the prophecy of the coming of Elijah. It was to be thirteen years later that the next major chapter would open in this thread of scriptural and doctrinal history, and nearly twenty years would pass before the revelations would come which would give a greatly expanded explanation.

Section 2 of the Doctrine and Covenants is the Moroni rendering of Elijah's prophesied coming.

> Behold, I will reveal unto you the Priesthood, by the hand of Elijah the prophet, before the coming of the great and dreadful day of the Lord.
>
> And he shall plant in the hearts of the children the promises made to the fathers, and the hearts of the children shall turn to their fathers.
>
> If it were not so, the whole earth would be utterly wasted at his coming. (D&C 2:1-3.)

There seems to have been guidance in the selection and placement of that quotation as a section in the Doctrine and Covenants. Other references that Moroni quoted, from Isaiah or Joel or Acts or the "many other passages of scripture," were not thus honored.

Revelation Continuous

Revelation is a continuous principle in the Church. In one sense the Church is still being organized. As light and knowledge are given, as prophecies are fulfilled and more intelligence is received, another step forward can be taken. Consider this illustration:

When a contractor is to construct a building, he has beforehand, for careful study and then for bidding, the plans and specifications. It is common procedure for these to be complete in great detail. They show the elevation, or the drawing of the building, to indicate how it will appear from the front, and the sides, and the back. Not infrequently a colored elevation or painting of the building also is available to the contractor. He can then see how the architect envisions the building will look when it is completed. The plans are carefully and minutely drawn, with details included, as careful drawings or as symbols, for electrical outlets, parts of the plumbing and heating systems, etc. And then the book of specifications (which on a large building can be a heavy volume) also gives descriptions in detail of the kinds of material to be used, all that the architect and the owner will require of the contractor. With these details before him, the contractor then can see the end from the beginning, as it were. He can see the building as a whole, or can search out any detail of it to know what is expected of him.

This is not so with the prophets. When the Lord called Joseph Smith, He gave him line upon line, precept upon precept, here a little and there a little. Step by step Joseph was led with revelations and direction. Ordinarily these came in answer to inquiries by the Prophet. They came as answers to prayers. The First Vision was in response to a fervent prayer on the part of the boy prophet.

The theme that is more prominent in the scriptures perhaps than any other one is given in the Savior's words: "Ask, and it shall be given you; seek, and ye shall find; knock, and it shall be opened unto you: for everyone that asketh receiveth; and he that seeketh findeth; and to him that knocketh it shall be opened." (Matthew 7:7-8.) It is said in more ways in holy writ than almost any other message. "Behold, I stand at the door, and knock: if any man hear my voice, and open the door, I will come in to him, and will sup with him, and he with me." (Revelation 3:20.)

It was in response to the asking that Joseph Smith the Prophet received each line of the plans for the Church, each detail and each specification. Nor was it fully revealed in his lifetime. Nor has it been yet. The Restoration continues.

President Wilford Woodruff said: "The Church of God could not live twenty-four hours without revelation." (*The Discourses of Wilford Woodruff*, ed. G. Homer Durham [Salt Lake City: Bookcraft, 1969], page 61.) Speaking on the subject of redemption for the dead, he plainly said:

I want to say, as the President of The Church of Jesus Christ of Latter-day Saints, that we should now go on and progress. *We have not got through revelation. We have not got through the work of God.* But at this period we want to go on and fulfill this commandment of God given through Malachi — that the Lord should send *Elijah* the prophet, "and he shall turn the heart of the fathers to the children, and the heart of the children to their fathers lest I come and smite the earth with a curse." Ye sons of men, I say unto you, *in the name of Israel's God,* those very principles that God has *revealed are what have stayed the judgment of the Almighty on the earth.* Were it not for these principles, you and I would not be here today. We have had prophets and apostles. President Young who followed President Joseph Smith, led us here. He organized these Temples and carried out the purposes of his calling and office. He laid the foundation of this great Temple on this block, as well as others in the mountains of Israel. What for? That we might *carry out these principles of redemption for the dead.* He accomplished all that God required at his hands. But he did not receive all the revelations that belong to this work; neither did President Taylor, nor has Wilford Woodruff. There will be no end to this work until it is perfected. ("The Law of Adoption," *The Utah Genealogical and Historical Magazine* 13 [October 1922]: 147-48; italics added.)

In our day there has been a marvelous outpouring of revelations, setting in order this matter or that, and showing the way ahead as the fulness of the everlasting gospel is progressively restored to the earth.

The Turning of the Hearts

Elijah would return. Why? If that turning of the hearts of the fathers to the children and the children to the fathers were not accomplished, the Lord would "smite the earth with a curse," as the King James Version of the Old Testament says, or "the whole earth would be utterly wasted at his coming," as Moroni quoted it to the Prophet Joseph Smith.

We will follow that theme of the turning of the hearts of the fathers to the children and the children to the fathers, for it emerges again and again in the revelations. It draws us toward the day of transcendent importance when Elijah did at last appear.

The next recorded angelic appearance to follow Moroni's visits came in August of 1830. Four months after the Church was organized, the Prophet Joseph Smith was making arrangements for a meeting at which the sacrament was to be administered. When he went to procure the bread and wine he was met by a heavenly messenger from whom he received a commandment that he should "not purchase wine neither strong drink of your enemies." (D&C 27:3.) He learned that "it mattereth not what ye shall eat or what ye shall drink when ye partake of the sacrament, if it so be that ye do it with an eye single to my glory — remembering unto the Father my body which was laid down for you, and my blood which was shed for the remission of your sins." (D&C 27:2.)

These words began section 27 of the Doctrine and Covenants. The following month, in September, the Prophet received the balance of that section. It speaks of Moroni having come to reveal the Book of Mormon. It tells of "Elias, to whom I have committed the keys of bringing to pass the restoration of all things spoken by the mouth of all the holy prophets since the world began, concerning the last days." (D&C 27:6.) It tells of John the Baptist, who had been sent as *an* Elias.

> And also John the son of Zacharias, which Zacharias he (Elias) visited and gave promise that he should have a son, and his name should be John, and he should be filled with the spirit of Elias;
> Which John I have sent unto you, my servants, Joseph Smith, Jun., and Oliver Cowdery, to ordain you unto the first priesthood which you have received, that you might be called and ordained even as Aaron. (D&C 27:7-8.)

And then this golden thread again appears:

> And also Elijah, unto whom I have committed the keys of the power of turning the hearts of the fathers to the children, and the hearts of the children to the fathers, that the whole earth may not be smitten with a curse. (D&C 27:9.)

Elijah would return, and he would turn the hearts of the fathers to the children, and the hearts of the children to the fathers; and again comes the statement which carries some prophetic hope that, if this could be accomplished, "the whole earth may not be smitten with a curse."

President Joseph Fielding Smith wrote: *"Why would the earth be wasted? Simply because if there is not a welding link between the fathers and the children — which is the work for the dead — then we will all stand rejected; the whole work of God will fail and be utterly wasted.* Such a condition, of course, shall not be." (*Doctrines of Salvation,* 2:122.)

The Prophet Joseph Smith said:

> Elijah was the last Prophet that held the keys of the Priesthood, and who will, before the last dispensation, restore the authority and deliver *the keys of the Priesthood,* in order that all the ordinances may be attended to in righteousness. It is true that the Savior had authority and power to bestow this blessing; but the sons of Levi were too prejudiced. "And I will send Elijah the Prophet before the great and terrible day of the Lord," etc., etc. Why send Elijah? Because he holds the keys of the authority to administer in all the ordinances of the Priesthood; and without the authority is given, the ordinances could not be administered in righteousness. (*HC,* 4:211; italics added.)

It happened! This signal event went unheeded by the world, but it would influence the destiny of every soul who has ever lived or will live. Things began quietly to happen. The Church became a temple-building church.

In the world there emerged here and there, in a way thought to be spontaneous, people and organizations and societies interested in tracing genealogies. This has all taken place since the appearance of Elijah in the Kirtland Temple. I quote from President Joseph Fielding Smith:

> *Before* the year 1836 there was very little, if any, research being made anywhere in this world in behalf of the dead. It is true that here and there some man may have been searching out a genealogical record, but what was his object? To prove title to some estate.

There were no genealogical societies; there were no genealogical organizations; there were no genealogical researches of any systematic character anywhere in the world. . . .

. . . One year after this revelation was given and these keys were bestowed, we find in Great Britain the government passing laws compelling the preservation of duplicate records of the dead on the part of those who kept them. . . .

In the year 1844, the year of the martyrdom, the first organization for the purpose of gathering together the records of the dead, and compiling genealogical records, was formed in the city of Boston. It was the New England Historical and Genealogical Society. In 1869, in the city of New York, another society, the New York Genealogical and Biographical Society, was organized.

Since that day societies have sprung up all over the land. . . . The hearts of the children have *since* that day turned to their fathers, and they are searching out the records of their dead. . . .

In the year 1902 the Legislature of the State of Massachusetts passed a measure providing for the compiling of the vital records of all the towns of the state, from their settlement down to the year 1850, and the genealogical organizations have the privilege of making these compilations. . . .

Following this the people in Rhode Island, and I understood also Connecticut and other states, have followed the lead of Massachusetts and are providing for the publication of the vital records of all towns in those states, from the beginning to the year 1850. . . .

In Great Britain, genealogical societies have been organized in practically every county in that land and in Scotland. These records have been kept and filed also in other countries in Europe, the countries from which the Latter-day Saints have come. The spirit has taken hold of the people, not only in the Church, but also of many who are not of the Church, and they too are searching the records, and compiling them, of the dead. (*Doctrines of Salvation*, 2:124-26).

From that very day, April 3, 1836, the hearts of the children began to turn to their fathers.

Behold, mine house is a house of order, saith the Lord God, and not a house of confusion. (D&C 132:8.)

14

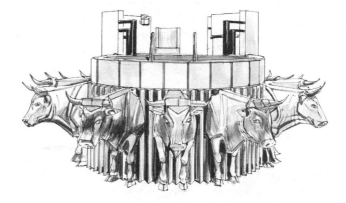

All Done in Order

Following the dramatic events at the Kirtland Temple, difficulties and persecutions required that the Saints move. Wherever they located, they made plans to build a temple. This was true in both Independence and Far West, Missouri. In this period persecution fell upon the Saints with unprecedented rage and eventually they fled to Nauvoo, Illinois. Here the revelation came again and the commandment to build a house of the Lord. The Lord gave the reason "for there is not a place found on the earth that he may come to and restore again that which was lost unto you, or which he hath taken away, even the fulness of the priesthood." (D&C 124:28.)

In describing some of the work that would be accomplished in the temple He further said, "for therein are the keys of the holy priesthood ordained, that you may receive honor and glory." (D&C 124:34.)

The Lord explained that the purpose of the building of the house was to reveal the ordinances. "And verily I say unto you, let this house be built unto my name, that I may reveal mine ordinances therein unto my people. For I deign to reveal unto my church things which have been kept hid from before the foundation of the world, things that pertain to the dispensation of the fulness of times." (D&C 124:40-41.)

He had mentioned that the temple would be a place for them to conduct "your anointings, and your washings, and your baptisms for the dead, and your solemn assemblies, and your memorials for your sacrifices by the sons of Levi, and for your oracles in your most holy places wherein you receive conversations, and your statutes and judgments, for the beginning of the revelations and foundation of Zion, and for the glory, honor, and endowment of all her municipals, . . . by the ordinance of my holy house, which my people are always commanded to build unto my holy name." (D&C 124:39.)

Order, Ordain, Ordinance

To explain something of the significance of the ordinances I begin with the Third Article of Faith. This states: "We believe that through the Atonement of Christ, all mankind may be saved, by obedience to the laws and ordinances of the Gospel."

The word *ordinance* means, "a religious or ceremonial observance"; "an established rite."

The *Oxford English Dictionary* (Oxford, England, 1970) gives as the first definition of the word *order*, "arrangement in ranks or rows," and as the second definition, "arrangement in sequence or proper relative position." At first glance that may not strike a person as having much religious significance, but indeed it has.

Among the ordinances we perform in the Church are these: baptism, sacrament, naming and blessing of infants, administering to the sick, setting apart to callings in the Church, ordaining to offices. In addition there are higher ordinances, performed in the temples. These include washings, anointings, the endowment, and the sealing ordinance, spoken of generally as temple marriage.

The word *ordinance* comes from the word *order*, which means, "a rank, a row, a series." The word *order* appears frequently in the scriptures. Some examples are: ". . . established the *order* of the Church" (Alma 8:1); ". . . all things should be restored to their proper *order*" (Alma 41:2); ". . . all things may be done in *order*" (D&C 20:68); "mine house is a house of *order*" (D&C 132:8). Mormon even defined depravity as being "without *order*" (Moroni 9:18).

The word *ordain*, a close relative to the other two words, has, as its first definition, "to put in order, arrange, make ready, prepare"; also, "to appoint or admit to the ministry of the Christian church . . . by the laying on of hands or other symbolic action."

From all of this dictionary work there comes the impression that an ordinance, to be valid, must be done in proper order.

Order

Ordain

Ordinance

Order—To put in ranks or rows, in proper sequence or relationship.

Ordain—The process of putting things in rows of proper relationship.

Ordinance—The ceremony by which things are put in proper order.

Authorized Gospel Ordinances Crucial

Now, what about the ordinances of the gospel? How important are they to us as members of the Church?

Can you be happy, can you be redeemed, can you be exalted without them? Answer: They are more than advisable or desirable, or even than necessary. More even than essential or vital. They are *crucial* to each of us.

We learn from the revelations:

> And this greater [Melchizedek] priesthood administereth the gospel and holdeth the key of the mysteries of the kingdom, even the key of the knowledge of God.
>
> Therefore, in the *ordinances* thereof, the power of godliness is manifest.
>
> And without the *ordinances* thereof, and the authority of the priesthood, the power of godliness is not manifest unto men in the flesh. (D&C 84:19-21; italics added.)

This chapter is not intended as a merely theoretical discussion. Rather I address it directly to you, the reader, with the intent, if I can, to induce in your mind and heart so serious an interest in the ordinances of the gospel that, if you have not yet received them, you will seek to qualify for each of the ordinances in proper sequence and to make and keep the covenants that are connected with each of them. If you have already received the ordinances, I hope these words stimulate within you a new resolve to observe strictly the covenants they embody. Make sure, in other words, that valid ordinances become a part of your life; that everything in this regard, for you, is in proper *order*.

Consider this illustration: Suppose that an agent comes to you offering a big bargain on insurance. He claims that his policy offers complete protection. He talks of generous coverage, very low premiums, no penalties for making a claim—even a heavy claim. Other features too make the policy look better than any you have considered before.

You are impressed by the insurance company the salesman names. You have heard of it as being completely reputable. As you study the policy your interest grows, for you find that it offers more to you, with less required of you, than any policy you have considered before.

Now you check carefully on the company and come away satisfied that they are reputable indeed. They do stand behind their policies. Some of your friends have dealt with them for years, and have always been satisfied. It appears, then, that you have found a real bargain. So you start paying premiums and you receive the completed policy.

But in this imaginary account there is one thing that you did not discover — there is, in fact, a hitch. The snag is that this salesman was never hired by that company. They have not authorized him to represent them. The company is not aware that he is using their name. He obtained copies of the policy and letterhead and adjusted the policy to give it wider appeal. He had some forms and letterheads printed and set himself up in business.

When he writes a policy and collects the premiums, they do not go to the head office. His copy of the policy goes into a drawer somewhere, the premium money into his pocket. Chances are, he figures, there will be no claim against the policy anyway — at least not while he is around. Since it is life insurance, certainly there will be no claim while the insured person is around. As the expression goes, you have been sold a bill of goods.

Meanwhile, you are comfortable with the thought that you are well insured. You feel content and suppose that, when the day comes, as it surely will, your claim will be paid. Too bad for you! Obviously the company will reject the claim. They cannot be compelled to honor policies except those written by authorized agents whom they have hired and certified. No matter how convinced you were that this man was a bona fide agent, he was not, and none of his agreements made in the company's name are valid.

Will you get sympathy? Yes. Full value of the policy? Not a chance! Would you not receive anything? Well, perhaps a little. As long as you didn't know the difference, you had the peace of mind for that period of time when you thought you were well insured — for whatever that is worth.

My wife has an aged aunt. She was one of fourteen children. Perhaps seventy-five years ago Millicent, in Brigham City, Utah, took her little brothers and sisters to town to see the Peach Days Parade.

With wonder and excitement they walked the long way to town. They hadn't been there long when a horse-drawn water wagon came along, sprinkling the streets to settle the dust. They watched it in awe; and when it had passed they went home, very impressed. They thought the parade was over. They were quite satisfied, until a year later they learned the difference.

If you had been sold the insurance policy we talked about, you too might be satisfied, even complacent, thinking you were well insured. What a shock when you discovered the truth! Somewhere in later conversations would come the sermon: "You ought to have been more careful about where you put your trust. You should have checked more carefully."

Now let me apply this illustration to the ordinances of the gospel.

With these ordinances there are no discounts. There is no credit buying. Nothing is ever put on sale at special reduced prices. There is never something for nothing. There is no such thing as a "bargain." You pay full value. Requirements and covenants are involved. And in due time you will get full value. But to obtain this full value you must, positively must, deal with an authorized agent.

Let me quote this meaningful scripture from section 132 of the Doctrine and Covenants:

> And verily I say unto you, that the conditions of this law are these: All covenants, contracts, bonds, obligations, oaths, vows, performances, connections, associations, or expectations, that are not made and entered into and sealed by the Holy Spirit of promise, of him who is anointed, both as well for time and for all eternity, and that too most holy, by revelation and commandment through the medium of mine anointed, whom I have appointed on the earth to hold this power (and I have appointed unto my servant Joseph to

hold this power in the last days, and there is never but one on the earth at a time on whom this power and the keys of this priesthood are conferred), are of no efficacy, virtue, or force in and after the resurrection from the dead; for all contracts that are not made unto this end have an end when men are dead.

Behold, mine house is a house of *order*, saith the Lord God, and not a house of confusion.

Will I accept of an offering, saith the Lord, that is not made in my name?

Or will I receive at your hands that which I have not appointed?

And will I appoint unto you, saith the Lord, except it be by law, even as I and my Father *ordained* unto you, before the world was?

I am the Lord thy God; and I give unto you this commandment — that no man shall come unto the Father but by me or by my word, which is my law, saith the Lord.

And everything that is in the world, whether it be ordained of men, by thrones, or principalities, or powers, or things of name, whatsoever they may be, that are not by me or by my word, saith the Lord, shall be thrown down, and shall not remain after men are dead, neither in nor after the resurrection, saith the Lord your God.

For whatsoever things remain are by me; and whatsoever things are not by me shall be shaken and destroyed. (D&C 132:7-14; italics added.)

That scripture is very clear. He will not, "saith the Lord," accept of an offering that is not made in His name. Nor will He receive at our hands that which He has not appointed. And things that are "ordained of men . . . shall not remain . . . in nor after the resurrection."

With these solemn words in mind, each Latter-day Saint needs to take inventory of his spiritual progress, and to ask himself the questions: Is my life in order? Do I have all of the ordinances of the gospel that I should possess by this time in my life? Are they valid?

If you can answer these questions affirmatively, and if the ordinances come under the influence of the sealing power and authority, they will remain intact eternally. In that case your life, to this point, is in proper order. You then would do well to think of your family, living and dead, with the same questions in mind.

Limits to Delegated Authority

Now I make another comparison as I explain something that is understood by relatively few. It is common in the world for institutions to delegate authority and at once strictly limit the extent of what is being delegated. For instance, in a branch bank the manager may have authorization to make loans up to a certain amount. If someone requests a loan larger than that amount, then a supervisor must approve it. For even larger amounts the regulations of the bank may require that only the president and chief executive officer himself may approve the loan.

If a commitment for a loan is made by a branch manager within the policy, the bank will honor it, even though that manager may later quit and go to work for a competing bank.

On one occasion I attended a meeting of the board of directors of a corporation. The board decided to give a certain employee authority to commit the company on some important matters. A motion was passed to this effect. One director then observed that a motion was not enough; it should have been a resolution, a formal one duly entered in the minutes. So the motion was replaced by a resolution, because delegating authority is serious business.

The practice of delegating authority, and at once limiting it, is so commonly demonstrated in business and education, in government, in cultural organizations, that we should not have difficulty in understanding that principle in the Church.

A missionary is given authority to teach and to baptize. Given certain approval, he can ordain someone to a priesthood office. If he is an elder, however, he cannot ordain someone to be a seventy or a high priest, for his authority is limited. Similarly, a bishop can call and release within the limits of his jurisdiction. But he could not, for instance, set apart a stake high councilor. Likewise a stake president can set apart a stake high councilor, but he cannot ordain a patriarch.

Those who hold the Aaronic Priesthood, or the preparatory priesthood, hold the authority, when specifically directed, to perform those ordinances that belong to that priesthood. They can baptize. They can bless the sacrament and perform every service relating to the lesser priesthood. They cannot confirm someone a member of the Church, however, for that takes a higher authority.

On the same principle, those who hold the Melchizedek Priesthood can perform the ordinances relating to the higher priesthood. But unless they are given special authorization they cannot endow, nor seal, nor perform those ordinances that pertain to the temple.

There are limits.

I heard President Kimball say on one occasion, as other Presidents of the Church have said, that, while he holds all of the keys that are held upon the earth, there are keys that he does not hold. There are keys that have not been given to him as President of the Church, because they are reserved to higher power and authority. For instance, he said that he does not hold the keys of the resurrection. The Lord holds them, but He has not delegated them — neither anciently, nor to modern prophets. President Kimball mentioned also the authority to command the elements, to walk on the water. The Lord has this power, but He has not given it to mortals, although there are times when righteous men have been inspired to command the forces of nature and have been obeyed.

Authority for All Ordinances

Nevertheless, in the Church we hold sufficient authority to perform all of the ordinances necessary to redeem and to exalt the whole human family. And, because we have the keys to the sealing power, what we bind in proper order here will be bound in heaven. Those keys — the keys to seal and bind on earth, and have it bound in heaven — represent the consummate gift from our God. With that authority we can baptize and bless, we can endow and seal, and the Lord will honor our commitments.

The Prophet Joseph Smith said he was frequently asked the question

"Can we not be saved without going through with all those ordinances, etc.?" I would answer, No, not the fullness of salvation. Jesus said, "There are many mansions in my Father's house, and I will go and prepare a place for you. *House* here named should have been translated kingdom; and any person who is exalted to the highest mansion has to abide a celestial law, and the whole law too. (*HC*, 6:184.)

On another occasion, talking on the same subject, he said:

There are mansions for those who obey a celestial law, and there are other mansions for those who come short of the law, every man in his own order. There is baptism, etc., for those to exercise who are alive, and baptism for the dead who die without the knowledge of the Gospel.

I am going on in my progress for eternal life. It is not only necessary that you should be baptized for your dead, but you will have to go through all the ordinances for them, the same as you have gone through to save yourselves. . . . Oh! I beseech you to go forward, go forward and make your calling and your election sure. (*HC*, 6:365.)

President Joseph Fielding Smith said:

I do not care what office you hold in this Church, you may be an apostle, you may be a patriarch, a high priest, or anything else, and you cannot receive the fulness of the priesthood unless you go into the temple of the Lord and receive these ordinances of which the prophet speaks. No man can get the fulness of the priesthood outside of the temple of the Lord.

He then said that there was a time when the Saints were unable to construct temples, when there was no house prepared in which to receive the ordinances, particularly when the persecutions were intense.

But now we have got temples, and you cannot get these blessings on the mountaintops, you will have to go into the house of the Lord, and you cannot get the fulness of the priesthood unless you go there. Do not think that because anybody has a higher office in the church than you have, that you are barred from blessings, because you can go into the temple of the Lord and get all the blessings there are that have been revealed, if you are faithful, have them sealed upon you as an elder in this Church, and then you have all that any man can get. There have to be offices in the Church, and we are not all called to the same calling, but you can get the fulness of the priesthood in the temple of the Lord. (*Elijah, the Prophet and His Mission,* pages 46-47.)

The Prophet Joseph Smith stated, "If there is no change of ordinance, there is no change of priesthood. Wherever the ordinances of the gospel are administered, there is the priesthood." (*Elijah, the Prophet and His Mission,* page 28.)

The Temple Ordinances

As mentioned previously, the ordinances of the temple include baptism, ordinations, endowments, marriages, and other sealing ordinances. I said earlier that in this book we would not discuss the ceremonies and ordinances of the temple beyond that which has previously been published by the Church. I include here a brief summary of the information that is available in print with reference to the temple ordinances.

To endow is to enrich, to give to another something long lasting and of much worth. The temple endowment ordinances enrich in three ways: (a) The one receiving the ordinance is given power from God. "Recipients are endowed with power from on high." (b) A recipient is also endowed with information and knowledge. "They receive an education relative to the Lord's purposes and plans." (*Mormon Doctrine,* page 227.) (c) When sealed at the altar a person is the recipient of glorious blessings, powers, and honors as part of his endowment.

There are two published definitions or descriptions of the endowment, the first by President Brigham Young:

> Let me give you a definition in brief. Your *endowment* is to receive all those ordinances in the House of the Lord, which are necessary for you, after you have departed this life, to enable you to walk back to the presence of the Father, passing the angels who stand as sentinels, being able to give them the key words, the signs and tokens, pertaining to the Holy Priesthood, and gain your eternal exaltation in spite of earth and hell. (*Discourses of Brigham Young,* comp. John A. Widtsoe [Salt Lake City: Deseret Book Co., 1971], page 637.)

Elder James E. Talmage described the endowment thus:

> The Temple Endowment, as administered in modern temples, comprises instruction relating to the significance and sequence of past dispensations, and the importance of the present as the greatest and grandest era in human history. This course of instruction includes a recital of the most prominent events of the creative period, the condition of our first parents in the Garden of Eden, their disobedience and consequent expulsion from that blissful abode, their condition in the lone and dreary world when doomed to live by labor and sweat, the plan of redemption by which the great transgression may be atoned, the period of the great apostasy, the restoration of the Gospel with all its ancient powers and privileges, the absolute and indispensable condition of personal purity and devotion to the right in present life, and a strict compliance with Gospel requirements. (*The House of the Lord*, pages 99-100.)

This statement from Brother Talmage makes it clear that when you receive your endowments you will receive instruction relative to the purpose and plans of the Lord in creating and peopling the earth. You will be taught what must be done for you to gain exaltation.

The Lord chastened the people for their hesitation in building the temple in Kirtland and said: "Yea, verily I say unto you, I gave unto you a commandment that you should build a house, in the which house I design to endow those whom I have chosen with power from on high; for this is the promise of the Father unto you." (D&C 95:8-9.)

The blessing of the endowment is required for full exaltation. Every Latter-day Saint should seek to be worthy of this blessing and to obtain it.

The ordinances of washing and anointing are referred to often in the temple as initiatory ordinances. It will be sufficient for our purposes to say only the following: Associated with the endowment are washings and anointings — mostly symbolic in nature, but promising definite, immediate blessings as well as future blessings. Concerning these ordinances the Lord has said: "I say unto you, how shall your washings be acceptable unto me, except ye perform them in a house which you have built to my name?" (D&C 124:37.)

And again: "I say unto you, that your anointings, and your washings . . . are ordained by the ordinance of my holy house." (D&C 124:39.)

In connection with these ordinances, in the temple you will be officially clothed in the garment and promised marvelous blessings in connection with it. It is important that you listen carefully as these ordinances are administered and that you try to remember the blessings promised and the conditions upon which they will be realized.

The sealing ordinance is that ordinance which binds families eternally. Temple marriage is a sealing ordinance. When a couple is sealed in the temple following a civil marriage the children born to them previous to that time, and therefore not born in the covenant, are sealed to them in a brief and sacred ordinance.

I have always been impressed that the ordinances of the temple are reverently and carefully administered. They are not complicated or extravagant, but are typical of the simplicity of the principles of the gospel.

Please be certain that your life is in complete order. This only comes from receiving your temple blessings, your ordinances, for "in the ordinances thereof, the power of godliness is manifest." (D&C 84:20.)

Now therefore, if ye will obey my voice indeed, and keep my covenant, then ye shall be a peculiar treasure unto me above all people: for all the earth is mine. And ye shall be unto me a kingdom of priests and an holy nation. (Exodus 19:5-6.)

15

Sacred Covenants

The Lord in the revelation now known as section 132 of the Doctrine and Covenants announces:

> For behold, I reveal unto you a new and an everlasting covenant; and if ye abide not that covenant, then ye are damned; for no one can reject this covenant and be permitted to enter into my glory.
>
> For all who will have a blessing at my hands shall abide the law which was appointed for that blessing, and the conditions thereof, as were instituted from before the foundation of the world. (D&C 132:4-5.)

President Joseph Fielding Smith defines the new and everlasting covenant in these words:

> What is the new and everlasting covenant? I regret to say that there are some members of the Church who are misled and mis-

informed in regard to what the new and everlasting covenant really is. *The new and everlasting covenant is the sum total of all gospel covenants and obligations,* and I want to prove it. In the 66th section of the *Doctrine and Covenants,* verse 2, I read:

"Verily I say unto you, blessed are you for receiving *mine everlasting covenant, even the fulness of my gospel,* sent forth unto the children of men, that they might have life and be made partakers of the glories which are to be revealed in the last days, as it was written by the prophets and apostles in days of old."

More definitely stated is the definition of the new and everlasting covenant given to us in section 132 of the *Doctrine and Covenants.* Now I am going to say before I read this that marriage is *not* the new and everlasting covenant. If there are any here that have that idea I want to say that right to them. Baptism is not the new and everlasting covenant. Ordination to the priesthood is not the new and everlasting covenant. In section 22 of the *Doctrine and Covenants* the Lord says that baptism is "a new and an everlasting covenant, even that which was from the beginning." Marriage in the temple of the Lord for time and for eternity is "a" new and everlasting covenant. (*Doctrines of Salvation,* 1:156.)

As to why it is called a new covenant, President Smith wrote:

> *Each ordinance and requirement given to man for the purpose of bringing to pass his salvation and exaltation is a covenant.* Baptism for the remission of sins is a covenant. When this ordinance was revealed in this dispensation, the Lord called it "a new and an everlasting covenant, even that which was from the beginning."
>
> This covenant was given in the beginning and was lost to men through apostasy, therefore, when it was revealed again, it became to man a *new covenant,* although it was from the beginning, and it is everlasting since its *effects* upon the individual endure forever. Then again, whenever there is need for repentance, baptism is the method, or law, given of the Lord by which the remission of sins shall come, and so *this law is everlasting.* (*Doctrines of Salvation,* 1:152.)

This covenant includes all ordinances of the gospel — the highest of which are performed in the temple. To quote President Smith again:

> Now there is a clear-cut definition in detail of the new and everlasting covenant. *It is everything — the fulness of the gospel.* So

marriage properly performed, baptism, ordination to the priest-hood, everything else — *every contract, every obligation, every performance that pertains to the gospel of Jesus Christ, which is sealed by the Holy Spirit of promise* according to his law here given, *is a part of the new and everlasting covenant. (Doctrines of Salvation, 1:158.)*

The Importance of Covenants

In the previous chapter we used the analogy of an insurance policy. It would be useless to buy insurance from a company if all claims had to be paid out of the pocket of the agent who sold the policies. You would not be very secure if your protection depended upon the financial resources of the salesman.

You should have some guarantee too that the company will honor the policies written by their agents. You should know what your policy requires the company to do, and what it re-quires *you* to do. For instance, how do you cancel out, if you decide not to continue? Remember, policies can be cancelled by the company as well. They cannot be obliged to keep their part of the contract forever if you willfully disregard yours.

This principle applies to spiritual matters. As was quoted above from President Joseph Fielding Smith, "Each ordinance and requirement given to man for the purpose of bringing to pass his salvation and exaltation is a covenant." With this in mind, we must be careful not to take the ordinances and covenants of the gospel lightly, nor to maintain them carelessly.

In the verse quoted previously (Doctrine and Covenants 132:4) the Lord spoke with unmistakable plainness: ". . . for no man can reject this covenant and be permitted to enter into my glory."

I learned a lesson regarding Church covenants many years ago. As a young married man I went ward teaching, as it was called in those days, to a very old man. He was a member of our high priests quorum and we occasionally worked together on projects. I can remember one day husking corn with him for a welfare canning project. On such occasions we would talk of spiritual things. One day he told me something that I shall always remember. It had great influence on me.

When he was a very young man he had attended a funeral. The man who had died had not been active in the Church, although he was regarded as "a good man." He was a very close relative of the President of the Church. The members of the tiny farming community who gathered for the funeral were surprised and felt greatly honored that the President of the Church, the prophet, had come a long distance to the funeral. The first speakers commented on the virtues of the departed brother. One told of some acts of charity that he had done. He had given flour to widows, for instance. Other kindnesses were mentioned.

When it came time for the President of the Church to speak, his sermon was very unsettling to some. This old brother told me that the President first made an expression of appreciation for his deceased relative. He acknowledged the good that the man had accomplished and said he placed full value on those things that had been mentioned by the previous speakers. But then he said, "All of this may be well and good, but the fact is he did not keep his covenants."

The President then soberly outlined the fact that this man had been to the temple, that he had made covenants. But he had not kept them. He had fallen into inactivity in the Church and had developed habits and attitudes not in keeping with the priesthood he held. Those things he had done this side of the veil that were not in harmony with his covenants, and those things that he had not done this side of the veil that were required by his covenants, stood in the way of his eternal progression. These matters would need to be settled before he could claim the blessings of his covenants. He had not kept his part of the promise.

It was an unusual funeral sermon, perhaps one that could only be given by the President of the Church. Although my friend told me the name of the deceased and his relationship to the President, it is not necessary to include that information to make a very sobering lesson of the incident as he described it to me. The experience had a profound effect on my friend. His conveying it to me had a similar effect on me. Perhaps my reciting it here will be sobering to you who read this and will motivate you to review and reevaluate your covenants and your observance of them.

Let me recount another interesting story, one from which we can draw an impressive analogy. Some years ago Elder O. Leslie Stone was in business in California. A prominent businessman called him to his office one day and told him that he was interested in starting a new business. This man had watched Brother Stone carefully, and he knew him to be a man of unusual talent in business. He had also come to admire him for his unquestioned integrity. To Brother Stone's surprise the man handed him a check made out to him for one million dollars.

The man explained that this was the amount he wanted to invest in the new business enterprise. The two men were to be partners. Brother Stone was to supply the management, his partner would supply the money. He did not dictate to Brother Stone how he should use the money; he was simply to start the business and operate as he pleased.

Did he not want to sign a contract? Did he not want a receipt for the money? No, Brother Stone's word was sufficient collateral for him. "If this business succeeds you'll get all the credit and if it fails you'll get all the credit."

But as Brother Stone left the office this wise man said to him: "Remember, if you fail, you stand to lose more than I do. All I will lose is the money, and I have more of that. You stand to lose your reputation."

That was an interesting covenant that those two entered into, essentially on a handshake. Those of us who know Elder Stone and have known him over the years know that there really was not a great deal of risk involved, for by supplying that money (and I remind you that the man had more) he tapped Brother Stone's resources of ingenuity, integrity, dependability, and decency, for all of those virtues characterize O. Leslie Stone.

With what little you have, how would you react to a similar invitation from someone who was known to possess a large fortune? Suppose he proposed a partnership in which he would supply the sustaining resource, you would supply your dedication, your personal attributes, and you each would share somewhat equally in the success of the venture. Who would not jump at such an opportunity? It would seem to be something of an unequal arrangement, with your partner supplying far more than you. But that is just the kind of arrangement the Lord makes with us when we make a covenant with Him.

The Temple Covenants

In 1831, before temple ordinances and covenants were available, the Lord commanded the early elders to "become instructed in the law of my church, and be sanctified by that which ye have received, and ye shall bind yourselves to act in all holiness before me—That inasmuch as ye do this, glory shall be added to the kingdom which ye have received." (D&C 43:9-10.)

Those who go to the temple have the privilege of taking upon themselves specific covenants and obligations relative to their exaltation and that of others. Elder James E. Talmage wrote:

> The ordinances of the endowment embody certain obligations on the part of the individual, such as covenant and promise to observe the law of strict virtue and chastity, to be charitable, benevolent, tolerant and pure; to devote both talent and material means to the spread of truth and the uplifting of the race; to maintain devotion to the cause of truth; and to seek in every way to contribute to the great preparation that the earth may be made ready to receive her King, — the Lord Jesus Christ. With the taking of each covenant and the assuming of each obligation a promised blessing is pronounced, contingent upon the faithful observance of the conditions.
>
> No jot, iota, or tittle of the temple rites is otherwise than uplifting and sanctifying. In every detail the endowment ceremony contributes to covenants of morality of life, consecration of person to high ideals, devotion to truth, patriotism to nation, and allegiance to God. (*The House of the Lord*, page 100.)

The Oxford Dictionary defines *covenant* as "a mutual agreement between two or more persons to do or refrain from doing certain acts; a compact, contract, bargain; sometimes, the undertaking, pledge, or promise of one of the parties." As a verb, *covenant* is defined as "to enter into a covenant or formal agreement; to agree formally or solemnly; to contract." And, interestingly enough, it provides a scriptural definition as "applied especially to an engagement entered into by the Divine Being with some other beings or persons." Thereafter the entry lists long columns of references relating to the subject of covenants in the Bible, reaching way back to ancient times when the Israelites carried with them the ark of the covenant. (*Oxford English Dictionary*, 2:1100-1102.)

The temple covenants are indeed "an engagement entered into by the Divine Being with some other beings or persons," and in human terms it is not always convenient when a call comes to honor the arrangement.

The Covenants Applied

Each year a number of men are called to preside over missions. In each case this requires the man's wife and family to accompany him to some distant place and live there for three years. This is a matter of great importance to the family. If the husband accepts the call he must leave his occupation, making such arrangements as he can to obtain a leave of absence from his employer or to find someone to carry on his business. Sometimes the later reentry into his employment is left unsettled. He gives up political preference, his other interests, his hobbies. He turns away from every worldly ambition in accepting the call.

His wife is equally affected. Her home, the garden, her social position, perhaps some of her family will be left behind for the years of the call. Frequently the call comes at a time when there is the promise of marriage for one of the children, or the coming of grandchildren. The probability is that the parents will not be present during these very important occasions in the lives of their children. Children who accompany the parents are affected too, sometimes more deeply and personally than are the parents. After several years of struggle a young man may have just made the athletic team. Or a young woman perhaps has achieved some position in the school or community that is very desirable to her.

What does a person do when he is asked to set aside every personal interest and go away for three years on call of the servants of the Lord? That depends on how he regards his covenants.

I have met mission presidents and their wives in the training session prior to their departure and have met them in the distant parts of the world in the mission field. I never fail to be impressed with one thought. We are here to receive a mortal body. We are here to be tested. Who will pass the test? Are there men and are there women and are there children in the world who will turn aside from all that they hold dear to respond to a call from the Lord? Is there such dedication in the world? Insofar as these mission presidents and their families are concerned, the question has to that time been answered.

We covenant with the Lord to devote our time, talents, and means to His kingdom. The faith of the members of the Church in earlier days was tested many, many times. In a Conference Report for 1856, we find the following. Heber C. Kimball, a counselor in the First Presidency, is speaking.

> I will present to this congregation the names of those whom we have selected to go on missions. Some are appointed to go to Europe, Australia, and the East Indies. And several will be sent to Las Vegas, to the north, and to Fort Supply, to strengthen the settlements there.

Assignments notified in this way often came as a complete surprise to those in the audience whose names were read out. Because of their faith, I suppose the only question they had on their minds in response to such a call was "When?" "When shall we go?" I am not so sure but that, should a similar call be made today, some would not respond "When?" but "Why?" "Why should *I* go?"

On one occasion I was in the office of a counselor in the First Presidency when a phone call he had placed earlier in the day came through. After greeting the caller, he said, "I wonder if your business affairs would bring you into Salt Lake City some-time in the near future? I would like to meet with you and your wife, for I have a matter of some importance that I would like to discuss with you."

Though they were many miles away, that man all of a sudden discovered that his business would bring him to Salt Lake City the very next day. I was in the same office the following day when the counselor announced to this man that he had been called to preside over one of the missions of the Church. "Now," he said, "we don't want to rush you into this decision. Would you call me in a day or two, as soon as you are able to make a determination as to your feelings concerning this call?"

The man looked at his wife and she looked at him, and with-out saying a word there was that silent conversation between husband and wife, and that gentle, almost imperceptible nod. He turned back to the member of the Presidency and said, "Well, President, what is there to say? What could we tell you in a few days that we couldn't tell you now? We have been called. What answer is there? Of course we will respond to the call."

Then the Presidency member said, rather gently, "Well, if you feel that way about it, actually there is some urgency about this matter. I wonder if you could be prepared to leave by ship from the West Coast on the thirteenth of March."

The man gulped, for that was just eleven days away. He glanced at his wife. There was another silent conversation, and he said, "Yes, President, we can meet that appointment."

"What about your business?" he was asked. "What about your grain elevator? What about your livestock? What about your other holdings?"

"I don't know," said the man, "but we will make arrangements somehow. All of those things will be all right."

Such is the great miracle that we see repeated over and over, day after day, among the faithful who have made covenants with the Lord.

The First Presidency frequently report to the Quorum of the Twelve that when they have called a man and his, wife in to counsel with them over whether or not they will accept a mission call the immediate answer is, "We've been to the temple!" Meaning: We are under covenant. That word *covenant* is a powerful, motivating word. It makes men and women and children rise above themselves, reach beyond themselves and come within grasp of celestial exaltation.

A Covenant People

Keeping our covenants will take courage on the part of each of us. It seems that, each generation or so, there comes a period of time when the faithful of the Church are under great criticism, even under attack. This has always been true of those who are under covenant with the Lord. We must expect, as part of our way of life, to stand condemned on occasion by those outside the Church who oppose the standards the Lord has directed us to keep.

Occasionally one inside the Church joins the ranks of the critics. It is one thing for nonmembers, who know little of ordinances or covenants, to criticize and attack the Church and its leaders. It is quite another when someone within the Church does so, after that person has entered into solemn and sacred covenants to do otherwise. It makes a very big difference indeed whether or not they do so in violation of sacred, specific covenants they have made.

Some years ago I attended a meeting at Ricks College with a group of seminary teachers. President Joseph Fielding Smith, who was then President of the Council of the Twelve, met with us. In the question-and-answer period one of the teachers asked about a letter that was being circulated about the Church from a dissident member who claimed that many of the ordinances were not valid because of some supposed mistake in procedure in conferring the priesthood. When President Smith was asked what he thought about the man's claim, he said, "Before we consider the claim, let me tell you about the man." He then told us several things about him and about the covenants he had not kept. He concluded with this statement: "And so you see, that man is a liar, pure and simple — well, perhaps not so pure."

Keeping covenants is a measure of those outside of the Church as well as those inside. Occasionally we find an individual who is seeking to hold high office in business, in education, or in government. Such a person may claim to be worthy of trust, may insist that he or she would not cheat the public, or misrepresent to them, or mislead them, or break faith with them. In assessing the sincerity of these expressions, the integrity of the person concerned, we may ask ourselves, What does that individual do with a private trust? A good measure is to determine how he keeps covenants relating to his family.

While one could not excuse, one perhaps could understand, that it would be somewhat easier to steal from, cheat on, or misrepresent to an anonymous stranger, or the "public," than it would be to do so to someone very close to you, someone with whom you live, someone with whom you have entered into covenants. But however that may be, one who is not faithful to his marriage partner and to his family is hardly worthy of confidence and trust. If he could cheat on marriage vows, counting perhaps on forgiveness and tolerance that may have been extended at times, surely he must stand unworthy of any great public trust. And he cannot reasonably claim that his dealings in this situation are a private matter, having no bearing on integrity before the public. They do indeed have a very great bearing.

So beware of covenant-breakers inside the Church and out. Beware of those who mock the prophets. When you have been to the temple you are under covenant to support the leaders of the

Church, your local officers and the General Authorities. Keep your covenants. Keep your faith. Be loyal.

In Civil War days a performer named Blondin astonished the country by crossing Niagara River on a tightrope. On one occasion President Abraham Lincoln faced a delegation of critics and said:

> Gentlemen, suppose all the property you possessed were in gold, and you had placed it in the hands of a Blondin to carry across the Niagara River on a rope. With slow, cautious steps he walks to the rope, bearing your all. Would you shake the cable and keep shouting at him, "Blondin, stand up a little straighter; Blondin, stoop a little more; go a little faster; lean more to the south; now lean a little more to the north?" Would that be your behaviour in such an emergency?
>
> No, you would hold your breath, every one of you, as well as your tongues. You would keep your hands off until he was safe on the other side.
>
> This government, gentlemen, is carrying an immense weight. Untold treasures are in its hands. The persons managing the ship of state in this storm are doing the best they can. Don't worry them with needless warnings and complaints. Keep silence; be patient, and we will get you safe across. (John Wesley Hill, *Abraham Lincoln: Man of God* [New York: G. P. Putnam's Sons], page 402.)

It is for each of us to be loyal and true, to keep our covenants. Keep your spiritual premiums paid up. Do not let your spiritual policy lapse. Do not cause it to be cancelled in some moment of rebellion. Extend your policy by adding endorsements as you qualify for the higher ordinances of the gospel. Make a list of them, keep them in mind, work to qualify for each of them. And pray earnestly for help to do so.

I was always impressed when President Joseph Fielding Smith was asked to pray. Invariably, he would make reference to the principles and ordinances of the gospel and always would include the expression, "May we remain faithful to our covenants and obligations."

On one occasion some years ago I served on an advisory committee to the Bureau of Indian Affairs in Washington, D.C.

I had gone to Washington to attend a meeting of the committee. Mrs. Hildegard Thompson, who was Chief of the Branch of Education, announced at the beginning of our meeting that the government had determined to develop an educational program for underprivileged citizens, particularly those from the minorities. A large amount of money had been budgeted to fund the study. The study was to be directed by a lovely black woman educator who held a doctor's degree and who had obvious interest in the education of children. She had asked for an interview with the committee to seek our suggestions on what might be done.

I said to her, "Since this is the Indian Bureau, I suppose you have a particular interest in Indian education." She consented that that was reasonable to suppose.

"Let me tell you," I said, "about a program we have to educate Indian youngsters." I began an explanation of our Indian student placement program.

Everyone there was intrigued by the program and asked many questions. I explained that many thousands of Indian children had been brought from government Indian reservations into the homes of Latter-day Saints. There they were accepted as members of the family and provided with all the blessings the family enjoyed—particularly including an education. These children would always return during the summer months to be with the natural parents.

Two hours after the interview began we were interrupted by our chairman, who indicated that the time allotted for it had long since passed and that we must go on with other business. The interviewer protested, saying, "Just one more question, just one more question. I must ask this." She said, "This is the perfect answer to our problem. This is what we will do to educate our underprivileged minorities. But I need one more answer."

The question she asked was this: "How much do you budget for such a program? What do you pay the foster parents? They take care of these Indian children in their own homes as members of their own families. What do you budget? How much a month do they receive by way of compensation?"

It was then that I realized that I had missed the very point central to the whole discussion. "We pay them nothing," was my reply. "They give freely. We could not operate the program if we should have to pay them. We may not have money enough, in the first place. But more important than that, we could not persuade them to do for material compensation what they will do willingly and freely without the thought of being paid."

Church members will do for nothing what they could not be persuaded nor compelled to do for pay. Why? The answer is dedication and testimony. The answer is *covenant*. We are a covenant people. We covenant to give of our resources in time and money and talent—all we are and all we possess—to the interest of the kingdom of God upon the earth. In simple terms, we covenant to do good. We are a covenant people, and the temple is the center of our covenants. It is the source of the covenant.

The Lord has said, "I, the Lord, am bound when ye do what I say; but when ye do not what I say, ye have no promise." (D&C 82:10.)

Our people are under covenant. We expect little more than the privilege of doing our part. We find always that the Lord blesses us far in excess of what we might have earned from him, so long as we do not serve merely because we expect the blessing. We do it because we are under covenant to do it.

Come to the temple. You ought to come to the temple. Here, acting as proxy for someone who has gone beyond the veil, you will have reviewed before you the covenants that you have made. You will have reinforced in your mind the great spiritual blessings that are associated with the house of the Lord.

Be faithful to the covenants and ordinances of the gospel. Qualify for those sacred ordinances step by step as you move through life. Honor the covenants connected with them. Do this and you will be happy.

Your lives will then be in order—all things lined up in proper sequence, in proper ranks, in proper rows. Your family will be linked in an order that can never be broken.

In the covenants and ordinances center the blessings that you may claim in the holy temple. Surely the Lord is pleased when we are worthy of the title: A keeper of the covenants.

Blessed are ye, when men shall revile you, and persecute you, and shall say all manner of evil against you falsely, for my sake.
Rejoice, and be exceeding glad: for great is your reward in heaven: for so persecuted they the prophets which were before you.
(Matthew 5:11-12.)

Not Without Opposition

Once the Brethren had the keys and knew what ordinance work was to be performed in the temples, the building of temples became a preoccupation with them. This was the first thing on their minds when they moved from one place to another. Before chapels or schools, sometimes even before they thought of adequate homes for themselves, they were laying plans for the building of temples.

A refining would take place—a testing. During the early period of the Church the Lord allowed the tangible things the people had been able to build to be taken away from them. They were persecuted and driven from place to place. Time after time they lost all they had.

If there is anything you would think the Lord would protect, it would be a temple. They built the temple in Kirtland, erected to the theme "Holiness unto the Lord." It was so filled with manifestations of the Spirit that on one occasion for miles around the people thought the building was in flames. You might think the Lord would protect His temple with thunderbolts or earthquakes, if necessary. He did not! The Saints lost the Kirtland Temple—that was to be something of a pattern for that generation. The Church does not have the Kirtland Temple now. But we have the keys we received within it.

Soon after the Latter-day Saints arrived in Missouri a temple site was selected, and this was dedicated at Independence, Jackson County, on August 3, 1831. The temple was never constructed. When the Saints were expelled from that area by the mobs in 1833 the site fell into other hands. Some day, however, in the Lord's own time, that site will be fully reclaimed and the house of the Lord built as we have been commanded to do it.

On July 3, 1837, ground was broken at Far West, Missouri. The cornerstones were laid on July 4, 1838. Nothing further was done until April 26, 1839, when the Twelve Apostles, in fulfillment of a revelation, quietly held a conference on the temple site and as a gesture rolled a large stone up to one of the corners as a symbol of beginning construction on the temple. The temple, which would have been 110 feet long and 80 feet wide according to the plan, was never built. The Saints were driven from Missouri at the end of 1838. After many years we repurchased the site and it is now owned by the Church.

Much of what happened at Kirtland was repeated in Nauvoo. We built a temple in Nauvoo. It was destroyed. It happened in Kirtland, in Independence, in Far West, and in Nauvoo. The Saints set about to build temples. In each case, either they were prevented from building the temple or it was taken away from them; and in Nauvoo the temple was defiled and destroyed.

Saints Retained What Mattered Most

Those who joined the unholy power to prevent temple work seemed to win. Time after time they had their way. They ended up, for a time at least, with the sites — leaving to the persecuted Saints nothing. Nothing? No! We have the keys, the ordinances. We have everything. *They* have nothing. They cannot baptize nor ordain. They cannot wash nor anoint nor endow nor seal. We came away with everything, and they have nothing. Our forebears were compelled, because of those deprivations in the early years, to focus on the things that mattered most.

In Nauvoo the temple was hardly completed when it was taken and defiled in the most offensive way by the mobs. But not before the Saints, in great numbers, had received their endowments.

Nauvoo, the city beautiful. An ideal place for the erection of a temple. The city of peace, the city of gathering. The ordinance work had been revealed there. There the blessings were at last made available to the people. Their washings, their anointings, their endowments, their sealings, were precious to them. Long before the temple was finished, the opposition and persecution came. This, we must understand, was not simply because the Latter-day Saints were a peculiar people, not because they were clannish or had different ideals or held strange new beliefs. There were other groups in other places with differences from the general population that were more extreme than those of the Latter-day Saints. The opposition was leveled at the Saints because the adversary was afraid of the temple. He would do anything to prevent their construction of it.

The Saints knew that they might not retain the temple. Even though they knew that, they gave of their means — not just of their surpluses — to the construction of the Nauvoo Temple. When it was ready for ordinance work they labored around the clock to give and to receive the blessings of the temple.

Brigham Young reported that, because of the pressures of persecution, it was felt necessary to close off the work. The Brethren had been working, performing endowments for endless hours with great fatigue. The Saints understood something of the significance of the temple. They stood by pleading with the Brethren not to stop. On February 3, 1846, only a day or two before the exodus from Nauvoo began, Brigham Young recorded:

> Notwithstanding that I had announced that we would not attend to the administration of the ordinances, the House of the Lord was thronged all day, the anxiety being so great to receive, as if the brethren would have us stay here and continue the endowments until our way would be hedged up, and our enemies would intercept us. But I informed the brethren that this was not wise, and that we should build more Temples, and have further opportunities to receive the blessings of the Lord, as soon as the saints were prepared to receive them. In this Temple we have been abundantly rewarded, if we receive no more. I also informed the brethren that I was going to get my wagons started and be off. I walked some distance from the Temple supposing the crowd would disperse, but on returning I found the house filled to overflowing.
>
> Looking upon the multitude and knowing their anxiety, as they were thirsting and hungering for the word, we continued at work diligently in the House of the Lord.
>
> Two hundred and ninety-five persons received ordinances. (*HC*, 7:579.)

Those who look back on Church history sometimes grind their teeth at the injustice of the persecutions or weep over the loss of the temples. They were taken away from us. But those who took the temples and defiled them have nothing, comparatively, and we have everything. They have a building or a site or two; we have the keys, we have the ordinances, we have the authority.

That testing and tempering of the Church in the early days has not, in the eternal scheme of things, injured the kingdom. The Saints who were unjustly dealt with, those who lost their property, their loved ones, or their lives, will find compensation. Each will be blessed far beyond anything he might otherwise have gained in mortality.

Opposition to Be Expected

On the other hand, those who are guilty of those transgressions against this sacred work have earned the retribution of the Lord. Until their repentance is complete and the uttermost farthing has been paid, they will not be free to progress toward their ultimate salvation.

Lehi told his son Jacob "For it must needs be, that there is an opposition in all things. If not so, my first-born in the wilderness, righteousness could not be brought to pass, neither wickedness, neither holiness nor misery, neither good nor bad." (2 Nephi 2:11.)

The Lord told Oliver Cowdery through the Prophet Joseph Smith that "it must needs be that the devil should tempt the children of men, or they could not be agents unto themselves; for if they never should have bitter they could not know the sweet." (D&C 29:39.)

Temples are the very center of the spiritual strength of the Church. We should expect that the adversary will try to interfere with us as a Church and with us individually as we seek to participate in this sacred and inspired work. The interference can vary from the terrible persecutions of the earlier days to apathy toward the work. The latter is perhaps the most dangerous and debilitating form of resistance to temple work.

When President Brigham Young announced that a temple was to be built in the Salt Lake Valley, many were afraid. They had experienced terrible persecutions and hardships. They thought another temple would be an invitation to call it all upon them again.

> Some say, "I do not like to do it, for we never began to build a Temple without the bells of hell beginning to ring." I want to hear them ring again. All the tribes of hell will be on the move, if we uncover the walls of this Temple. But what do you think it will amount to? You have all the time seen what it has amounted to. (*Discourses of Brigham Young*, page 410.)

All the angels in heaven are looking at this little handful of people, and stimulating them to the salvation of the human family. So also are the devils in hell looking at this people, too, and trying to overthrow us, and the people are still shaking hands with the servants of the devil, instead of sanctifying themselves and calling upon the Lord and doing the work which he has commanded us and put into our hands to do. When I think upon this subject, I want the tongues of seven thunders to wake up the people. (*Discourses of Brigham Young*, pages 403-4.)

I think there is a work to be done then which the whole world seems determined we shall not do. What is it? To build temples. We never yet commenced to lay the foundation of a temple but what all hell was in arms against us. That is the difficulty now: we have commenced the foundation of this temple. (*Discourses of Brigham Young*, page 402.)

The Devil will fight hard to hinder us, and we shall not take an inch of ground except by obedience to the power of, and faith in, the Gospel of the Son of God. (*Discourses of Brigham Young*, page 401.)

Temple work brings so much resistance because it is the source of so much spiritual power to the Latter-day Saints, and to the entire Church. Elder John A. Widtsoe said:

In view of this great temple activity, we may well prepare ourselves for opposition. There never yet has been a time in the history of the world when temple work has increased without a corresponding increase in the opposition to it. Some three or four years after the pioneers came to this valley, President Brigham Young said that it was time to begin the building of a temple; and some of the old timers here will probably remember that thousands of the Saints dreaded the command, because they said, "Just as soon as we lay the cornerstone of a temple, all hell will be turned loose upon us and we will be driven out of the valleys." President Young thought that was true, but that they also would have, if temple work were undertaken, a corresponding increase in power to overcome all evil. Men grow mighty under the results of temple service; women grow strong under it; the community increases in power; until the devil has less influence than he ever had before. The opposition to truth is relatively smaller if the people are engaged actively in the ordinances of the temple. ("Temple Worship," page 51.)

At the dedication of the Logan Temple, President George Q. Cannon made this statement:

> Every foundation stone that is laid for a temple, and every temple completed according to the order the Lord has revealed for His holy priesthood, lessens the power of Satan on the earth, and increases the power of God and godliness, moves the heavens in mighty power in our behalf, invokes and calls down upon us the blessings of eternal gods, and those who reside in their presence. (George Q. Cannon, Logan Temple Dedication, 1877.)

From the dedicatory prayer for the Kirtland Temple, March 27, 1836, comes the following:

> For thou knowest that we have done this work through tribulation; and out of our poverty we have given of our substance to build a house to thy name, that the Son of Man might have a place to manifest himself to his people. (D&C 109:5.)

No one takes hold of this work without being susceptible to the blessings of the Lord. If you have problems with your own immediately living family, do all you can for them. Begin working in behalf of the Lord's family and good things will start to happen. We should not shrink from trials and opposition. President Joseph F. Smith set the spirit for the Saints in this counsel to Church leaders.

> Leaders must be courageous. One of the highest qualities of all true leadership is a high standard of courage. When we speak of courage and leadership we are using terms that stand for the quality of life by which men determine consciously the proper course to pursue and stand with fidelity to their convictions. There has never been a time in the Church when its leaders were not required to be courageous men; not alone courageous in the sense that they were able to meet physical dangers, but also in the sense that they were steadfast and true to a clear and upright conviction.
>
> Leaders of the Church, then, should be men not easily discouraged, not without hope, and not given to forebodings of all sorts of evils to come. Above all things the leaders of the people should never disseminate a spirit of gloom in the hearts of the people. If

men standing in high places sometimes feel the weight and anxiety of momentous times, they should be all the firmer and all the more resolute in those convictions which come from a God-fearing conscience and pure lives. (*Gospel Doctrine* [Salt Lake City: Deseret Book Co., 1966], page 155.)

Opposition, as I have said, can be collective — directed at the Church — or focused on the individual. We must view the temple as the source of abundant spiritual strength.

Spiritual Blessings of the Temple

On one occasion I went to a Salt Lake City hospital to see a young man who was near death. I gave him a blessing and visited for some time with his wife. The doctors had told her that he could not recover. They have a large family; the oldest was then deacon's age. This brave little woman, soon to be widowed, showed great courage. "I have told the children what is about to happen," she said. "Last week I took them all to Temple Square." Although her children were too young to enter the temple, she wanted them to be near that source of strength and spiritual power. She continued: "There we saw the film, 'Man's Search for Happiness.' " This film depicts the cycle of life, with the death of a family member. "I think the children will accept it," she said. "I think we are ready for whatever may happen."

A few days later I received word that the husband had passed away. I talked with her again. She was determined to face with courage the responsibility of raising her little brood without her companion.

It is not without significance that when she faced a great trial she went to Temple Square.

When members of the Church are troubled or when crucial decisions weigh heavily upon their minds, it is a common thing for them to go to the temple. It is a good place to take our cares. In the temple we can receive spiritual perspective. There, during the time of the temple service, we are "out of the world."

A large part of the value of these occasions is the fact that we are doing something for someone that they cannot do for themselves. As we perform the endowment for someone who is dead, somehow we feel a little less hesitant to pray fervently to the Lord to assist us. When young married couples have decisions to make, if they are near a temple there is great value in attending a session. There is something cleansing and clarifying about the spiritual atmosphere of the temple.

Sometimes our minds are so beset with problems, and there are so many things clamoring for attention at once, that we just cannot think clearly and see clearly. At the temple the dust of distraction seems to settle out, the fog and the haze seem to lift, and we can "see" things that we were not able to see before and find a way through our troubles that we had not previously known.

On many occasions I heard President Harold B. Lee repeat the expression, "In the temple we are close to the Lord. Where is He more likely to be than here in His house."

Consider these words of Elder John A. Widtsoe:

> Men may rise through temple work to high levels of character and spiritual joy. Once only may a person receive the temple endowment for himself, but innumerable times may he receive it for those gone from the earth. Whenever he does so, he performs an unselfish act for which no earthly recompense is available. He tastes in part the sweet joy of saviorhood. He rises toward the stature of the Lord Jesus Christ who died for all. Men who thus serve the dead go out of the temple into the marts of men with renewed power to deal fairly with others, to put into practice the golden command "Do ye unto others as ye would have them do unto you."
>
> Yet there are immediate rewards for such vicarious service. Every time a person receives the temple endowment for another, he reviews the eternal journey of man, is reminded of the conditions of eternal progress and of his own covenants to obey God's law, is impressed anew with the necessity of making truth alive by use, and beholds again the glorious destiny of righteous man. His memory is refreshed, his conscience warned, his hopes lifted heavenward. Temple repetition is the mother of daily blessings. Wherever one turns, temple service profits those who perform it. (*Improvement Era* 39 [April 1936]: 228.)

The Prophet Joseph Smith, speaking of salvation for the dead, said "This glorious truth is well calculated to enlarge the understanding, and to sustain the same under troubles, difficulties, and distress."

I have the conviction that the Lord will bless us as we attend to the sacred ordinance work of the temples. Blessings there will not be limited to our temple service. We will be blessed in all of our affairs. We will be eligible to have the Lord take an interest in our affairs both spiritual and temporal.

Accomplishing the Work

In the face of the opposition we have described one might wonder how we will ever succeed in bringing the sacred ordinances of the temple to all the spirits of the world. But when the servants of the Lord determine to do as He commands, we move ahead. As we proceed, we are joined at the crossroads by those who have been prepared to help us.

They come with skills and abilities precisely suited to our needs. And we find provisions — information, inventions, help of various kinds — set along the way waiting for us to take them up. It is as though someone knew we would be traveling that way. We see the invisible hand of the Almighty providing for us.

President Brigham Young said:

> To accomplish this work there will have to be not only one temple but thousands of them, and thousands and tens of thousands of men and women will go into those temples and officiate for people who have lived as far back as the Lord shall reveal. (*Discourses of Brigham Young,* page 394.)

I heard President Spencer W. Kimball, at the dedication of the temple in Washington, D. C., and again at the rededication of the St. George Temple, say:

> The day is coming not too far ahead of us when all temples on this earth will be going day and night. There will be shifts and people will be coming in the morning hours and in the night hours and in the day hours, and we must reach the time when we will have no vacations, that is, no temple vacations. . . .

But there will be a corps of workers night and day almost to exhaustion, because of the importance of the work and the great number of people who lie asleep in the eternity and who are craving, needing the blessings we can bring them.

When there were just two or three thousand members in the Church, the Lord gave a commandment to Joseph Smith that they should build a temple. They built temples in those days before they built chapels. Wherever the Saints settled, the first concern was the building of a temple.

Brigham Young's first act in the Salt Lake Valley was to set his cane to mark the temple site. In 1838, when there were but 20,000 members of the Church, already four temple sites had been selected. By 1880, with 160,000 members, there were four temples in operation or nearing completion.

Today, at the same ratio, we would need hundreds of temples to represent the same emphasis, and that would be but the beginning.

If we face difficulties and frustrations and opposition, even persecution—both individually and as a church—it is of little moment in the eternal scheme of things. Do not let opposition deter you from your genealogical or temple work.

To those who sense the size of this challenge to provide temple ordinance work for all, both living and dead, and are overwhelmed by it, I say, "Have faith. We will win the day, and the Lord will provide." To those who are hesitant to move, I say, "Wake up and see the vision of it. We can accomplish the things we have been commanded, if we will but get started."

President J. Reuben Clark, Jr., said in a general priesthood meeting:

I have said to you brethren, over and over again, and I repeat it tonight, that if we were really united, if we really saw eye to eye, and then would move in unison, there is nothing in the world, in righteousness, that we might not do in accordance with the will of the Lord and not to defeat his purposes. (J. Reuben Clark, Jr., Conference Report, April 1949, page 184.)

Some years ago I learned a lesson that I shall never forget.

I had been called as an Assistant to the Council of the Twelve, and we were to move to Salt Lake City and find an adequate and permanent home. President Henry D. Moyle assigned someone to help us.

A home was located that was ideally suited to our needs. Elder Harold B. Lee came and looked it over very carefully and then counseled, "By all means, you are to proceed."

But there was no way we could proceed. I had just completed the course work on a doctor's degree and was writing the dissertation. With the support of my wife and our eight children, all of the resources we could gather over the years had been spent on education.

By borrowing on our insurance, gathering every resource, we could barely get into the house, without sufficient left to even make the first monthly payment.

Brother Lee insisted, "Go ahead. I know it is right."

I was in deep turmoil because I had been counseled to do something I had never done before—to sign a contract without having the resources to meet the payments.

When Brother Lee sensed my feelings he sent me to President David O. McKay, who listened very carefully as I explained the circumstances.

He said, "You do this. It is the right thing." But he extended no resources to make the doing of it possible.

When I reported to Brother Lee he said, "That confirms what I have told you."

I was still not at peace, and then came the lesson. Elder Lee said, "Do you know what is wrong with you—you always want to see the end from the beginning."

I replied quietly that I wanted to see at least a few steps ahead. He answered by quoting from the sixth verse of the twelfth chapter of Ether: "Wherefore, dispute not because ye see not, for ye receive no witness until after the trial of your faith."

And then he added, "My boy, you must learn to walk to the edge of the light, and perhaps a few steps into the darkness, and you will find that the light will appear and move ahead of you."

And so it has—but only as we walked to the edge of the light.

And so it is with this work. We can build those thousands of temples and we can work for the redemption of our dead by the thousands and tens of thousands and millions.

We have not yet moved to the edge of the light, either as individuals or as a church. We have not used all of the resources yet available to us.

I am confident that as we move to the edge of the light, like the cloud that led the Israelites, or like the star that led the wise men, the light will move ahead of us and we can do this work.

Each a Savior

The keys are to be delivered, the spirit of Elijah is to come, the Gospel to be established, the Saints of God gathered, Zion built up, and the Saints to come up as saviors on Mount Zion.

But how are they to become saviors on Mount Zion? By building their temples, erecting their baptismal fonts, and going forth and receiving all the ordinances, baptisms, confirmations, washings, anointings, ordinations and sealing powers upon their heads, in behalf of all their progenitors who are dead, and redeem them that they may come forth in the first resurrection and be exalted to thrones of glory with them; and herein is the chain that binds the hearts of the fathers to the children, and the children to the fathers, which fulfills the mission of Elijah.

———————

(Joseph Smith.)

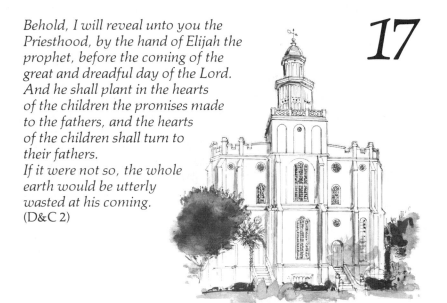

*Behold, I will reveal unto you the
Priesthood, by the hand of Elijah the
prophet, before the coming of the
great and dreadful day of the Lord.
And he shall plant in the hearts
of the children the promises made
to the fathers, and the hearts
of the children shall turn to
their fathers.
If it were not so, the whole
earth would be utterly
wasted at his coming.*
(D&C 2)

Turning the Hearts

Between the Prophet Joseph Smith himself and the administration of President Spencer W. Kimball, when new vigor and dimension were given to temple building, perhaps no man in this dispensation has made so strong an impression upon temple work and the supporting genealogical research as President Wilford Woodruff.

If I were to describe President Woodruff in one word that would best characterize him, I would choose the word *spirituality*. A man of deep spiritual attunement, from the days of his youth he had received and responded to spiritual guidance; and it was this trait, perhaps above any other, that qualified him for a call to be a member of the Quorum of the Twelve Apostles.

Here we can give only a few insights into the life of this Church President. But that life was such that I recommend for inspirational reading the book *Wilford Woodruff* by Matthias Cowley, a biography that attests to the humility and obedience of one of the great prophets of this dispensation.

The baptism of Wilford Woodruff was attended with divine power. George Q. Cannon recorded in his history:

> In view of all that has since occurred, it is a remarkable fact that the Prophet recorded in his journal of the 31st of December, 1833, the fact that "Wilford Woodruff was baptized at Richland, Oswego County, New York, by Zera Pulsipher," and this was before the Prophet and the future apostle and president had ever met in the flesh. This is not the only mention of Wilford Woodruff in Joseph's diary prior to their meeting. In one place the Prophet notices that Wilford had been ordained a teacher. (Matthias F. Cowley, *Wilford Woodruff: History of His Life and Labors* [Salt Lake City: Bookcraft, 1964], page 37.)

That ordination to the office of teacher took place on January 25, 1834, when Zera Pulsipher organized the Saints in Richland, New York, into a branch of the Church. After ordaining Wilford Woodruff a teacher he gave him a written license, and what Wilford Woodruff wrote of that experience gives insight into the spiritual depths of this great man.

> I felt that I could truly exclaim with the prophet of God, "I had rather be a door-keeper in the house of my God than to dwell in the tents of wickedness." The fulness of the everlasting gospel had come at last. It filled my heart with great joy. It laid the foundation of a greater and more glorious work than I ever expected to see in this life. I pray God in the name of Jesus Christ to guide my future life, that I may live to His honor and glory, and be a blessing to my fellowmen, and in the end be saved in His celestial kingdom, even so, Amen. (*Wilford Woodruff,* page 36.)

It was not until April 25, 1834, that Wilford Woodruff met the Prophet Joseph Smith, at Kirtland. From that time until the Prophet's martyrdom they were intimately associated. It was on July 8, 1838, at Far West, Missouri, that the Prophet received a revelation which concluded, "Let my servant John Taylor, and also my servant John E. Page, and also my servant Wilford Woodruff, and also my servant Willard Richards, be appointed to fill the places of those who have fallen, and be officially notified of their appointment." (D&C 118:6.)

One month later Wilford Woodruff was holding a meeting with the Saints at North Vinyl Haven, an island off the coast of Maine (then called the Fox Islands), when a letter arrived from President Thomas B. Marsh of the Quorum of the Twelve Apostles. Brother Woodruff recorded in his journal the contents of this letter, including the final comment, "Know then, Brother Woodruff, by this, that you are appointed to fill the place of one of the Twelve Apostles, and that it is agreeable to the word of the Lord, given very lately, that you should come speedily to Far West, and, on the 26th of April next, take your leave of the Saints here and depart for other climes, across the mighty deep."

Then Brother Woodruff added this very significant statement in his journal. "The substance of this letter had been revealed to me several weeks before, but I had not named it to any person." (*Wilford Woodruff*, page 93.)

I make a point of this spiritual qualification, for it was President Woodruff who was directed by the Lord to set in place the foundation of genealogical and temple work that would function in the Church to this day.

Progressive Revelation of Temple Doctrine

The Prophet Joseph Smith had set the foundation of the doctrine relating to temple work and the place it holds in the redemption of both the living and the dead. He had received the revelations (sections 124, 127, 128, and 132) which pertain directly to this work. And during the last part of his life he said, "This subject was upon my mind more than any other."

The cruel martyrdom left the work unfinished. Others must take up the task. From what the Prophet Joseph Smith had been given, the early Brethren knew that there should be baptism for the dead, that there should be a linking of the generations. They knew that the sealings were to take place. The full instructions had not been given, however, at the time the Prophet Joseph Smith was martyred.

Brigham Young, who succeeded the Prophet Joseph as the President of the Church, led the people through persecutions and danger to the relative safety of the West.

President John Taylor, his successor, might be described as an architect of priesthood government. He gave direction to the organization of the priesthood and to setting in order the functions of the Church. Then came Wilford Woodruff, who at the time of his appointment as Church President had served as an Apostle for half a century.

President Woodruff carried with him a restless concern for the matter of the temples and the ordinances carried on in them. He was deeply interested also in genealogical work, which is crucial to the support of the temple. He participated in the erection of temples. He gave the dedicatory prayer at the St. George Temple and later dedicated the Salt Lake Temple.

Some time after the dedication of the Salt Lake Temple President Woodruff prepared and signed a brief testimony concerning the St. George Temple. He wanted certain things to be remembered. I quote his statement:

> President Brigham Young requested me to take charge of the Temple, which I did. He also requested me to write all the ordinances of the Church from the first baptism and confirmation through every ordinance of the Church. G. Q. Cannon assisted some in this writing, and when I had finished it to the satisfaction of the President, he said to me, "Now you have before you an ensample to carry on the endowments in all the temples until the coming of the Son of Man." (As quoted in Janice Force DeMille, *The St. George Temple First 100 Years* [Hurricane, Ut.: Homestead Publishers, 1977], pages 71-72.)

It may be that prior to that time the ordinances had been memorized and performed from memory or from other notes or records that we do not now have. Brother Woodruff was assisted in this work by President Brigham Young himself, and the

records indicate that President Young carefully scrutinized the
writing and counseled with Elder Woodruff on the preparation of
the sacred documents.

It was at the St. George Temple that President Woodruff was
visited by a congregation from the spirit world, many of whom
had been prominent in the history of the United States of
America. In a discourse given in the Salt Lake Tabernacle on
September 16, 1877, he said:

> In order that this work may be done, we must have Temples in
> which to do it; and what I wish to say to you, my brethren and
> sisters, is that the God of heaven requires us to rise up and build
> them, that the work of redemption may be hastened. Our reward
> will meet us when we go behind the vail.
>
> "Blessed are the dead which die in the Lord from henceforth:
> Yea, saith the Spirit, that they may rest from their labors; and their
> works do follow them."
>
> We have labored in the St. George Temple since January, and
> we have done all we could there; and the Lord has stirred up our
> minds, and many things have been revealed to us concerning the
> dead. President Young has said to us, and it is verily so, if the dead
> could they would speak in language loud as ten thousand thunders,
> calling upon the servants of God to rise up and build Temples,
> magnify their calling and redeem their dead. This doubtless sounds
> strange to those present who believe not the faith and doctrine of
> the Latter-day Saints; but when we get to the spirit-world we will
> find out that all that God has revealed is true. We will find, too,
> that everything there is reality, and that God has a body, parts and
> passions, and the erroneous ideas that exist now with regard to him
> will have passed away. I feel to say little else to the Latter-day
> Saints wherever and whenever I have the opportunity of speaking
> to them, than to call upon them to build these Temples now under
> way, to hurry them up to completion. The dead will be after you,
> they will seek after you as they have after us in St. George. They
> called upon us, knowing that we held the keys and power to re-
> deem them.
>
> I will here say, before closing, that two weeks before I left St.
> George, the spirits of the dead gathered around me, wanting to
> know why we did not redeem them. Said they, "You have had the
> use of the Endowment House for a number of years, and yet

nothing has ever been done for us. We laid the foundation of the government you now enjoy, and we never apostatized from it, but we remained true to it and were faithful to God." These were the signers of the Declaration of Independence, and they waited on me for two days and two nights. I thought it very singular, that notwithstanding so much work had been done, and yet nothing had been done for them. The thought never entered my heart, from the fact, I suppose, that heretofore our minds were reaching after our more immediate friends and relatives. I straightway went into the baptismal font and called upon brother McCallister to baptize me for the signers of the Declaration of Independence, and fifty other eminent men, making one hundred in all, including John Wesley, Columbus, and others. (*Deseret News,* 27 March 1878.)

The others included nearly every president of the United States.

I should explain here that the Saints knew they were to perform baptisms for the dead. They knew that there was to be a linking of the generations. They knew that families were to be united through sealings or "adoptions." They were baptized for the dead, but kept only sparse records of this ordinance work. They were in some cases sealed or adopted to prophets of this dispensation.

During the several years that the Saints were on the move to the West and preoccupied with the troubles of the period, these matters were not clarified. When the Saints were established and temples (for the first time in the plural) were under construction, it was time to have these matters set in order. It was during the closing years of the ministry of President Wilford Woodruff that this instruction was given by revelation.

President Woodruff was a prophet uniquely qualified to accomplish this setting in order. In 1894, near the end of his ministry, having received instruction through revelation, he laid the foundation for genealogical work in the Church.

President Woodruff kept a meticulous journal. His pattern of writing was something between printing and a script. His diary might be referred to as a red-letter edition, for on important matters he would change the color of the ink to red.

Under the date of April 5, 1894, there appears a remarkable entry. "I met with the Presidency and Twelve Apostles on the subject of endowments and adoption, and the following is a revelation to Wilford Woodruff upon the subject." There followed more than a page of blank space obviously left to record the revelation. But, as is often the case, the revelation was not framed in scriptural language as many of the sections of the Doctrine and Covenants are framed.

While the space in the diary stands empty, the revelation was not lost to us. In the *Deseret Evening News* of April 9, 1894, there is a brief report on the annual conference. It was the sixty-fourth anniversary of the organization of the Church and the third day of the conference. The newspaper records:

> President Wilford Woodruff addressed the conference. After he had made a few preliminary remarks upon the necessity of the servants of God being influenced by the power of His spirit in their ministrations, he announced that President George Q. Cannon would read from the 128th Section of the book of Doctrine and Covenants. This revelation treats upon the power of the priesthood to bind on earth and it is bound in heaven; also of the means of salvation or redemption of the living and the dead. After the reading President Woodruff resumed his remarks and delivered an important instructive discourse, throwing additional light upon the process, and of the law of adoption, by which the children and the fathers are to be united and bound together by the indissoluble ties. The method of the procedure for the accomplishment of this great purpose had been manifest by the Lord to the president and his counselors in the First Presidency, and also the Twelve Apostles had received a witness on the same subject. The presidents of the temples, their associates were to be henceforward governed by the principles of adoption enunciated by President Woodruff in their labors in that department. *The subject is too important to admit of the presentation of a mere synopsis of the discourse in which it was embodied.*

In President Woodruff's diary under the date of April 12, 1894, appears this sentence: "The Presidency met and read the discourse of Wilford Woodruff and made such corrections as were necessary before publication."

On April 21 the entire sermon was published in the *Deseret Weekly*. One month later it was printed in England in the *Millennial Star*. This attests to the great significance the Brethren placed on the sermon, for it would have been necessary for someone to take the text to England for it to appear that soon in print there.

The sermon contains the revelation that the President did not record in his diary.

As Latter-day Saints we are under commandment to listen to the prophet. Not all revelation is yet in the standard works. Three revelations have been added to the Doctrine and Covenants in recent years — the first in over a century. It is not without great significance that two of them — the Prophet Joseph Smith's vision of the celestial kingdom, and President Joseph F. Smith's vision of the redemption of the dead — relate directly to the subject of temple work.

The third new section in the Doctrine and Covenants announced the authorization to confer the priesthood upon all worthy male members of the Church regardless of race or national origin. This too has significance for temple work, since it makes these blessings available to all who will live for them, without restriction. That revelation was not included in the Doctrine and Covenants, but only the announcement of it. Such was true of the Manifesto given by President Wilford Woodruff in 1890.

President Woodruff's Sermon

Because of the signal importance of President Woodruff's sermon at the April 1894 General Conference, we will include here the substance of his words on that occasion. To set it apart from other sizable quotations in this book, we show his words in regular type with quotation marks. Here is the text of his sermon.

"I feel thankful for the privilege of meeting with so many of the Latter-day Saints this morning. In order to present my position before the Saints I wish to say that I have been a member of The Church of Jesus Christ of Latter-day Saints over sixty years, a member of the quorum of the Apostles fifty-five years, and the President of the Church for a short time. During all these years, and in all my travels, I have never seen a moment when I have had the power to preach the Gospel of Jesus Christ or to administer in any of the ordinances of the House of the Lord, acceptable to God or to myself, only by the assistance of the Holy Ghost; and I do not know of any other man that could ever do this. Even the Son of God, in referring to His work, said: 'I do nothing of myself, but as my Father hath taught me, I speak these things.' So it has been with all the prophets and patriarchs in every age of the world; they have had to be assisted by the power of God. I occupy that position today before this assembly. Therefore, as the Lord commanded us not to speak only as we are moved upon by the Holy Ghost, I desire that, and in order to obtain it I want the prayers and faith of the Latter-day Saints.

"I have some things resting upon me that I wish to present before the Latter-day Saints, and in order to do this I will call upon President George Q. Cannon to read from the book of Doctrine and Covenants concerning the subject which I wish to speak upon. (President Cannon read from Sec. 128, of Doc. and Cov. Resuming, President Woodruff said:)

"Thus you have before you the subject which is resting upon us, and which we wish to present to the Latter-day Saints. Let me say that age has very little to do with revelation. In an early age of the world, old Father Adam, three years previous to his death—he being nearly one thousand years of age—called together his posterity in the valley of Adam-ondi-Ahman, and he stood upon his feet for hours, clothed with the power of God and the revelations of heaven, and blessed his posterity, some seven of whom, each representing a generation, were High Priests. Among them were Enoch and Methusaleh, both great men of their day and generation. He prophesied upon them what should transpire with their posterity unto the end of time. His old age did not have any effect whatever upon the revelations of God to him. Joseph Smith, when fourteen years of age, while calling upon God in the wilderness, had the heavens opened unto him. Both the Father and the Son presented themselves unto him in the clouds of heaven, and the Father said, 'This is my Beloved Son; hear Him.' The age of man is very short indeed in this day to what it was in ancient days. Men anciently lived to a very great age. When four or five hundred years old they took wives, begat children, and raised up posterity. Today our age is limited to something like three score years and ten.

"I wish to say to the Latter-day Saints that we live in a very important generation. We are blessed with power and authority, holding the Holy Priesthood by the commandment of God, to stand upon the earth and redeem both the living and the dead. If we did not do it, we should be damned and cut off from the earth, and the God of Israel would raise up a people who would do it. The Lord would not permit me to occupy this position one day of my life, unless I was susceptible to the Holy Spirit and to the revelations of God. It is too late in the day for this church to stand without revelation. Not only the President of the Church should possess this gift and give it unto the people, but his counselors and the Apostles and all men that bear the Holy Priesthood, if they magnify their calling, although they may not be called to give revelations to lead and direct the Church. The spirit of revelation belongs to the priesthood.

"But to come to the subject before us. Perhaps it may be said by the inquiring or the objecting mind, what have you to say about redeeming the dead, or about baptism for the dead, or the work of the Temples of our God, that is not already revealed? I will say this: When the Prophet Joseph had this revelation from heaven, what did he do? There are witnesses here of what he did. He never stopped till he got the fulness of the word of God to him concerning the baptism for the dead. But before doing so he went into the Mississippi river, and so did I, as well as others, and we each baptized a hundred for the dead, without a man to record a single act that we performed. Why did we do it? Because of the feeling of joy we had, to think that we in the flesh could stand and redeem our dead. We did not wait to know what the result of this would be, or what the whole of it should be. Finally the Lord told the prophet: 'When any of you are baptized for your dead, let there be a recorder, and let him be eye witness of your baptisms; let him hear with his ears, that he may testify of a truth, saith the Lord; that in all your recordings it may be recorded in heaven; whatsoever you bind on earth may be bound in heaven; whatsoever you loose on earth, may be loosed in heaven.' [D&C 127:6-7.] That was the beginning of this work.

"Joseph Smith, instead of living to be nearly a thousand years of age, as Adam did, lived to be about thirty-eight years of age. He brought forth the record of the stick of Joseph in the hands of Ephraim—the history of the ancient inhabitants of this continent. By the power of God he translated that, and it has been published in many languages. Besides this, he organized The Church of Jesus Christ of Latter-day Saints upon the foundation of apostles and prophets, Christ Jesus being the chief corner stone. Men were ordained to the Priesthood and sent forth, from the various occupations of life, to carry this gospel to the world. God informed Joseph Smith that he was called to prune the vineyard once more for the last time before the coming of the Son of Man. Since that, thousands of Elders of Israel have been sent into the world to preach the Gospel. Joseph Smith did all this during the fifteen years he held the Priesthood. Let any man read the revelations in the Book of Doctrine and Covenants, which were given through him during the little time he spent here in the flesh. It is one of the greatest records that any man ever gave to the human family. Not only this, but he organized the endowments and did a great deal of other work. Who could expect him, during the short time he lived in the flesh, to do more than he did? I received my endowment from under his hands. He brought forth all these ordinances that have been given unto the Latter-day Saints. In fact, it is a marvel and a wonder that he performed as much as he did.

"I want to say, as the President of The Church of Jesus Christ of Latter-day Saints, that we should now go on and progress. We have not got through revelation. We have not got through the work of God. But at this period we want to go on and fulfill this commandment of God given through Malachi—that the Lord should send Elijah the prophet, 'and he shall turn the heart of the fathers to the children, and the heart of the children to their fathers lest I come and smite the earth with a curse.' Ye sons of men, I say unto you, in the name of Israel's God, those very principles that God has revealed are what have stayed the judgment of the Almighty on the earth. Were it not for these principles, you and I would not be here today. We have had prophets and apostles. President Young who followed President Joseph Smith, led us here. He organized these temples and carried out the purposes of his calling and office. He laid the foundation of this great Temple on this block, as well as others in the mountains of Israel. What for? That we might carry out these principles of redemption for the dead. He accomplished all that God required at his hands. But he did not receive all the revelations that belong to this work; neither did President Taylor, nor has Wilford Woodruff. There will be no end to this work until it is perfected.

"I want to lay before you what there is for us to do at the present time; and in doing this I desire particularly the attention of President Lorenzo Snow, of the Salt Lake Temple; President M. W. Merrill, of the Logan Temple; President J. D. T. McAllister of the Manti Temple, and President D. H. Cannon, of the St. George Temple, and those associated with them. You have acted up to all the light and knowledge that you have had; but you have now something more to do than you have done. We have not fully carried out those principles in fulfillment of the revelations of God to us, in sealing the hearts of the fathers to the children and the children to the fathers. I have not felt satisfied, neither did President Taylor, neither has any man since the Prophet Joseph who has attended to the ordinance of adoption in the temples of our God. We have felt that there was more to be revealed upon the subject than we had received. Revelations were given to us in the St. George Temple, which President

Young presented to the Church of God. Changes were made there, and we still have more changes to make, in order to satisfy our Heavenly Father, satisfy our dead and ourselves. I will tell you what some of them are. I have prayed over this matter, and my brethren have. We have felt as President Taylor said, that we have got to have more revelation concerning sealing under the law of adoption. Well, what are these changes? One of them is the principle of adoption. . . .

"Now, what are the feelings of Israel? They have felt that they wanted to be adopted to somebody. President Young was not satisfied in his mind with regard to the extent of this matter; President Taylor was not. When I went before the Lord to know who I should be adopted to (we were then being adopted to prophets and apostles), the Spirit of God said to me, 'Have you not a father, who begot you?' 'Yes, I have.' 'Then why not honor him? Why not be adopted to him?' 'Yes,' says I, 'that is right.' I was adopted to my father, and should have had my father sealed to his father, and so on back; and the duty that I want every man who presides over a Temple to see performed from this day henceforth and forever, unless the Lord Almighty commands otherwise, is, let every man be adopted to his father. When a man receives the endowment, adopt him to his father; not to Wilford Woodruff, nor to any other man outside the lineage of his fathers. That is the will of God to this people.

"I want all men who preside over these temples in these mountains of Israel to bear this in mind. What business have I to take away the rights of the lineage of any man? What right has any man to do this? No; I say let every man be adopted to his father; and then you will do exactly what God said when he declared He would send Elijah the prophet in the last days. Elijah the prophet appeared unto Joseph Smith and told him the day had come when this principle must be carried out. Joseph Smith did not live long enough to enter any further upon these things. His soul was wound up with this work before he was martyred for the word of God and testimony of Jesus Christ. He told us that there must be a welding link of all dispensations and of the work of God from one generation to another. This was upon his mind more than most any other subject that was given to him.

"In my prayers the Lord revealed to me, that it was my duty to say to all Israel to carry this principle out, and in fulfillment of that revelation I lay it before this people. I say to all men who are laboring in these temples, carry out this principle, and then we will make one step in advance of what we have had before. Myself and counselors conversed upon this and were agreed upon it, and afterwards we laid it before all the Apostles who were here (two were absent—Brothers Thatcher and Lund, the latter being in England), and the Lord revealed to every one of these men—and they would bear testimony of it if they were to speak—that that was the word of the Lord to them. I never met with anything in my life in this Church that there was more unity upon than there was upon that principle. They all feel right about it, and that it is our duty. That is one principle that should be carried out from this time henceforth. 'But,' says one, 'suppose we come along to a man who perhaps is a murderer.' Well, if he is a murderer, drop him out and connect with the next man beyond him. But the Spirit of God will be with us in this matter. We want the Latter-day Saints from this time to trace their genealogies as far as they can, and to be sealed to their fathers and mothers. Have children sealed to their parents, and run this chain through as far as you can get it. . . . This is the will of the Lord to his people, and I think when you come to reflect upon it you will find it to be true.

"Another principle connected with this subject I want to talk about. A man has married a woman, and they have a family of children. The man lays down in death without ever hearing the Gospel. The wife afterwards hears the Gospel and embraces it. She comes to the temple and she wants to be sealed to her husband, who was a good man. The feeling has been to deny this and to say, 'No, he is not in the Church, and you cannot be sealed to your husband.' Many a woman's heart has ached because of this, and as a servant of God I have broken that chain a good while ago. I have laid before every woman this principle and let her have her choice. Why deprive a woman of being sealed to her husband because he never heard the Gospel? What do any of us know with regard to him? Will he not hear the Gospel and embrace it in the spirit world? Look at Joseph Smith. Not one of Joseph Smith's fathers or brothers or sisters were in the covenant when he received the keys of the kingdom of God and translated the Book of Mormon. They afterwards received it. Every brother and sister that he had, and his father and his father's brothers, except Uncle Jesse Smith, embraced the Gospel. Now, suppose that any of these had died before they had the opportunity of entering into the covenant with the Lord through the Gospel, as his brother Alvin did; they would have been in the same position as Alvin, concerning whom the Lord, when Joseph saw him in the celestial kingdom, said: 'All who have died without a knowledge of this Gospel, who would have received it if they had been permitted to tarry, shall be heirs of the celestial kingdom of God; also all that shall die henceforth without a knowledge of it, who would have received it with all their hearts, shall be heirs of that kingdom, for I, the Lord, will judge all men according to their works, according to the desire of their hearts.'

"So it will be with your fathers. There will be very few, if any, who will not accept the Gospel. Jesus, while his body lay in the tomb, went and preached to the spirits in prison, who were destroyed in the days of Noah. After so long an imprisonment, in torment, they doubtless gladly embraced the Gospel, and if so they will be saved in the kingdom of God. The fathers of this people will embrace the Gospel. It is my duty to honor my fathers who begot me in the flesh. It is your duty to do the same. When you do this, the Spirit of God will be with you. And we shall continue this work, the Lord adding light to that which we have already received. I have had friends adopted to me. We all have, more or less. But I have had peculiar feelings about it, especially lately. There are men in this congregation who wish to be adopted to me. I say to them, if they can hear me, Go and be adopted to your fathers, and save your fathers, and stand at the head of your father's house, as saviors upon Mount Zion and God will bless you in this. This is what I want to say, and what I want carried out in our temples.

"The Almighty is with this people. We shall have all the revelations that we will need, if we will do our duty and obey the commandments of God. When any of us get so that we cannot receive these revelations, the Lord will take us out of the way and put someone in our places who can. I am here today, on borrowed time, I may say. I would have been in the spirit world today, mingling with the spirits in the presence of God, had it not been for the cry of this people for my life when I lay at the gates of death a year ago. I have been preserved by the power of God. How long I shall live I do not know. It does not make any difference to me. But while I do live I want to do my duty. I want the Latter-day Saints to do their duty. Here is the Holy Priesthood in these mountains. Their responsibility is great and mighty. The eyes of God and all the holy prophets are watching us. This is the great dispensation that has been spoken of ever since the world began. We are gathered together in these mountains of Israel by the power and commandment of God. We are doing the work of God. This is not our home. As far as mortality is concerned, we shall soon pass away. But while here let us fill our mission. I want to say to Brother L. Snow, Brother M. W. Merrill, Brother J. D. T. McAllister and Brother D. H. Cannon, and all associated with you, carry these things before the Lord and see for yourselves. If you are not satisfied with this order of things, go and ask the Lord about it, and the Holy Ghost will reveal to you the truth of these principles.

"This is all I ought to say at this time, perhaps upon this subject. I am glad to meet with you. I have had a great anxiety over this matter. I have had a great desire that I might live to deliver these principles to the Latter-day Saints, for they are true.

They are one step forward in the work of the ministry and in the work of the endowment in these temples of our God. . . . A man may say, 'I am an Apostle, or I am a High Priest, or I am an Elder in Israel, and if I am adopted to my father, will it take any honor from me.' I would say not. If Joseph Smith was sealed to his father, with whom many of you were acquainted, what effect will that have upon his exaltation and glory? None at all. Joseph Smith will hold the keys of this dispensation to the endless ages of eternity. It is the greatest dispensation God ever gave to man, and he was ordained before the world was to stand in the flesh and organize this work. He was martyred for the word of God and testimony of Jesus, and when he comes in the clouds of heaven he will wear a martyr's crown. Those of you who stand here—I do not care whether you are apostles or what you are— by honoring your father you will not take any honor from your heads; you will hold the keys of the salvation of your father's house, as Joseph Smith does. You will lose nothing by honoring your fathers and redeeming your dead. It is a glorious work.

"When I returned from England in 1841 and heard Joseph Smith give this revelation, that we had power to redeem our dead, one of the first things I thought was, 'I have a mother in the spirit world.' My father was in the flesh. I baptized and ordained him and brought him up to Zion, where he is buried. But I never saw my mother to know her. She died when I was an infant. I had power to seal my mother to my father. Was that not a satisfaction? It was to me. I have gone to work with the assistance of my friends and redeemed my father's and my mother's house. When I went to inquire of the Lord how I could redeem my dead, while I was in St. George, not having any of my family there, the Lord told me to call upon the Saints in St. George and let them officiate for me in that temple, and it should be acceptable unto Him. Brother McAllister and the brethren and sisters there have assisted me in this work, and I felt to bless them with every feeling of my heart. This is a revelation to us. We can help one another in these matters, if we have not relatives sufficient to carry this on, and it will be acceptable unto the Lord.

"Brethren and sisters, lay these things to heart. Let us go on with our records, fill them up righteously before the Lord, and carry out this principle, and the blessings of God will attend us, and those who are redeemed will bless us in days to come. I pray God, that as a people our eyes may be opened to see, our ears to hear, and our hearts to understand the great and mighty work that rests upon our shoulders, and that the God of heaven requires at our hand. Great and glorious are these principles which God has revealed to us concerning the redemption of our dead. I tell you when the prophets and apostles go to preach to those who are shut up in prison, and who have not received the Gospel, thousands of them will there embrace the Gospel. They know more in that world than they do here. I pray God that as a people we may have power to magnify our calling in this great and mighty dispensation while we dwell in the flesh that when our work is done we may be satisfied with this life and this work. This is my prayer and the desire of my heart, in the name of Jesus Christ. Amen." (Wilford Woodruff, "The Law of Adoption," pages 146-52.)

Genealogical Research Essential to Temple Work

Thus the fundamental principles for temple sealings and for genealogical research were announced. It was established that thenceforth sealings should be done according to family lineage. We are to be sealed to our parents, they to their parents, and so on.

So it was established that we should search the records for the names of our kindred dead. We are to run that chain of lineage sealings back as far as we can obtain the information. We are to do the ordinance work for our progenitors.

The Church was prompt in following through on President Woodruff's revelation. Archibald F. Bennett, who devoted his entire life to genealogical and temple work, gave the following historical summary:

> On the thirteenth of November [1894], a meeting was held in the old historian's office. That office was located across the street south from the present Church Administration Building and just a little to the east, where the Medical Arts Building now stands. There were present on that occasion all members of the First Presidency, Wilford Woodruff, George Q. Cannon, Joseph F. Smith, the president of the Twelve, Franklin D. Richards, and other apostles, and a few others. They organized the Genealogical Society of Utah. It was incorporated under the laws of Utah and it was to be "benevolent, educational, and religious" in purpose — benevolent in gathering together into a library books that would help the people trace their ancestry; educational in teaching the people how to trace their ancestry and do temple work properly, including the sealings, and to avoid duplication; religious in that they would do all in their power to encourage the people to perform in the temples all the necessary ordinances to make it possible for people everywhere, if they were willing, to obtain the greatest gift of God, eternal life.

> The president of the Society, according to the articles of incorporation, was to be appointed by the First Presidency.

Brother Bennett continued with this important clarification:

> It should be emphasized that the Genealogical Society is not an auxiliary. I have some words here from President Anthon H. Lund when he was president of the Society: "The work done by the Genealogical Society cannot be classed as an auxiliary. It is a basic part of the work of the Church. Take away the power of the priesthood to seal for time and eternity husbands, wives, and children; take away the binding power of the families of the nations, past, present, and future; and the bringing to the dead the ordinances of the gospel; and you will take away the means of a perfect salvation for us all." (Address to seminary and institute faculty, Brigham Young University, 2 July 1958.)

Someone wrote and asked President Joseph Fielding Smith if the Genealogical Society was an auxiliary of the Church — someone in the correspondent's stake had said it was. President Smith replied as follows: "Genealogical work is part of the regular temple work. This work is not auxiliary. We do not look upon it as auxiliary, except in the sense it is an aid to temple work. The Genealogical Society is not an auxiliary organization."

Over the years the Genealogical Society or the Genealogical Department of the Church has been directed by a member of the First Presidency. It has been generously funded. The Temple Index Bureau was organized to give system to the processing of names for ordinance work and to avoid duplication insofar as possible. Enormous effort has gone into the microfilming and collecting of records from all over the world. Local genealogical libraries have been established. The forms and procedures for recording genealogical information have been developed. Negotiations continue around the world for access to the records of the human family. Worldwide conferences have been held to exchange information and to promote an interest in this work.

In accordance with changing legal requirements, the Genealogical Society was reorganized into the Genealogical Department of the Church. It is one of the largest departments of the Church, measured both by the size of the budget and the number of employees.

Every piece of equipment that becomes available that is useful in genealogical work is carefully studied with the hope of speeding up the work. Every system and procedure that can help with the collecting, the processing, and the recording of genealogical information is tested for use in this work.

As the years have passed since Elijah restored the keys of the sealing power, the determination of the Latter-day Saints to turn their hearts to their fathers has become increasingly evident.

This is not just a philosophical idea to be debated. It is a work to be performed.

We receive further light and knowledge as the work requires. We can each receive inspiration—the spirit of Elijah—as we involve ourselves in this sacred labor of love.

Will not a man who keeps the commandments of the Lord, who is faithful and true so far as he himself is concerned, receive perfection? Yes, provided his worthy dead also receive the same privileges, because there must be a family organization, a family unit, and each generation must be linked to the chain that goes before in order to bring perfection in family organization. (Joseph Fielding Smith.)

18

The Spirit of Elijah

On January 21, 1844, the Prophet Joseph Smith recorded: "Preached at the southwest corner of the temple to several thousand people, although the weather was somewhat unpleasant. My subject was the sealing of the hearts of the fathers to the children, and the hearts of the children to the fathers." (*HC*, 6:183.)

Wilford Woodruff recorded that sermon and the Prophet Joseph Smith included in his history the following from Brother Woodruff's record:

> The Bible says, "I will send you Elijah the Prophet before the coming of the great and dreadful day of the Lord; and he shall turn the hearts of the fathers to the children, and the hearts of the children to their fathers, lest I come and smite the earth with a curse."

Now, the word *turn* here should be translated *bind* or *seal*. But what is the object of this important mission? or how is it to be fulfilled? The keys are delivered. *The spirit of Elijah is to come*, the Gospel to be established, the Saints of God gathered, Zion built up, and the Saints to come up as saviors on Mount Zion. (*HC*, 6:183-84.)

The spirit of Elijah spoken of by the Prophet here and on other occasions is something very real. When a member of the Church comes under its influence, it is a powerful, compelling force which motivates him with a desire to be attending to genealogical and temple work. It leaves him anxious over the well-being of his forebears. When that spirit comes, somehow we desire to know more about those forebears — we desire to *know* them.

If we can literally be "caught up" in any work in the church, it is this work relating to genealogical research and to the temples. This, because there is the spirit of Elijah. The prophets have spoken of it. The Saints have felt it; and following the inspiration of it they have come to the temple to do the sacred work for both the living and the dead.

Persistence Despite Overwhelming Assignment

Somewhere I heard of an incident that happened in World War II. A group of commandos were sent across the English Channel to accomplish a military mission. They were sent ashore at night in high seas and had to make their way across a treacherous reef.

When the first of them reached the beach, led by a sergeant, they heard a companion calling for help. He was caught up on the reef and was unable to free himself. If left to himself he would be dashed to pieces by the heavy seas against the reef.

The sergeant pulled off his gear in preparation for an attempt to rescue the man. One of those on the beach said, "Don't go out there — it's too dangerous and difficult. If you go out there you'll never come back."

The sergeant replied, "I don't have to come back. I just have to go out there."

This illustrates something of our position with regard to our doing the work of the Lord. We are commanded to preach the gospel to all the living, for example. We see no way to accomplish this task in our lifetime. Many refuse to listen, some turn away, others resent and even persecute us. Nevertheless we are not released from the assignment to try. We are to do the best we can. If we do, the honest in heart can be found and sifted out of the world.

As for those who have died, there seems no way we can find them all. We have no way of knowing whether they will accept the work we do for them. We are sure some will reject it. There may be those who are not eligible to receive it. We can only do as we do in missionary work—set our hand to the task, be about the work, do all we can to seek out the names of our kindred dead and prepare these names for temple work. Insofar as we can, too, we gather the identifying data of all who have lived in mortality.

Those who would have received the gospel had they heard it in this life surely will accept it. As for the others, the Lord will provide a reward and a kingdom that pays full regard to both justice and mercy. Many are hung up on the reef, as it were. They cannot free themselves. It is for us to go to them.

They are otherwise described as being in prison. We can assist in setting them free. We can be their saviors.

We in the Church must not retreat before the overwhelming assignment of extending the gospel message to all men, both living and dead. Not all those living to whom we preach the gospel may accept it. Not all of the dead for whom we do work may claim it. But we are obliged to extend it to them. If we go out to do it, that part which is consistent with the will of the Lord will be accomplished and we will stand approved of Him. President Spencer W. Kimball emphasized the importance of this work in these words:

We are a Church that is actively engaged in temple and genealogy work for ourselves and for the infinite numbers of our Father's children who have the promise, but not as yet the opportunity, for the ordinances of salvation. This is a work that makes even more meaningful the great corresponding missionary work being carried out in the spirit world. ("The Things of Eternity—Stand We in Jeopardy?" *Ensign* [January 1977]:4.)

Speaking of the redemption of those in the spirit world, President Woodruff said:

They are shut up in prison, awaiting the message of the Elders of Israel. We have only about a thousand millions of people on the earth, but in the spirit world they have fifty thousand millions; and there is not a single revelation which gives us any reason to believe that any man who enters the spirit world preached the Gospel there to those who lived after him; but they all preach to men who were in the flesh before they were. Jesus himself preached to the antediluvian world, who had been in prison for thousands of years. So with Joseph Smith and the Elders—they will have to preach to the inhabitants of the earth who have died during the last seventeen centuries; and when they hear the testimony of the Elders and accept it there should be somebody on the earth, as we have been told, to attend to the ordinances of the house of God for them. (*Discourses of Wilford Woodruff,* page 151.)

The Prophet Joseph Smith said, "It is not only necessary that you should be *baptized* for your dead, but you will have to go through *all* the ordinances for them, the same as you have gone through to save yourselves." (*HC,* 6:365; italics added.)

President Joseph Fielding Smith outlined the conditions under which all were to receive the gospel:

The Lord has made it known that his mercy extends to the uttermost bounds and that every soul is entitled to hear the gospel plan, either in this life or in the spirit world. *All who hear and believe, repenting and receiving the gospel in its fulness, whether living or dead, are heirs of salvation in the celestial kingdom of God.*

Those who reject the gospel, but who live honorable lives, shall also be heirs of salvation, but not in the celestial kingdom. The Lord has prepared a place for them in the terrestrial kingdom.

Those who live lives of wickedness may also be heirs of salvation, that is, they too shall be redeemed from death and from hell *eventually*. These, however, must suffer in hell the torments of the damned *until* they pay the price of their sinning, for the blood of Christ will not cleanse them. This vast host will find their place in the telestial kingdom where their glories differ as the stars of the heavens in magnitude.

Sons of perdition are those who have rejected the light and the truth after having received the testimony of Jesus, and they are the only ones who are not redeemed from the dominion of the devil and his angels. (*Doctrines of Salvation*, 2:133-34.)

We cannot know the full outcome of our efforts. We are commanded to bring the gospel message to the living, and to make provision for ordinance work to be performed for those who have died. We do not know how many of them will be redeemed in the celestial kingdom. We only make it possible for those to progress who can qualify.

It might be likened to putting spiritual resources in a bank to be held in escrow under the name of an ancestor. When and how much he will be eligible to withdraw and claim we do not know. We just know that we are to provide the account for the use of the worthy.

The Lord commanded His Apostles, "Go ye therefore, and teach all nations, baptizing them in the name of the Father, and of the Son, and of the Holy Ghost." (Matthew 28:19.)

There is no doubt that His commandment meant everyone, for He included "all nations, kindreds, tongues and people." (See D&C 42:58, Revelation 14:6, Mosiah 3:13.) That was an all-inclusive assignment. It was clear that not all may accept, but those who did believe, repent, and submit to baptism would be eligible for salvation. Those who would not believe but would reject His word would be damned.

There was reluctance, even resistance on the part of some early Christian leaders to expand their vision as wide as humanity is wide. Were they not Israel? Were they not the Lord's chosen people? Were they not the children of the covenant? Was not the gospel for them, to the exclusion of the others? Because the Lord sent the Apostles first to the "lost sheep of the house of Israel"

(Matthew 10:6), they were not willing to include all. Later, when they asked the Lord if it was time for Him to restore again the kingdom to Israel, He told them that it was not for them to know the times and the seasons "but ye shall receive power, after that the Holy Ghost is come upon you: and ye shall be witnesses unto me both in Jerusalem, and in all Judaea, and in Samaria, and unto the uttermost part of the earth." (Acts 1:8.)

His specific reference to Samaria, whose inhabitants the Jews resented, was a lesson to them. And later, when contention arose on the matter of Jewish Christians mixing with Gentiles, Peter told of a vision in which he had resisted the commandment of the Lord because he wanted only that which was chosen. "But the voice answered me again from heaven, What God hath cleansed, that call not thou common." (Acts 11:9.)

They were the chosen people. They were chosen to assist with the redemption of all nations. They were to be prepared to bring the saving message and the saving ordinances to every living soul.

Chosen to Be Saviors

President Joseph Fielding Smith pointed out that not all of the dead will be eligible to receive the effect of all of the ordinances.

> *We are going to do the temple work for those who are entitled, through their faith and their repentance, to enter into the celestial kingdom.* But somebody says, "How do we know? We search our records for hundreds of years and do the work for all of them." Of course we do, because we cannot judge. I do not know whether one man is worthy and another is not.
>
> The Lord has given us the privilege of doing the work for all of *our kindred,* with the hope, of course, on our part that all of them will receive the truth. (*Doctrines of Salvation,* 2:191.)

Brigham Young preached the same doctrine:

> Never have I seen to so great an extent that willingness to labor for the cause of righteousness, as was witnessed in the Temple, at St. George, last winter. The Spirit of God pervaded the hearts of the brethren and sisters, and how willing they were to labor! This

work will continue, and the brethren and sisters will go into the Temples of the Lord, to officiate for those who have died without the Gospel from the days of Father Adam to the winding-up scene, until every one is officiated for who can or will receive the Gospel, so that all may have the opportunity and privileges of life and salvation. (*Discourses of Brigham Young*, page 419.)

Wilford Woodruff had the same understanding. He stated:

God is no respecter of persons; he will not give privileges to one generation and withhold them from another; and the whole human family, from father Adam down to our day, have got to have the privilege, somewhere, of hearing the Gospel of Christ; and the generations that have passed and gone without hearing that Gospel in its fullness, power and glory, will never be held responsible by God for not obeying it, neither will he bring them under condemnation for rejecting a law they never saw or understood; and if they live up to the light they had they are justified so far, and they have to be preached to in the spirit world. But nobody will baptize them there, and somebody has got to administer for them by proxy here in the flesh, that they may be judged according to men in the flesh and have part in the first resurrection. (*Discourses of Wilford Woodruff*, page 149.)

Elder John A. Widtsoe expressed in an impressive way the spirit with which we approach this work, which is the spirit relating to all of the gospel. He stated:

The least of us, the humblest, is in partnership with the Almighty in achieving the purpose of the eternal plan of salvation.

That places us in a very responsible attitude towards the human race. By that doctrine, with the Lord at the head, we become saviors on Mount Zion, all committed to the great plan of offering salvation to the untold numbers of spirits. To do this is the Lord's self-imposed duty, this great labor his highest glory. Likewise, it is man's duty, self-imposed, his pleasure and joy, his labor, and ultimately his glory.

There is no place for forgetting the other man, in the Gospel of the Lord Jesus Christ. There stands my brother. It was for him that the whole plan was made, for him the Church was organized, for him all these blessings were given — not for me alone. Oh, I stand there too. The Church was made for me . . . but my brother is entitled to them just as much as I am. He and I together and all of us must unitedly work together to fulfill the greater purposes of the Almighty Father.

Under the Gospel what is man's highest ideal? Under the Gospel it must be to become like the Father. If the Lord's concern is chiefly to bring happiness and joy, salvation, to the whole human family, we cannot become like the Father unless we too engage in that work. There is no chance for the narrow, selfish, introspective man in the kingdom of God. He may survive in the world of men; he may win fame, fortune and power before men, but he will not stand high before the Lord unless he learns to do the works of God, which always point toward the salvation of the whole human family.

In our preexistent state, in the day of the great council, we made a certain agreement with the Almighty. The Lord proposed a plan, conceived by him. We accepted it. Since the plan is intended for all men, we became parties to the salvation of every person under that plan. We agreed, right then and there, to be not only saviors for ourselves but measurably, saviors for the whole human family. We went into a partnership with the Lord. The working out of the plan became then not merely the Father's work, and the Savior's work, but also our work. (John A. Widtsoe, "The Worth of Souls," *Utah Genealogical and Historical Magazine* 25 [October 1934]:189-90.)

If all were to be eligible for baptism, and if baptism is the gate to the celestial kingdom, and if all in the Church are commanded to seek after their kindred dead and to find them and to bind them to them by the sacred ordinances, then the mighty work of the salvation and exaltation of all the human family rests upon that church which bears the name of Jesus Christ with full authority.

The Prophet Joseph Smith was martyred at the time he was unfolding the doctrine and procedures relating to the redemption of the dead. He described it as "this most glorious of all subjects." (D&C 128:17.) The intensity of the persecution at the time of the martyrdom and during the generation that followed was accompanied by the determination of the Latter-day Saints to receive by revelation the instruction with reference to temple work. It is evident that the work relating to temples bothers the adversary the most.

When they received instruction that they could baptize for their dead, they went forth with great joy and baptized more or less without organization or order or records, as we learned from the sermon of President Wilford Woodruff. That was set in order by revelation. (See D&C 127:6.)

At first they made no distinction as to who would be baptized for whom, and males were baptized for females and vice versa. That was also corrected later.

They knew that there was to be a linking of the generations. They knew that they were to have their families put in proper order, both here and beyond the veil. Remember, the word *order* means to put in rows or in proper relationship. Ordaining is the process of doing it, and ordinance is the ceremony by which it is done.

The early Latter-day Saints seemed to understand, too, that the turning of the hearts to the fathers meant turning to the ancient ones, to Abraham and the prophets—the ancient fathers—for those prophets held the keys. Moses appeared in the Kirtland Temple to commit the keys of the gathering of Israel. The gathering of the people is done so that the temples can be built; we gather to build temples. Elias committed to Joseph Smith and Oliver Cowdery the keys to the dispensation of the gospel of Abraham, saying "that in us and our seed all generations after us should be blessed." (D&C 110:12.) The early Saints understood that they should be tied somehow to the prophets, that their hearts should be turned to "the fathers."

And so, without further light the Saints began the practice of being adopted—or sealed—to the prophets, the leaders of the Church. The revelation given to Wilford Woodruff recorded in the previous chapter corrected this practice and instructed that they were to be sealed to *their* fathers.

Thus, the revelation had a general meaning relating to the Church and the priesthood and the prophets. It had also a specific, individual meaning relating to our own families. President Wilford Woodruff said:

When I went before the Lord to know who I should be adopted to (we were then being adopted to prophets and apostles), the Spirit of God said to me, "Have you not a father, who begot you?" "Yes, I have." "Then why not honor him? Why not be adopted to him?" "Yes," says I, "that is right." I was adopted to my father, and should have had my father sealed to his father, and so on back; and the duty that I want every man who presides over a Temple to see performed from this day henceforth and forever, unless the Lord Almighty commands otherwise, is, let every man be adopted to his father. ("The Law of Adoption," page 148.)

So it was established. We were to be sealed to our own fathers. So it was established that our hearts are to be true to "the fathers," the prophets.

"If it were not so, the whole earth would be utterly wasted at his coming." While it may seem overwhelming that we have the responsibility to extend the gospel to the entire human family, that responsibility rests upon us. Through us and our posterity, all the nations of the earth can be blessed.

The Prophet Joseph Smith said:

Elijah! what would you do if you were here? Would you confine your work to the living alone? No: I would refer you to the Scriptures, where the subject is manifest: that is, without us, they could not be made perfect, nor we without them; the fathers without the children, nor the children without the fathers.

I wish you to understand this subject, for it is important; and if you will receive it, this is the spirit of Elijah, that we redeem our dead, and connect ourselves with our fathers which are in heaven, and seal up our dead to come forth in the first resurrection; and here we want the power of Elijah to seal those who dwell on earth to those who dwell in heaven. This is the power of Elijah and the keys of the kingdom of Jehovah. (*HC*, 6:252.)

Our Father's Business

In 1964 I was on assignment in South America and I went with President A. Theodore Tuttle of the First Quorum of the Seventy to Cuzco in Peru. It is a large city in a valley in the Andes, about thirteen thousand feet in elevation. The mountains rise above that high valley at every view. We were unable to get a regular room in a hotel, and finally arrangements were made that we would sleep on mattresses on the basement floor of an old house adjoining the hotel. They were not very inviting quarters, but we were grateful for the accommodations.

Our first stop in the city was to visit the missionaries. One of the missionaries had been ill for a long period of time. We went to the humble apartment, up several flights of stairs at the back of a large building. There we found him in bed, his companion nursing him and studying during his free time. We administered to the elder and blessed him to be healed. That night he came to the meeting.

At the meeting that night we had a most interesting experience. When I returned I told Elder Spencer W. Kimball of it. Since he has subsequently made reference to it in a conference sermon and on other occasions, I feel I can include it here. Perhaps his feeling for the experience is that it is somehow symbolic of the seeking for every soul to the very least and last. I include here an account of this incident as it was presented in a talk at a Brigham Young University Indian Week meeting.

> Whenever I'm in South America, and that seems to be very often, I'm always looking for someone. I saw him first fourteen years ago. Brother Tuttle and I were in Cuzco at a meeting of the branch.
>
> The meeting was held in a little room, and a door opened onto the street. At Cuzco, at an elevation of thirteen thousand feet, it is bitterly cold at night. The room was packed and the door was open to let a little air in.
>
> Brother Tuttle was speaking. There were several chairs against the wall and I was sitting there. To our left, against the wall was a little sacrament table.
>
> As Brother Tuttle was speaking, I saw a little Indian boy, perhaps six years old, come in the back door, perhaps for the warmth. He had on a ragged shirt and that was all. His little feet were so calloused that it was hard to tell that he had toes that were separated from one another.
>
> Then he saw the sacrament table and the bread. He was inching along the wall and was almost to the sacrament table when an

Indian woman, sitting in about the third row, saw him from the corner of her eye.

Without saying a word, but with just a look, and a shake of her head, she conveyed the message: "Get out of here! You don't belong here!"

That little fellow turned and ran out into the night.

Before Brother Tuttle had finished, the little boy appeared again at the door, and again, I suppose driven by that same hunger, he edged along the wall. He was almost to the place where that Indian woman would see him again. He was studying us very carefully.

I held out my arms to him, and he came willingly. I picked him up and held him. And then, to teach our Lamanite members in Cuzco a lesson, I sat him in the chair that had been reserved for Brother Tuttle.

When the meeting closed, the little boy darted out into the night before I could talk to him or do anything for him.

So every time I'm in South America I am looking for him. He's old enough now, I'm sure, to be married. When I am in a missionary meeting I look for him and wonder, could it be, could this elder be that boy, or could that one?

I watch for him in the market place as we travel. I look for him in the streets. And some say that it is a futile search, that I will never find him. But in this Church we will find him, if we have to sift through every soul in South America.

Some will say, "Perhaps he has died; you will never find him." To them we say, "We will find him. We will gather the names of every soul who ever lived and bring them to the temple. Perhaps his son will bring his name. We will find him."

Others will say, "Perhaps no record was kept." In that case we will depend on revelation.

We're looking for him with all the resources we can find. We send tens of missionaries, and hundreds of missionaries, and thousands of missionaries to find him. *You* must look for him.

Some of you have already been on missions, others will go. Some of you will go there to preside, perhaps in Cuzco or in Otavalo, or at Coban, or any of the other places among these missions. You have the power that can redeem them.

It was mentioned earlier that Joseph Smith was not given the complete plan for organizing the Church at the beginning of his ministry. Instructions on the progressive process of organization continue to be received to our day.

This principle governs all the operations of the kingdom. We do not now see how we can preach the gospel to every living soul. Nor do we yet know how we can find the names of those who did not have the opportunity to hear the gospel in mortality. But we can do what we can do now. And when we stand in need of further light and knowledge or more developed means of doing the work, the need will be supplied. Direction may be given on how we can hasten both the acquisition of names and the performing of the necessary vicarious ordinance work.

We will one day know more of how this work will be accomplished. In the meantime we move ahead, seeking out both the living and the dead. We extend to them an opportunity to accept baptism and qualify for the higher ordinances.

In it all, we are being tested. It would be well for all of us to be about our Father's business.

19

Again: The doctrine or sealing power of Elijah is as follows: — If you have power to seal on earth and in heaven. . . . The first thing you do, go and seal on earth your sons and daughters unto yourself, and yourself unto your fathers in eternal glory. (Joseph Smith.)

Claiming Your Own

The Prophet Joseph Smith said:

> I would advise all the Saints to go to with their might and gather together all their living relatives to this place, that they may be sealed and saved, that they may be prepared against the day that the destroying angel goes forth; and if the whole Church should go to with all their might to save their dead, seal their posterity, and gather their living friends, and spend none of their time in behalf of the world, they would hardly get through before night would come, when no man can work. (*HC*, 6:184.)

We repeat the instruction of President Wilford Woodruff.

We want the Latter-day Saints from this time to trace their genealogies as far as they can, and to be sealed to their fathers and mothers. Have children sealed to their parents, and run this chain

through as far as you can get it. . . . This is the will of the Lord to
His people, and I think when you come to reflect upon it you will
find it to be true. (General Conference Address, April 8, 1894.)

Many members of the Church live at great distance from
temples. In many places the economy of the countries is such, or
the means available to the individuals may be such, that there is
little apparent hope that they will be able to go to the temple
very soon. These members of the Church are not deprived of
activity in the work to redeem the dead in fulfillment of their
individual obligations. Indeed, there is a very substantial work
that they can do. That work is in genealogical research, in the
preparing of family records and family histories.

The records of the family are most available to the family. If
you will start wherever you are in the world, no matter how far
distant from the temple, you can contribute to the salvation of
your kindred dead. Others may do the actual ordinance work,
but the sealing of ancestral families and the linking of the generations cannot be done without what you are able to give.

Work for the Dead an Individual Responsibility

You should be about your genealogical research. No member
of the Church needs to be left out of this work. If you wonder
where to begin, begin with yourself. Complete your own records.

You cannot have regard for temple ordinance work without
having great respect for genealogical work as well. Genealogical
work is the fundamental service for the temples. The temples
could not stay open without success in the genealogical program.
The same spirit that characterizes the patrons and employees of
the temples should be characteristic of the patrons and employees
of the Genealogical Department of the Church. Members of the
Church cannot touch this work without becoming affected spiritually. The spirit of Elijah permeates it. Many of the little intru-
sions into our lives, the little difficulties and the petty problems

that beset us, are put into proper perspective when we view the linking of the generations for the eternities. We become much more patient then. So if you want the influence of dignity and wisdom and inspiration and spirituality to envelop your life, involve yourself in temple and genealogical work.

All that I have learned from the revelations and from reading the statements of the prophets has fixed two things in my mind. First, we are individually responsible to seek after our kindred dead and see that the temple ordinances are performed for them. Second, once those names have been found, we are to establish family relationships. Genealogical and temple work is lineage-linked. We are linking the generations together.

Our purpose for doing genealogical work is a proper one, a worthy one. The scriptures contain condemnation of "endless genealogies," rebuking the ancients for seeking their ancestry for the wrong purposes. Those things happen today when a search is made into the past to find some basis for prestige, to make connections with the "right" family, to run the thread of relationship simply to tie to royalty or to prominence, or to lay claim to properties in an unworthy way. We should be careful of this. The purpose for seeking the names of our kindred and running the chain back as far as we can find it is to give something to our progenitors, not to get something from them. We do it so that they can receive the sacred ordinances in the holy temple. Eventually the linking of the generations will be complete and the family of man will be sealed together. This is the obligation of this Church and kingdom.

The Prophet Joseph Smith said emphatically:

> The greatest responsibility in this world that God has laid upon us is to seek after our dead. The apostle says, "They without us cannot be made perfect" [Hebrews 11:40]; for it is necessary that the sealing power should be in our hands to seal our children and our dead for the fulness of the dispensation of times — a dispensation to meet the promises made by Jesus Christ before the foundation of the world for the salvation of man. (*HC*, 6:313.)

He also said:

> This doctrine presents in a clear light the wisdom and mercy of God in preparing an ordinance for the salvation of the dead, being baptized by proxy, their names recorded in heaven and they judged according to the deeds done in the body. This doctrine was the burden of the scriptures. Those Saints who neglect it in behalf of their deceased relatives, do it at the peril of their own salvation. (*HC*, 4:426.)

The Prophet made a similar statement concerning missionary work — preaching the gospel to the living. "After all that has been said, the greatest and most important duty is to preach the Gospel." (*HC*, 2:478.)

On occasions you hear one or the other of these quoted in a sermon. How can each of them be the greatest responsibility?

They are, of course, both parts of the overall work we are commanded to do. Genealogical and temple work may well be missionary work for the dead, and missionary work may constitute the initial part of genealogical and temple work for the living.

President Joseph Fielding Smith made this explanation:

> The Lord has given *to the Church* the responsibility of preaching the Gospel to the nations of the earth. This *is* the greatest responsibility *of the Church*. Men are to be taught the Gospel and called to repentance and warned. When they refuse to heed the warning they must be left without excuse.
>
> The Lord has also placed upon the *individual members* of the Church a responsibility. It is our duty as *individuals* to seek after *our* immediate dead — those of our own line. This is the *greatest* responsibility that we have and we should carry it through in behalf of our "fathers" who have gone before. ("Thoughts on Temple Work and Salvation," *The Utah Genealogical and Historical Magazine* 20 [January 1929]:42-43.)

By this definition, missionary work is primarily a Church responsibility, with members being called to labor individually. Work for the redemption of the dead, on the other hand, is primarily an individual responsibility, with the Church assuming some of it when it can be done best collectively.

The Prophet Joseph Smith put these subjects together when he said: "We ought to have the building up of Zion as our greatest object." (*HC*, 3:390.)

The Church builds and maintains temples. This we could not do as individuals. That is why the people are gathered. The Prophet said:

> It was the design of the councils of heaven before the world was, that the principles and laws of the priesthood should be predicated upon the gathering of the people in every age of the world. Jesus did everything to gather the people, and they would not be gathered, and He therefore poured out curses upon them. Ordinances instituted in the heavens before the foundation of the world, in the priesthood, for the salvation of men, are not to be altered or changed. All must be saved on the same principles.
>
> It is for the same purpose that God gathers together His people in the last days, to build unto the Lord a house to prepare them for the ordinances and endowments, washings and anointings, etc. (*HC*, 5:423-24.)

There was a day when people were gathered to "Zion" to build up the Church, to build temples. Now temples are being constructed in many parts of the world.

The gathering now is not from the far reaches of the world to Nauvoo or to Salt Lake City; the gathering now is out of the world into the Church: the Saints of Mexico to gather in Mexico, into the Church; those in Japan to gather out of the world but to remain in Japan. And so it is for all the world to gather into the Church to build temples.

There are other things we can do collectively as a church. We microfilm records worldwide. We establish libraries for use of members and nonmembers. We build vaults to store records. As a Church we develop forms and procedures to help in research. We prepare research manuals. We program conferences, meetings and seminars to motivate, instruct, and inspire.

Nevertheless genealogical and temple work are basically *individual* responsibilities.

The name extraction program consists of reviewing records such as copies of parish registers and recording the required data for every name. That data then is processed for temple ordinance work. Name extraction becomes an important part of genealogical work. However, this does not relieve each member from the responsibility to seek after his own kindred dead. We are all responsible, individually, to link our families in proper order.

Consider this comparison. In the welfare program we have been counseled for generations by the leaders of the Church to secure for ourselves a year's supply of food and clothing, and if possible fuel, and to be concerned for our shelter. This is a responsibility laid upon the individual members of the Church, upon each family. The commodities are to be stored at home. They are to be privately purchased, privately stored, and in time of crisis privately used.

There also has been developed in the Church a system of bishop's storehouses. Here commodities are collected which are distributed by the bishop of the ward in times of emergency need. This is a collective or Church way of solving the problem. Welfare farms are maintained and members of the Church donate their labor to produce the various commodities that find their way into the bishop's storehouse.

It is not ever suggested that because we have bishop's storehouses there would be no need for the individual families to maintain their year's supply. The counsel for the individual to protect himself and his family has never been withdrawn. It has been continually emphasized.

There is something of a comparison in genealogical research. Name extraction is a collective way of contributing to the gathering of names. We have mentioned other examples of collective Church-sponsored and Church-funded answers to our obligation to seek the dead. But this does not excuse the individual member of the Church from the responsibility laid upon each one of us personally to see to it that our kindred dead are sought out and that proper ordinances are ultimately performed for them.

The Lord through His prophet has made this work an individual responsibility. We are to move forward with such information and records as we have or can obtain, whether or not we are assisted by the Church either locally or from Church headquarters.

Something of the spirit with which we should approach this work is illustrated by an incident I recall hearing from President Joseph T. Bentley, who presided over the Mexican Mission. It happened, I think, somewhere in Mexico. An eleven-year-old boy had been seriously injured in an automobile accident. By the time they got him to the doctor, he was dying from loss of blood. In looking for a donor for an emergency transfusion they decided on his seven-year-old sister. The doctor explained to the little girl that her brother was dying and asked whether she would be willing to donate her blood in order to save his life. The little girl turned pale with fright, but in a moment she consented to do it.

The transfusion was made. The doctor came to the little girl. "The color is coming back into his face," he said. "It looks as though he is going to be all right." She was happy her brother would be all right, but she asked, "But doctor, when am I going to die?" She had thought all the time that she was not just giving blood but literally her life to save an older brother. We learn great lessons from our youth.

There are several basic component parts to genealogical and temple work. Over the years, they may be rearranged somewhat in emphasis, or the approach in programming Church participation may change somewhat. But the responsibilities stay about the same.

1. Each of us is to compile his own life history.
2. Each of us is to keep a Book of Remembrance.
3. As individuals and families we are each to seek out our kindred dead, beginning first with the four most recent generations on each line, and then going back as far as we can.
4. We are each to participate in other programs such as name extraction when asked to do so.
5. We are to organize our families and hold meetings and reunions.

6.   If we have access to a temple, each of us should go to the temple as often as possible to do ordinance work—first for ourselves, then for our progenitors, then for all the names that have been gathered by means other than our own.

Genealogical Work for Every Church Member

There somehow seems to be the feeling that genealogical work is an all-or-nothing responsibility. That is not so. Genealogical work is *another* responsibility for every Latter-day Saint. And we may do it successfully along with all the other callings and responsibilities that rest upon us.

The bishop can do it without neglecting his flock. A stake missionary can do it without abandoning his mission. A Sunday School teacher can accomplish it without forgetting his lesson. A ward Relief Society president can do it without forsaking the sisters in her ward.

You can fulfill your obligation to your kindred dead and to the Lord without forsaking your other Church callings. You can do it without abandoning your family responsibilities. You can do this work. You can do it without becoming a so-called "expert" in it.

As mentioned before, many Church members live far from a temple. Some are never able to attend, and others can do so only rarely. And yet Latter-day Saints have a feeling for the word *temple* and are drawn to it. Somehow temples and temple work are such a part of us that we find very few, if any, in the Church who object to the work, who resist it, or who are against it.

So it is not likely that you need to be converted to genealogical work. There are very few in the Church who are in this position. Most of us really don't understand the procedures, but somehow we sense that it is an inspired, spiritual work.

But many of us don't get started because, never having done any of the work, we don't feel we know how to. We just don't quite know how to take hold of it or where to begin. And those who have become experts in it are not always able to get down to the level of the beginner and wisely introduce this work to him.

Many a beginner has gone to a class with the feeling that he wants to start in this work, only to be confronted with a pedigree chart extending across the blackboard or taped to the wall, plus stacks of forms with blanks and numbers and spaces, lists of procedures and regulations, and so on. He has been overwhelmed. "Surely this is too difficult for me," he decides. "I could never be expert at it."

Genealogical work has, I fear, sometimes been made to appear too difficult, too involved, and too time-consuming to really be inviting to the average Church member.

Elder John A. Widtsoe said on one occasion:

> In many a science, the beginning courses are so taught as if the whole class were intending to become candidates for the Ph.D. degree in the subject. Students fall out in despair . . . the beginning courses . . . are crowded with difficult, remote problems . . . until the freshman loses interest in the whole subject.

Brother Widtsoe concluded:

> It took some time to make them understand that a good teacher does such work as to enable his students to pass, with ordinary diligence. (John A. Widtsoe, *In a Sunlit Land* [Salt Lake City: Deseret News Press, 1952], pages 90, 150.)

It is easy for one teaching a subject like genealogical research, which can become very involved, to assume that because he understands it everyone else understands it. There is the tendency for him to want everybody in the class to know everything about it all at once. But the beginner frequently doesn't follow it all. And as the little girl said, "it becomes complicateder and complicateder."

How to Begin

There is a way that it can be done. And there is a place to begin. You don't need to begin with the pedigree charts or the stacks of forms, or the blank spaces, or the numbers, or the procedures, or the regulations. You can begin with *you*, with who you are and with what you have right now.

It is a matter of getting started. You may come to know the principle that Nephi knew when he said, "And I was led by the Spirit, not knowing beforehand the things which I should do." (1 Nephi 4:6.)

If you don't know where to start, start with *yourself*. If you don't know what records to get, and how to get them, start with what you have.

If you can start with what you have and with what you know, it's a little hard to find an excuse to delay. And it may be spiritually dangerous to delay it too long.

The General Authorities attending stake quarterly conferences have carried with them the message that all Latter-day Saints are to prepare a life history and to make a record of events which have occurred in their lives. The responsibility to lead out in this work was placed on the priesthood bearers. They are to do it and see that all others are encouraged and helped to do it.

There are two very simple instructions for those who are waiting for a place to begin. Here's what you might do:

Get a cardboard box. Any kind of a box will do. Put it some place where it is in the way, perhaps on the couch or on the counter in the kitchen — anywhere where it cannot go unnoticed. Then, over a period of a few weeks, collect and put into the box every record of your life, such as,

> your birth certificate,
> your certificate of blessing,
> your certificate of baptism,
> your certificate of ordination,
> your certificate of graduation.

Collect diplomas, all of the photographs, honors or awards, a diary if you have kept one, everything that you can find pertaining to *your* life; anything that is written, or registered, or recorded that testifies that you are alive and what you have done.

Don't try to do this in a day. Take some time on it. Most of us have these things scattered around here and there. Some of them are in a box in the garage under that stack of newspapers; others are stored away in drawers, or in the attic, or one place or another. Perhaps some have been tucked in the leaves of the Bible or elsewhere.

Gather all these papers together and put them in the box. Keep it there until you have collected everything you think you have. Then make some space on a table, or even on the floor, and sort out all that you have collected. Divide your life into three periods. The Church does it that way. All of our programming in the Church is divided into three general categories—children, youth, and adult.

Start with the childhood section and begin with your birth certificate. Put together every record in chronological order: the pictures, the record of your baptism, etc., up to the time you were twelve years of age.

Next assemble all that which pertains to your youth, from twelve to eighteen, or up until the time you were married. Put all of that together in chronological order. Line up the records—the certificates, the photographs, and so on—and put them in another box or envelope. Do the same with the records on the rest of your life.

Once you have done this, you have what is necessary to complete your life story. Simply take your birth certificate and begin writing: "I was born September 10, 1924, the son of Ira W. Packer and Emma Jensen Packer, at Brigham City, Utah. I was the tenth child and the fifth son in the family." Etc. etc. etc.

It really won't take you long to write, or dictate into a tape recorder, the account of your life, and it will have an accuracy because you have collected those records.

Now, don't say that you can't collect them. All you are asked to do is to collect that information that you have and what you know. It is your obligation.

What then? After you've made the outline of your life history to date, what do you do with all of the materials you have collected?

That, of course, brings you to your Book of Remembrance. Simply paste them lightly on the pages so that they can be taken out if necessary from time to time, and you have your Book of Remembrance.

Once you begin this project, very interesting and inspiring things will happen. You cannot do this much without getting something of the spirit of it, and without talking about it, at least in your family circle. Some very interesting things will start to happen once you show some interest in your own genealogical work. It is a firm principle. There are many, many testimonies about it. It will happen to you.

Aunt Clara will tell you that she has a picture of you with your great-grandfather. You know that cannot be so, because he died the year before you were born. But Aunt Clara produces the picture. There is your great-grandfather holding you as a tiny baby. As you check through the records you find that he died the year *after* you were born, an important detail in your family history.

That accurate data means something. The middle name written on the back of the picture means something too. You may not know it at the moment, but it is a key; the beginning of ordinance work in the temple for some of your ancestors.

You believe in the resurrection. You must know that baptism for someone who is dead is quite as essential as baptism for someone who is living. There is no difference in the importance of it. One by one it must happen. They must do it here while living or it must be done for them here after they die.

The whole New Testament centers on the resurrection of the Lord. The message is that *all* are to be resurrected. Every scripture and every motivation that applies to missionary work has its application to ordinance work for the dead.

Now you have your own family history written and you have your Book of Remembrance assembled. It sounds too easy —well it is, almost. But it does mean that you have to get started. Like Nephi, you will be "led by the Spirit, not knowing beforehand the things which [you] should do." (1 Nephi 4:6.)

Several years ago Sister Packer and I determined that we should get our records in order. However, under the pressure of Church responsibilities with my travels about the world, and the obligations with our large family and a home to keep up both indoors and outdoors, there just was not enough time. But we were restless about this genealogical responsibility, and finally we determined that somehow we would have to make more time in the day.

During the Christmas holidays when we had a little extra time, we started. Then as we moved back to a regular schedule after the holidays, we adopted the practice of getting up an hour or two earlier each day.

We gathered together everything we had, and in the course of a few weeks we were amazed at what we were able to accomplish. The thing that was most impressive, however, was the fact that we began to have experiences that told us somehow that we were being guided, that there were those beyond the veil who were interested in what we were doing. Things began to fall into place.

As I have traveled about the Church and paid particular attention to this subject, many testimonies have come to light. Others who assemble their records together are likewise having similar experiences. It was as though the Lord was waiting for us to begin.

We found things we had wondered about for a long time. It seemed as though they came to us almost too easily. More than this, things that we never dreamed existed began to show up. We began to learn by personal experience that this research into our families is an inspired work. We came to know that an inspiration will follow those who move into it. It is just a matter of getting started.

There is an old Chinese proverb which states: "Man who sit with legs crossed and mouth open, waiting for roast duck to fly in, have long hunger!"

Once we started, we found the time. Somehow we were able to carry on all of the other responsibilities. There seemed to be an increased inspiration in our lives because of this work.

Paths Open When We Start

But the decision, the action, must begin with the individual. The Lord will not tamper with our agency. If we want a testimony of genealogical and temple work, we must do something about that work.

Someone paraphrased Proverbs 4:7 in this way. "Wisdom is the principal thing; therefore get wisdom: and with all thy getting, *get going!*" Here is an example of what can happen when you do.

I once attended a conference in the Hartford Stake. An assignment had been made three months earlier to all members of the stake presidency to speak on this subject of genealogical work. One had been a counselor in the stake presidency but became stake patriarch at that conference. He told this interesting incident.

He had not been able to get started in genealogical work, although he was "converted" to it. He just didn't know where to start. When he received the assignment to prepare a life history from his own records, he was unable to find anything about his childhood and youth except his birth certificate. He was one of eleven children born to Italian immigrants. He is the only member of his family in the Church.

In fulfilling the assignment he tried to put together everything he could find on his life. At least he was started, but there just didn't seem to be anywhere to go. He could get his own life story put together from his own memory and from what few records he had.

Then a very interesting thing happened. His aged mother, who was in a rest home, had a great yearning to return once more to her homeland in Italy. Finally, because she was obsessed with this desire, the doctors felt nothing would be gained by denying her this request, and the family decided to grant their mother her dying wish. And for some reason they all decided that this brother (the only member of the family in the Church) should be the one to accompany his mother to Italy.

All at once, then, he found himself returning to the ancestral home. A door was opening! While in Italy he visited the parish church where his mother was baptized, and also the parish church where his father was baptized. He met many relatives. He learned that the records in the parish go back for five hundred years. He visited the town hall to look into the records and found the people very cooperative there. The town clerk told him that the previous summer a seminarian and a nun had been there together looking for records of this brother's family name, and they had said they were collecting the genealogy of the family. He was given the name of the city where they lived, and he now could follow that lead. He learned also that there is a city in Italy bearing the family name.

But this is not all. When he came to Salt Lake City to general conference he returned by way of Colorado, where many of his family live. There, with very little persuasion, a family organization was effected and a family reunion was planned, which soon afterwards was held.

And then, as always happens, some of his relatives, his aunts and uncles, his brothers and sisters, began to provide pictures and information about *his* life that he never knew existed. And, as always happens, he learned that this is a work of inspiration.

The Lord will bless you once you begin this work. This has been very evident to my family. Since the time we decided that we would start where we were, with what we had, many things have opened to us.

On one occasion I took to the Genealogical Society eight large volumes, manuscript genealogical work, consisting of six thousand family group sheets of very professional genealogical work, all on the Packer family. All of it was compiled by Warren Packer, originally from Ohio, a schoolteacher, a Lutheran. He has spent thirty years doing this work, not really knowing why. There are two more volumes now added to the others. He senses now why he has been involved in this work over the years and very much has the spirit of the work.

We have had the opportunity, too, of locating and visiting the ancestral Packer home in England. Many of the large manor houses in England in recent years have been opened to the public. This one is not. It is about a fifteen-minute drive from the London Temple and it is built on the site of an ancient castle, with a moat around it. It stands just as it was finished in the early sixteen hundreds. The portraits of our ancestors are hanging where they were placed nearly three hundred years ago. On the estate is a little chapel. In it is a stained glass window with the Packer coat of arms, put there in 1625.

Things began to emerge once we got to work. We still are not, by any means, experts in genealogical research. We are, however, dedicated to our family. And it is my testimony that if we start where we are—each of us with ourselves, with such records as we have—and begin putting those in order, things will fall into place as they should.

You can get started now! Find a cardboard box and put it in the way and begin to put things in it, and as the things unfold you will sense something spiritual happening and not be too surprised at that.

There is a common expression when some unusual good fortune befalls a person. They respond with, "Someone up there likes me," and credit to some divine providence the good thing that has come into their lives.

As the Heart Turns

Sometimes this work may become a little discouraging. How can we seek out all of our progenitors—and all the others? One day while pondering prayerfully on this matter I came to the realization that there is something that any one of us can do for all who have died. I came to see that any one of us, by himself, can care about them, all of them, and love them. That came as a great inspiration, for then I knew there was a starting point.

Whatever the number, we can love them and desire to redeem them. Any one of us has within him the power to expand his concern to include them all. If a billion more are added, we can *care* about them also. At least we can do that.

If the assignment seems impossible, we must move ahead. If the process is tedious, we must move ahead anyway. If the records have been lost, if the obstacles and opposition seem overwhelming, we will move ahead anyway. When we determine to do as the Lord commands, we move ahead.

As we proceed, we are joined at the crossroads by those who have been prepared to help us. They come with skills and abilities precisely suited to our needs. And we find provisions: information, inventions, help of various kinds, set along the way waiting for us to take them up. It is as though someone knew we would be traveling that way. We see the invisible hand of the Almighty providing for us.

Elder LeGrand Richards said: "Brethren, the Lord has inspired men to invent these great tools. Now, if we don't use them to teach His gospel, Satan will use them to lead the people astray." We must get the vision of this, for where there is no vision the people perish, and the dead go unredeemed.

Genealogical work has the power to do something *for* the dead. It has an equal power to do something *to* the living. Genealogical work of Church members has a refining, spiritualizing, tempering influence on those who are engaged in it. They understand that they are tying their family together, their living family here with those who have gone before.

Genealogical work in one sense would justify itself, even if one were not successful in clearing names for temple work. The process of searching, the means of going after those names, would be worth all the effort you could invest. The reason: You cannot find names without knowing that they represent people. You begin to find out things about people. When we research our own lines we become interested in more than just names or the number of names going through the temple. Our interest turns our hearts to our fathers—we seek to find them and to know them and to serve them.

In doing so we store up treasures in heaven.

Has the day of miracles ceased?
Or have angels ceased to appear unto the
children of men? Or has he withheld
the power of the Holy Ghost from
them? Or will he, so long
as time shall last, or the earth
shall stand, or there shall be
one man upon the face thereof
to be saved?
Behold I say unto you, Nay.
(Moroni 7:35-37.)

Help from Beyond

I know of no work in the Church more conducive to spiritual refinement and communication than temple and genealogical work. In this work our hearts and our minds are turned to those beyond the veil. Such a work helps us to sharpen our spiritual sensitivities.

Each of us has the right to receive revelation concerning his personal affairs. The Prophet Joseph Smith said:

> The spirit of revelation is in connection with these blessings. A person may profit by noticing the first intimation of the spirit of revelation; for instance, when you feel pure intelligence flowing into you, it may give you sudden strokes of ideas, so that by noticing it, you may find it fulfilled the same day or soon; (i.e.) those things that were presented unto your minds by the Spirit of

God, will come to pass; and thus by learning the Spirit of God and understanding it, you may grow into the principle of revelation, until you become perfect in Christ Jesus. (*HC,* 3:381.)

Elder John A. Widtsoe has counseled us in these words:

The seen and the unseen worlds are closely connected. One assists the other. Those who fail to partake of the privileges and blessings of temple work deprive themselves of some of the choicest gifts within the keeping of the Church. ("The Urgency of Temple Service," *The Utah Genealogical and Historical Magazine* 28 [January 1937]:5.)

President Heber J. Grant said:

I am sure, if we were to collect the various experiences that people have had in obtaining information that has led them to get a record of their forefathers, that it would be one of the most faith-promoting things that we could have. ("Service, the True Key to Happiness," *The Utah Genealogical and Historical Magazine* 23 [January 1932]:10.)

Spiritual communication and inspiration and miracles are a vital evidence of the Lord's church upon the earth. Moroni, presenting the teachings of his father, Mormon, wrote:

And now, my beloved brethren, if this be the case that these things are true which I have spoken unto you, and God will show unto you, with power and great glory at the last day, that they are true, and if they are true has the day of miracles ceased?

Or have angels ceased to appear unto the children of men? Or has he withheld the power of the Holy Ghost from them? Or will he, so long as time shall last, or the earth shall stand, or there shall be one man upon the face thereof to be saved?

Behold I say unto you, Nay; for it is by faith that miracles are wrought; and it is by faith that angels appear and minister unto men; wherefore, if these things have ceased wo be unto the children of men, for it is because of unbelief, and all is vain.

For no man can be saved, according to the words of Christ, save they shall have faith in his name; wherefore, if these things have ceased, then has faith ceased also; and awful is the state of man, for they are as though there had been no redemption made.

But behold, my beloved brethren, I judge better things of you, for I judge that ye have faith in Christ because of your meekness;

for if ye have not faith in him then ye are not fit to be numbered among the people of his church. (Moroni 7:35-39.)

Spiritual Guidance in the Work

It will be our purpose to consider the spiritual guidance that attends this work and to reverently explore the past for a few examples of help beyond the veil. Before we do so I wish to say something about spiritual experiences.

I have come to know that deeply spiritual experiences are usually given to us for our individual edification and it is best not to talk of them generally. Alma told Zeezrom: "It is given unto many to know the mysteries of God; nevertheless they are laid under a strict command that they shall not impart only according to the portion of his word which he doth grant unto the children of men, according to the heed and diligence which they give unto him." (Alma 12:9.) We may be prompted on occasion to tell of our spiritual experiences, but generally we should regard them as sacred. It is not out of order, however, to present some experiences from those who have lived in years past.

The fact that sacred spiritual experiences are not discussed widely—for instance, by the General Authorities—should not be taken as an indication that the Saints do not receive them. Such spiritual gifts are with the Church today as they were in years past.

Experiences which involve dreams or visions or visitations might be recorded and put away in family records to serve as a testimony and an inspiration to our descendants in the generations ahead.

I have been interested to see the continued indication of spiritual inspiration in temple and genealogical work, as evidenced by the large number of such experiences recorded in Church history, in Church publications, and in personal records. I began to gather them from these sources and found there is an abundance of them.

Here I will present a few examples. Earlier it was mentioned that the return of Elijah generated a worldwide awakening of interest in genealogical records. As further evidence that there is a special motivation in this work, I include the following report of "guidance" in genealogical research outside the Church. Such incidents are testimony that Elijah did return.

The average research genealogist who becomes either a successful amateur or professional investigator of family history, often meets with remarkable and unusual experiences. The writer knows one of the most successful research workers in this line in the country whose experiences would fill a book with marvelous tales of a most fascinating kind. Let us begin with one that has been duplicated but seldom, if at all.

Considerable correspondence with a woman in the South about the ancestry of a client of this investigator brought only word that they knew nothing more than they had already given, but would keep it in mind, as they felt later on they might obtain that which was asked for. Three, nearly four years passed before further word was received; and in the meantime, this individual had been forgotten and correspondence ceased with her.

One day the postman brought a rather heavy package addressed to this genealogical investigator, which, upon opening, was found to contain the name plate from the coffin of the ancestor buried nearly two generations ago, on which appeared his full name, date, and place of birth and death. In fact, it gave all the details sought for and which existed nowhere else but in the person's grave. A letter accompanying the plate stated that the remains had been moved to another burial ground, and that as a new coffin was used, the old plate was forwarded.

Again this research genealogist, who had been nearly forty years trying to find out the date of death of her own great-grandmother, and had never succeeded, one day when recently clearing a number of old magazines in her own home was looking through a copy of Scribners or Harpers. In snapping through the pages, suddenly her eye saw something that caused her to stop and take a second look. To her astonishment, she saw at the heading of one page the words:

In Memory of _____

Who Died _____

To her further amazement she found that the poem had been written in memory of her great-grandmother, and the date of the grandmother's death was given as part of the heading. One would hardly expect to find genealogical material in a publication devoted exclusively to current literature. Nor would one expect to find it in a grave—at least find it accessible; but such instances go to prove one cannot actually place a limit on where such facts may finally be located.

Recently she unearthed an even more interesting case. In New York state there is a family association that is devoting a great deal of time and money to unearthing information to carry their family back to the Mayflower passengers. For years they had been stuck and could make no headway. In working out the lineage for a client this consulting research genealogist came in touch with this family association, and ran up against the same wall that was halting them. However, not to be daunted, she began to investigate the land records and finally located the old farm of the last known ancestor.

Following clews from the tax and other records of the times, she decided that if some one was to personally interview the oldest of the living persons at the farm, or near it, some information might be obtained. Making the suggestion to the head of the family association, who took kindly to it, a personal call by auto was made there. Questioning brought to light that the old woman still living on the farm was the grandchild of the ancestor last known, but she could offer nothing more, and so no family Bible or other records were in the place.

Disappointed, the interviewer arose to go. When at the door the old lady said, "Wait a moment," and with that went to the attic and from an old chest brought out a quilt on which the names of the members of the family, dates and locations by birth, marriage and death were first written, then sewed into it, not only the person sought for, but for several of the earlier generations as well, and many of the collateral lines of descent that had at this late date not been able to connect with what all evidence pointed to that of all being in one family. Needless to say, photographs and affidavits of this valuable find were secured without delay.

This is one of the most remarkable genealogical discoveries of its kind in late years and has opened up a tremendous field of family research for several thousand descendants belonging to the Standish family. (Pierson W. Banning, "Strange Experiences of a Genealogist," *The Utah Genealogical and Historical Magazine* 13 [October 1922]: 179-80.)

Elder John A. Widtsoe recorded this experience:

I know of no work that I have done in the Church which has been so filled with testimonies of the divinity of this work as the little I have done in behalf of the salvation of our dead. I could tell you a number of experiences, but the one that impressed me most happened a few years ago when I accompanied Brother Reed Smoot to Europe.

We came to Stockholm; he had his work to do; I decided to see what I could do in the way of finding books on Swedish genealogy. I knew the names of the two big bookstores in Stockholm. I went to the one, made my selections, and then started across the city to the other bookstore in the hope that I might find some more suitable books. As I hurried along the street filled with people, I was stopped suddenly by some voice which said to me: "Go across the street and down that narrow side street." I looked across the street and saw a little narrow street. I had not been in Stockholm before. I thought: This is all nonsense, I have little time to spend here. I am not going down that street, I have to do my work, and I walked on.

Almost at once the voice came again, as distinctly as any voice I have ever heard. Then I asked myself: What is your business in this city? Are you not on the Lord's errand? And I crossed over; went down the little narrow street, and there, half-way down, found a little bookstore that I had known nothing about. When I asked for books on genealogy the lady said: "No, we do not carry books on genealogy. When we get such books we send them to the bookstore" — naming the store for which I was headed. Then, just as I was leaving in disappointment, she said: "Stop a minute. A leading book collector, a genealogist, died about a month ago, and we bought his library. Many of his genealogical books are in the back room ready to be sent to the bookstore, but if you want to buy them you may have them."

Thus we secured the foundation of Swedish genealogy in our library. I could relate many such experiences. ("Genealogical Activities in Europe," *The Utah Genealogical and Historical Magazine* 22 [July 1931]:101.)

President Charles W. Penrose spoke of revelation attending this work.

Let us think over these things, and pray to the Lord to open the way, and the way will be opened by which we will learn about our ancestors. And when the time comes that we have done all we can in a natural way, the veil will be drawn aside, and the Priesthood behind the veil will minister to the Priesthood in the flesh, and reveal many things that we could not ordinarily obtain knowledge of here; but we will get them by this kind of revelation. ("Salvation for the Dead," *The Utah Genealogical and Historical Magazine* 4 [January 1913]: 1-18.)

Elder Rudger Clawson spoke in General Conference of such an experience.

Some years ago, a brother approached me, and he said: "Brother Clawson, I am sixty-seven years of age; I have been a strong and active man in my life, and have done a great deal of hard work, but now I am somewhat feeble; I cannot engage in manual labor as heretofore. How shall I spend my time?" I said to him, "Go to the house of the Lord." "Thank you," he replied, "I will take your counsel."

About eight years later, I met this brother again. He appeared to be very happy indeed; and there was an expression of joy in his countenance. "Brother Clawson," he said, "during the past eight years I have been working for my ancestors, in the house of the Lord. After that conversation with you, I went east and I gathered up eight hundred names of my relatives; and during the past eight years I have personally officiated for three hundred of my ancestors, and I propose to continue on with the good work; I am happy for the Lord has blessed me."

He further said, "I saw in a vision, upon one occasion, my father and mother, who were not members of the Church, who had not received the Gospel in life, and I discovered that they were living separate and apart in the spirit world, and when I asked them how it was that they were so, my father said: 'This is an enforced separation, and you are the only individual that can bring us together; you can do this work; will you do it?' " —meaning that he should go into the house of the Lord and there officiate for his parents who were dead, and by the ordinance of sealing bring them together and unite them in the family relation beyond the veil; and he informed me that he had attended to the work, and I rejoiced with him and congratulated him. (Conference Report, October 1908, page 74.)

At the rededication of the Logan Temple in 1979 I recounted an incident in the life of my wife's grandfather, which I include here.

The Logan Temple is sacred to our family, for there my wife and I were married, and my wife's grandfather responded to the call and helped to construct that temple.

C. O. Law, the superintendent of construction for that temple, wrote on February 25, 1884: "This letter certifies that Brother Julius Smith of Brigham City has worked faithfully and honorably on the Logan Temple for nearly two years, and as the temple nears completion, his branch of the labor being terminated, he is now honorably released and we sincerely trust that Brother Smith may become a participant in the blessings of the House of the Lord which he has assisted to erect."

Brother Smith with his wife, Josephina, lived on a few acres of ground in Brigham City. There they raised fourteen children, my wife's father being the youngest. When the call came for workers to assist in the building of the temple, he responded.

Each Monday morning he left his family in the care of his wife and hiked up through Flat Bottom Canyon, down Dry Canyon to the south end of Cache Valley, and on to Logan. After his week's work on Saturday, he walked home to spend Sunday with his family.

He was not a young man, just over five feet tall, and very slight in build. He was, nevertheless, assigned as a hod carrier. For the younger readers I explain that a hod carrier would fill a V-shaped wooden box full of mortar or plaster. He would lift it to his shoulder and carry it to where the masons were working, often carrying this very heavy weight up long ladders.

On the afternoon of August 11, 1883, Brother Smith was supplying two plasterers who were finishing the ceiling a hundred feet above the ground in the northwest tower of the temple. Suddenly the scaffolding gave way, tipped to one side, and fell. The projections for the spiral staircase had been installed. The three men tumbled through these projections and landed at various levels amid the rubble. The record states that they were removed to their homes and soon returned to their work, having sustained only minor injuries.

The hope "that Brother Smith would participate in the blessings of the House of the Lord which he had assisted to erect" was amply fulfilled. He went there often.

As a young man he had lived among the Indians. In later years when Indian bands would visit Brigham City, one of the Indians would go to the home of Brother Smith. His visits were not welcomed by the rest of the family, for he would peer in every window intently until he determined that Brother Smith was home. And only then would he knock at the door.

One night, some years after the completion of the temple, Brother Smith was reading his newspaper. He heard a noise at the window, and he saw his Indian friend peering in with an unusually sad expression. He went to the door and found no one there, and the snow beneath the window had not been disturbed.

This incident bothered him greatly, and during the following week he tried to locate and get some information about this Indian friend. He learned that he had died.

In due time, he recorded, "Today I have taken care of his work in the temple." That very evening he was looking through the mail and again heard a sound at the window. When he looked up he saw his Indian friend, this time smiling. He counted that a very sacred experience, and in the record of a great amount of work done by this faithful grandfather in this temple is found the name Be-a-go-tia.

I have wondered over the years about the meaning of the scripture recorded three times in the Book of Mormon, that "the course of the Lord is one eternal round." (1 Nephi 10:19, Alma 7:20, Alma 37:12.)

I can see one meaning as it relates to our work for the dead. Genealogical work, the essential preparation for temple work, puts us to seeking through the records for those who have lived in the past. We look back to the past to find them. We perform temple ordinance work for them and then we look forward to the future to meet them. Something sacred is consummated when we have safely recorded, in the list of ordinances completed, the names of those who *lived* in our past and who yet *live* in our future. This ordinance work is crucial to us and to the Church.

Elder Harold B. Lee spoke at a genealogical research seminar and gave the following account of an experience of President George Albert Smith:

I remember the story that President George Albert Smith used to tell us. Now, as you remember Brother Smith, he was one of the friendliest men that I think we ever had in the Church. No one was a stranger to him. He'd get on a plane and within five minutes the man in the seat next to him was like an old friend. When he arrived in Chicago during the Chicago World's Fair he learned that the president of the fair was a man by the name of Dawes. He had been to Harvard University with a man named Dawes. He wondered if this could be his old class mate. So, prompted by this spirit of friendliness, he called up the office and asked the secretary if he could have an appointment to see Mr. Dawes.

There were three brothers—Charles Dawes who was the vice-president of the United States, you will recall; Henry Dawes; and Rufus Dawes. Now, he wasn't sure of the first name of his friend, and this smart young secretary said, "Well, there are 125 people lined up outside to see him, but I guess if you want to come and stand in line you can see him." "Well," said President Smith, "I didn't want anything; I'm just an old schoolmate and just wanted to pass the time of day." "Well," she said, "wait a minute. I think he'd want to meet somebody who doesn't want anything. All the rest of these people want something. You come around to the side door and I'll let you in to see him." So, President Smith caught a taxi and went out there.

Just as he got to the side door, as indicated, this man was ushering out a couple who had been in conference with him. One look told him this wasn't the man he knew. Now, here he was ushered into the busy man's office without a thing to say to him. He rubbed his hands a little bit and finally said, "Mr. Dawes, where do your people come from?" President Smith said, "Wasn't that an asinine thing to ask him." Mr. Dawes looked at him for a minute and asked, "Are you interested in genealogy?"

Well, here was President Smith's cue. He told him about the genealogical library, our great interest in genealogical research. Mr. Dawes said, "Let me show you something." He went into the back room and came out with a volume, a beautifully bound volume, and said, "This is the genealogy of my mother. I loved my mother and I was curious about her ancestors. So I had researchers go over to the old country and search out her genealogy. It cost me somewhere between $30,000 to $40,000 to make this research. And now that I have it done and have satisfied my curiosity I have no further use for it. How would you like if it I gave it to you to take back and put in your wonderful library?"

"My," President Smith said, "I think that would be a treasure."

This was the genealogy of the Gates family — one of our pioneer families. And that genealogy linked with many of the pioneer families. Within 15 minutes President Smith walked out of this man's office, within his arms $40,000 worth of research from a man he had never seen before. You tell me the Lord isn't opening the doors to genealogy work? It means merely that when you do all that you can, then you can expect the Lord to open the doors beyond our own efforts. (*Genealogical Devotion Addresses — 1970*, Fifth Annual Priesthood Genealogical Research Seminar, Brigham Young University, 1970, pages 31-32.)

There is much evidence that the work goes on beyond the veil. From his vision of October 3, 1918, President Joseph F. Smith records:

And as I wondered, my eyes were opened, and my understanding quickened, and I perceived that the Lord went not in person among the wicked and the disobedient who had rejected the truth, to teach them;

But behold, from among the righteous, he organized his forces and appointed messengers, clothed with power and authority, and commissioned them to go forth and carry the light of the gospel to them that were in darkness, even to all the spirits of men; and thus was the gospel preached to the dead. (D&C 138:29-30.)

There is an incident in which President Lorenzo Snow raised a young girl from the dead. She gave a vivid account of her visit in the spirit world — including a meeting with her grandfather, who was so busy working on records that he had little time for her.

In the early days of Brigham City a stake conference was being held. President Lorenzo Snow, of the Box Elder Stake, a member of the Quorum of the Twelve Apostles, was speaking in the meeting. Behind him on the stand was Elder Rudger Clawson. A note was delivered to the meeting and handed to President Snow at the pulpit. He read the note. It asked that he announce the funeral services for Ella Jensen, who had passed away that morning.

Instead of making the announcement, President Snow announced to the audience that there was trouble in the community and he and Brother Clawson would be excused from the meeting for a time.

They went by buggy the several miles to the Jensen home. There they found the grieving parents and the body of the nineteen-year-old girl washed and laid out for burial.

President Snow told the parents not to be troubled, and these two Brethren blessed the girl. They stood around for some time, but nothing happened; and then they left.

Some time after they had gone, the girl stirred and opened her eyes and said, "Where is he? Where is he?"

"Where is who?" the parents asked.

"Where is President Snow? He called me back."

She then left a detailed account of her experiences in the spirit world, including a meeting with her grandfather, whom she confronted with great joy. He, in turn, greeted her with polite affection, but was very busy and excused himself because of the weight of responsibility he was carrying.

A detailed account of this miraculous experience, including the testimonies of President Snow and Elder Clawson, was published in the *Improvement Era* in two issues (32 [September, October 1929]:881-86, 972-80.)

Brother Widtsoe reaffirmed that "those who give themselves with all their might and main to this work [genealogical work] receive help from the other side. Whoever seeks to help those on the other side receives help in return in all the affairs of life." ("Genealogical Activities in Europe," page 104.)

Of course, you cannot force spiritual things. The Lord said that such things as these come in His own time and in His own way and according to His own will; and if we will live as we should and endeavor to keep His commandments, what ought to happen to us can happen to us.

President Wilford Woodruff left this testimony of help from beyond the veil:

> Joseph Smith continued visiting myself and others up to a certain time and then stopped. The last time I saw him was in heaven. In the night vision I saw him at the door of the Temple in heaven. He came and spoke to me. He said he could not stop to talk to me because he was in a hurry. The next man I met was Father Smith; he couldn't talk to me because he was in a hurry. I met a half a dozen brethren who held high positions on earth, and none of them could stop to talk with me because they were in a hurry. I was much astonished.
>
> By and by I saw the Prophet again, and I got the privilege to ask him a question. "Now," said I, "I want to know why you are in a hurry? I have been in a hurry all my life, but I expected my hurry would be over when I got into the Kingdom of Heaven, if I ever did."
>
> Joseph said, "I will tell you, Brother Woodruff, every dispensation that has had the priesthood on earth and has gone into the celestial kingdom, has had a certain amount of work to do to prepare to go to the earth with the Savior when he goes to reign on earth. Each dispensation has had ample time to do this work. We have not. We are the last dispensation, and so much work has to be done and we need to be in a hurry in order to accomplish it."
>
> Of course, that was satisfactory with me, but it was new doctrine to me. (Discourse delivered at Weber Stake Conference, Ogden, 19 October 1896; as published in *Deseret News Weekly*, vol. 53, no. 21.)

On one occasion when Elder Harold B. Lee spoke to the seminary and institute teachers, he was stressing to us the reality of spiritual communication and of the help and guidance we may receive from beyond the veil. But, he warned, we must be attuned in order to receive it.

Here is an excerpt from his address:

> A few weeks ago, President McKay related to the Twelve an interesting experience, and I asked him yesterday if I might repeat it to you this morning.
>
> He said it is a great thing to be responsive to the whisperings of the Spirit, and we know that when these whisperings come it is a

gift and our privilege to have them. They come when we are re-laxed and not under pressure of appointments. The President then took occasion to relate an experience in the life of Bishop John Wells, former member of the Presiding Bishopric.

A son of Bishop Wells was killed in Emigration Canyon on a railroad track. Brother John Wells was a great detail man and pre-pared many of the reports we are following up now. His boy was run over by a freight train. Sister Wells was inconsolable. She mourned during the three days prior to the funeral, received no comfort at the funeral, and was in a rather serious state of mind.

One day soon after the funeral services while she was lying on her bed relaxed, still mourning, she says that her son appeared to her and said, "Mother do not mourn, do not cry. I am all right." He told her that she did not understand how the accident happened and explained that he had given the signal to the engineer to move on, and then made the usual effort to catch the railing on the freight train; but as he attempted to do so his foot caught on a root and he failed to catch the hand rail, and his body fell under the train. It was clearly an accident.

Now, listen. He said that as soon as he realized that he was in another environment he tried to see his father, but *he couldn't reach him. His father was so busy with the duties in his office he could not respond to his call.* Therefore he had come to his mother. He said to her, "You tell father that all is well with me, and I want you not to mourn any more."

Then the President made the statement that the point he had in mind was that when we are relaxed in a private room we are more susceptible to those things; and that so far as he was concerned, his best thoughts come after he gets up in the morning and is re-laxed and thinking about the duties of the day; that impressions come more clearly, as if it were to hear a voice. Those impressions are right. If we are worried about something and upset in our feelings, the inspiration does not come. If we so live that our minds are free from worry and our conscience is clear and our feelings are right toward one another, the operation of the Spirit of the Lord upon our spirit is as real as when we pick up the telephone; but when they come, we must be brave enough to take the suggested actions. The Lord will approve it and the Brethren will approve it, and we know it is right. He said, it is a great consolation in this upset world today to know that our Savior is directing this work. Then the President concluded: "I value that testimony." If you forget all else I have said, you remember that lesson and that admonition. (Address to seminary and institute faculty, Brigham Young University, 6 July 1956.)

A Work Pleasing to the Lord

Temple and genealogical work constitutes a living testimony of the ministry of the Lord Jesus Christ. He wrought the Atonement, He set in operation the resurrection.

If men were really "dead" when they die, why concern ourselves? Why the vast resources of time and money and effort directed at this work? If there were no resurrection, why would we do it?

But there is life beyond the veil. Every thought or word or act we direct at this sacred work is pleasing to the Lord. Every hour spent on genealogical research, however unproductive it appears, is worthwhile. It is pleasing to the Lord. It is our testimony to Him that we accept the doctrine of the resurrection and the plan of salvation. It draws us close to those who have gone before. It welds eternal links in family associations and draws us closer to Him who is our Lord and stands in the presence of Him who is our Eternal Father.

*Shall we not go on in so great
a cause? Go forward and not
backward. Courage,
brethren; and on, on to the
victory!*
(D&C 128:22.)

21

Toward the Veil

I have a letter that I read periodically. It is now nearly a hundred years old. It was written from Safford, Arizona, to Martha Packer Pierce, a sister of my grandfather. It was written by her sister-in-law, Mary Ann Packer, wife of William J. Packer. She wrote to report the condition of her dying father-in-law, Johnathan Taylor Packer. He was my great-grandfather and the first of my progenitors to join the Church. When he was eighteen years old he with two of his brothers journeyed from Ohio to Nauvoo to meet the Prophet Joseph Smith. There he was baptized, and from then on, through his entire hard, eventful life, he followed the Brethren.

Through this letter more than through any other record I came to know my great-grandfather. The letter is dated January 17, 1889. He died twelve days later.

Safford Graham Co.
Jan. 17th 1889

Dear Sister Martha

As your Father is not able to answer your most welcome letter I will do so instead. He is living with me he is very sick and have been for some five weeks. Do not know exactly what is the matter with him but dropsy is one complaint and he is troubled very much for breath and such a disstress in his Stomach and unless their is a change in him before long I do not think he will stand it much longer for he grows weaker everyday. But I will do all I can for him for I consider it my duty. I will do for him as I would like someone to do for my dear Mother for I am afraid I shall never see her again in this World.

Tell your Mother I often think of her, If I do not write, and of the comforting words she have spoken when I lay on my bed of sickness. I have good health this winter the best for the last six years. I trust your Mothers health will be good and that she will enjoy life. I so often look at her picture and it looks like it might talk. I wish I had yours also the boys. It would be a great comfort to me to have a picture to look at if I cannot see you all but I hope we will meet again. I am glad you enjoyed yourselves Holiday. We did not have much enjoyment on Christmas. Annie got a dinner invite all their and on News Years. *Your Father says for you all to be faithful to the principles of the Gospel and asks the blessings of Abraham Isaac and Jacob upon you all and bid you all good bye until he meets you in the morning of the resurrection.* Well Martha I can't hardly see the lines for tears so I will stop writing give my love to yourself from your loving sister.

Mary Ann Packer

I guess you know Aleathea my sister she live about eighty miles from here she stayed with me two months last summer she has four children.

It is quite an ordinary letter. But I see in it things that are extraordinary in importance. The most valuable message of the letter is from my great-grandfather, his parting message: "Your

Father says for you all to be faithful to the principles of the Gospel and asks the blessings of Abraham Isaac and Jacob upon you all." His heart was turned to *the* fathers, the ancient ones, the prophets.

More than once I have shared Mary's deep feelings as she concludes: "Well Martha I can't hardly see the lines for tears."

Consider the note to Martha about her mother—my great-grandmother—and her "comforting words she have spoken when I lay on my bed of sickness."

The letter is dominated by the theme of family love strengthened in time of trouble. How the significance of such family feelings is deepened by time and experience!

It is so also with the temple ordinances. They have different meanings to the young and to the old. I often think, when I perform the sealing for a young couple, that it is a beginning for them; their hearts and minds are set upon those parts of the covenant that have to do with their marriage which is just beginning. A young husband and wife accept one another, not quite knowing what life holds for them. They do not know at this point how many children they will have or whether they will have any at all. They do not know where circumstances will lead them. They are not sure where the husband will be employed or what their fortunes will be. They move ahead in faith.

I always look around the sealing room for a grandmother or a grandfather, one perhaps whose partner has gone ahead. The sealing ordinance means something much different to the older ones. They too are looking ahead. But they are more interested in resurrection than they are in the creating of a family. Some uncertainty is present with them, too. But there is a serenity about them, a confidence and a faith. Words that held little meaning for a person as he or she first came to the altar as bride or groom now shine brightly as a beacon and a promise. The words "the Holy Spirit of Promise" take on a depth and a dimension that the person could not have felt in youth.

Care for Parents

Mary gave to her father-in-law a tender care; for she hoped someone would treat her mother with equal tenderness. My wife and I have learned from that, and we have tried—really tried— to care for our parents with tender regard in their declining years.

When I was a boy my grandfather came to live with us—my father's father, Joseph Alma Packer. He was having problems with his eyesight. He always walked with a cane. He was a typical old man. I did not appreciate what had to be done to order the household for Grandpa. As I look back now, that was one of the choice experiences of my life, to have an intimate relationship and memory with my grandfather. He died in our home.

When my wife's father became incapacitated after major surgery, and it was clear that he would need a great deal of care, we brought him to our home. He only lived for a short time, but the experience we had was a great blessing to our family. Our children helped to care for their grandfather, administer to his every need. I am sure this experience will be a great influence for good in their lives.

When we say *temple* I would list what in essence are Latter-day Saint synonyms for the word: Marriage, family, children, happiness, joy, eternal life, resurrection, redemption, exaltation, inspiration, revelation. All of these words in their own way are synonyms for the word *temple*. The word *temple* to the Latter-day Saint suggests a reverence for life. It embraces a concern for the young and the very old in the family. The world now fosters another view of these family connections. There is a growing tendency to establish centers for the care of the very young and of the very old. This responsibility is being shifted outside the home and family. There may be times when institutional help is needed for the care of the infirm. But we are becoming too free nowadays to shift from the family the privilege (I call it a privilege rather than a burden) of caring for family members. It is wrong. We should not disconnect the generations in this way. We should not unlink ourselves from our generations.

On one occasion Alex Haley the noted author was in our home. As we went over our family records he commented on the influence of the Church in holding the generations together.

Although he was being sought after to speak to large and prominent groups, he told me he preferred to speak to elementary school children because he took a message to the young people. The message: "Talk to the older people." He said he wanted to help his people, and that his people particularly had been threatened by the dissolution of the family. He said to us, "I like to tell the young people that they will not get bad advice from the old people." He said that from his experience in his own life, and from the experience that he'd observed in others, good comes from tying the young to the old. Tying the little folks with the older folks is a great and powerful tool to preserve and to protect the family and the individual.

Some of our most comforting memories of our parents for my wife and myself center around the service we were able to extend to them in their final years. We have not felt to send them away for others to care for. It is good to have the older ones around. They move toward the veil. Where they are now, surely we shall be.

When we know what we ought to know we will seek to weld those links, not just in genealogical research on paper, but here in mortality with our family, with our parents and our grandparents, with our children, and with our grandchildren.

Care for Children

I remember well the dedication of the Oakland Temple, particularly the remarks of Elder Harold B. Lee. When we returned to Salt Lake City I went to his office and talked with him about his comments. "You were inspired," I told him. He replied that he had felt that and said he had another subject prepared but felt prompted to speak as he did. In his address, after quoting the prophecy of Malachi that Elijah would return to turn the hearts of the fathers to the children and the hearts of the children to the fathers, he said:

> I ask you to consider a Church-wide family teaching program about which we're talking today. Under the direction of President McKay we are sending throughout the Church a program to strengthen the relationship of parents and children in the home. Not that it is something new. It has been talked about, to use President McKay's language, "for fifty years" since President Joseph F. Smith and his counselors promised Church members that if they would gather their children around them once a week and instruct them in the gospel, those children in such homes would not go astray.
>
> And so today there is being prepared instruction to do what? Is it not to turn here upon the earth the hearts of the parents to children and the hearts of the children to parents? Can you conceive that when parents have passed beyond the veil that that is the only time when parents should have their hearts turn to their children?
>
> . . . I'd have you consider seriously whether or not that binding with your family will be secure if you have waited until you have passed beyond the veil before your hearts then yearn for your children whom you have neglected to have helped along the way. It is time for us to think of turning the hearts of parents to children now while living, in order that after they have gone to the beyond there might be the bond between parents and children that will last beyond death. (Harold B. Lee, talk at dedication of the Oakland Temple.)

There is a principle of great importance in what Brother Lee said on that occasion. As we move toward the veil we can prepare ourselves and our families.

President Kimball has continually recommended that there be a picture of a temple in the children's room. From their earliest day they should look forward to the temple.

If we do these things, as we progress through life we may look forward with faith, with our covenants made and kept.

There is another important thing we learn as we become acquainted with our forefathers. We develop a respect for the decency, integrity, and goodness of many of our ancestors who did not have the gospel. We find how proud we can be of them, living as well as they did with so little to go on, relatively speaking. We can come to develop a great sympathy and love and respect for our ancestors, and for all of God's children.

Mary Ann Packer wrote, "It would be a great comfort to have a picture to look at if I cannot see you all." A picture is a record—an important one.

Notes like her mention of Aleathea, giving a clue as to where she lived and the number of her children, have provided many a researcher with a clue which has opened the way to find hundreds, sometimes thousands, of names which after verification have been sent to the temples.

Understanding Comes Through Obedience

Not long before President McKay died, he spoke to the General Authorities in the Temple meeting just prior to a general conference. He talked of the temple ordinances and quoted at length from the ceremonies. He explained them to us. (That was not inappropriate, considering that we were in the temple.) After he had spoken for some time, he paused and stood gazing up to the ceiling in deep thought.

I remember that his big hands were in front of him with his fingers interlocked. He stood gazing as people sometimes do when pondering a deep question. Then he spoke: "Brethren, I think I am finally beginning to understand."

Here he was, the prophet—an Apostle for over half a century and even then he was learning, he was growing. His expression "I think I am finally beginning to understand," was greatly comforting to me. Perhaps if he was learning still, I might not be quite so much condemned for my state of relatively little understanding on many spiritual matters, provided that I'm still striving and learning.

Brigham Young said it well: "I will not say, as do many, that the more I learn the more I am satisfied that I know nothing; for the more I learn the more I discern an eternity of knowledge to improve upon." (*Discourses of Brigham Young,* page 250.)

Consider these verses from the Pearl of Great Price:

> And he gave unto them commandments, that they should worship the Lord their God, and should offer the firstlings of their flocks, for an offering unto the Lord. And Adam was obedient unto the commandments of the Lord.
>
> And after many days an angel of the Lord appeared unto Adam, saying: Why dost thou offer sacrifices unto the Lord? And Adam said unto him: I know not, save the Lord commanded me.
>
> And then the angel spake, saying: This thing is a similitude of the sacrifice of the Only Begotten of the Father, which is full of grace and truth.
>
> Wherefore, thou shalt do all that thou doest in the name of the Son, and thou shalt repent and call upon God in the name of the Son forevermore. (Moses 5:5-8.)

The angel explained to Adam the purpose of the sacrifice. He would thereafter not only obey the commandment, but he would know *why* it was required of him.

I can imagine that after Adam knew why the sacrifices were given to him by way of commandment he went forward with greater determination. I can imagine that he began to see a meaning and a purpose and a necessity for the commandment. It is quite possible that thereafter he approached his duty with great reverence and dedication — even determination.

We also should be obedient! The fact that we have received a commandment from God is reason enough in itself to go and do as we have been directed to do.

I have come to know that if we will do so, even though we may not understand at first, the Lord will tell us, as he told Adam, why we are so commanded.

We must gain some feeling for why we build temples, and why the ordinances are required of us. Thereafter we are continually instructed and enlightened on matters of spiritual importance. It comes line upon line, precept upon precept, until we gain a fullness of light and knowledge. This becomes a great protection to us—to each of us personally. It is a protection also for the Church.

Nephi in a vision saw the Lord's church in our day. He saw that "its numbers were few." He saw the Saints "upon all the face of the earth." He also saw that "their dominions upon the face of the earth were small." He described the assembling of the powers of evil:

> And it came to pass that I beheld that the great mother of abominations did gather together multitudes upon the face of all the earth, among all the nations of the Gentiles, to fight against the Lamb of God. (1 Nephi 14:13.)

To counterbalance these monstrous forces of evil the Lord did not arm his people with weapons or military forces. But arm them he did, as Nephi said:

> And it came to pass that I, Nephi, beheld the power of the Lamb of God, that it descended upon the saints of the church of the Lamb, and upon the covenant people of the Lord, who were scattered upon all the face of the earth; and they were armed with righteousness and with the power of God in great glory. (1 Nephi 14:14.)

No work is more of a protection to this Church than temple work and the genealogical research which supports it. No work is more spiritually refining. No work we do gives us more power. No work requires a higher standard of righteousness.

Our labors in the temple cover us with a shield and a protection, both individually and as a people.

Blessings Both Here and Beyond

It is in the ordinances of the temple that we are placed under covenant to Him—it is there we become the covenant people.

If we will accept the revelation concerning temple ordinance work, if we will enter into our covenants without reservation or apology, the Lord will protect us. We will receive inspiration sufficient for the challenges of life.

For a number of years the Church had negotiated with the government of Israel for permission to microfilm the archives of that nation. These records, including many carefully kept genealogies, are priceless records of the human family and have a tie to great events in the history of the world.

The officials had learned all they wanted to know about the Church storage procedures and were impressed. They insisted however that someone be sent to talk to them about the doctrine relating to our desire for their records. They wanted to know *why* we wanted their records.

In 1977 I received the assignment to go to Israel and meet with their official archivists and scholars on the matter. I went in company with Brother Ted Powell, the director of acquisitions of records for the Genealogical Department of the Church.

A meeting was held in the Peace Building at Hebrew University on Mount Scorpius. Nine archivists and scholars represented the Israelis. I explained to them our great interest in the Old Testament and our kinship with Israel. We talked of family, of patriarchal lineage and blessings. We talked of the doctrine of agency.

But all of these things were not central to the point. It might seem that in order to obtain a favorable decision we would have to be "diplomatic" and not mention ordinances — especially baptism.

But we were on the Lord's errand, and so I told them — plainly, bluntly — that we desired their records in order to provide baptism, Christian baptism, for their forebears and for ours. The reaction was immediate and intense.

The meeting thereafter was most interesting! We came away uncertain as to the outcome. But we were on the Lord's errand. We were serving the work of redemption for the dead. We had told the truth without any shade of misrepresentation.

In due time the answer came. We received approval to microfilm and preserve those records which were sanctified by the suffering of our brethren of the house of Israel.

On many occasions I have been present — when sealings were to be performed, when temple ordinance work was being done, when funeral sermons were being preached — in circumstances when the veil was very thin. The gratitude of those who have gone beyond found its way through that misty barrier and was communicated as spiritual things are communicated.

The time will come when each one of us will be invited to pass through that separating veil. If we have done our duty in this great work for those who have passed on, well might we look forward with great anticipation to that time, for a great reward awaits us there. With all assurance, it awaits. I will meet my forebears and you will meet yours.

I cannot close this chapter and this book without bearing you my testimony concerning temple work and the genealogical work associated with it.

I have long since learned that there are no special compelling words set aside to be used only by the Brethren in the bearing of testimony. We use the ordinary words. They are often very inadequate to convey the very depth of feelings. I feel deeply — very, very deeply — this inspiration in the work of the temples. I have a profound regard for it.

I know as surely as I know that I live that the work relating to the temples is true. I know that it was revealed from beyond the veil. I know that that revelation continues.

I know also that revelation may come to each member of the Church individually concerning temple work. It has been my privilege to work very closely with the First Presidency of the Church in preparation for the announcement of small temples. My part, however meager, however insignificant, I have regarded with a greater depth of reverence and a deeper feeling of gratitude than any assignment of which in my ministry I have had a part. Once again ponder these verses:

> Brethren, shall we not go on in so great a cause? Go forward and not backward. Courage, brethren; and on, on to the victory! Let your hearts rejoice, and be exceedingly glad. Let the earth break

forth into singing. Let the dead speak forth anthems of eternal praise to the King Immanuel, who hath ordained, before the world was, that which would enable us to redeem them out of their prison; for the prisoners shall go free.

Let the mountains shout for joy, and all ye valleys cry aloud; and all ye seas and dry lands tell the wonders of your Eternal King! And ye rivers, and brooks, and rills, flow down with gladness. Let the woods and all the trees of the field praise the Lord; and ye solid rocks weep for joy! And let the sun, moon, and the morning stars sing together, and let all the sons of God shout for joy! And let the eternal creations declare his name forever and ever! And again I say, how glorious is the voice we hear from heaven, proclaiming in our ears, glory, and salvation, and honor, and immortality, and eternal life; kingdoms, principalities, and powers!

Behold, the great day of the Lord is at hand; and who can abide the day of his coming, and who can stand when he appeareth? For he is like a refiner's fire, and like a fuller's soap; and he shall sit as a refiner and purifier of silver, and he shall purify the sons of Levi, and purge them as gold and silver, that they may offer unto the Lord an offering in righteousness. Let us, therefore, as a church and a people, and as Latter-day Saints, offer unto the Lord an offering in righteousness; and let us present in his holy temple, when it is finished, a book containing the records of our dead, which shall be worthy of all acceptation. (D&C 128:22-24.)

Come to the temple — come and claim your blessings. It is a sacred work. Of this I give my witness.

Index